VISION AND VALUES IN MANAGING EDUCATION

Successful Leadership Principles and Practice

edited by
Judith Bell and Bernard T. Harrison

David Fulton Publishers
London

David Fulton Publishers Ltd
2 Barbon Close, London WC1N 3JX

First published in Great Britain by David Fulton Publishers 1995

Note: The right of Judith Bell and Bernard T. Harrison to be identified as the editors of this work has been asserted by them in accordance with the Copyright, Designs and Patents Act 1988.

Copyright © David Fulton Publishers

British Library Cataloguing in Publication Data

A catalogue record for this book is available from the British Library

ISBN 1–85346–359–0

Typeset by The Harrington Consultancy Ltd
Printed in Great Britain by the Cromwell Press Ltd, Melksham

Contents

Notes on the Editors and Contributors

The Editors

Judith Bell has worked as a university lecturer, head of department and vice principal in colleges of further education, senior counsellor and course team writer for the Open University, and as one of Her Majesty's Inspectors of Schools specialising in continuing education. She works now as a freelance writer, lecturer and consultant, and holds honorary fellowships in the Universities of Lancaster, Sheffield and Warwick.

Bernard T. Harrison is Professor of Education in the Division of Education, University of Sheffield, where he is director of research and teaching programmes in Educational Management, and of the Teacher Professional Development Research Centre. He is a member of the BEMAS Research Committee. Recent works include *The Literate Imagination* (1994), and studies in educational management and leadership.

The Contributors

Mike Bottery is Senior Lecturer in Education in the School of Education, University of Hull. His books include *The Ethics of Educational Management* (1992) and *Lessons for Schools? A Comparison of Business and Educational Management* (1994).

Marie Brown and **Sue Ralph** both teach in the School of Education, University of Manchester. They lecture and research in Educational Management and Administration and in Education and the Mass Media. They have researched and published extensively on the effects of stress on teachers.

Esmeralda Brodeth is former Director of the Library at the University of Bethlehem, and is now completing research in the Division of Education, University of Sheffield, on the career experience of senior academic leaders in higher education.

Mike Calvert lectures in the Division of Education, University of Sheffield; his research and publications include studies of pastoral care, and of curriculum development in personal/social education and modern languages. He is engaged on a long-term study of pastoral provision in schools.

Brian Chaplin was formerly Divisional Inspector of Her Majesty's Inspectorate in the North West of England. He is now Director of Inspection Services at the Didsbury School of Education, Manchester Metropolitan University.

Terry Cowham is Senior Vice Principal at Manchester College of Arts and Technology, and is active in Management Training and Development. He has published a study (1994) of Strategic Planning for FE Colleges, and has written course materials for the Open University.

Tony Dobell is an Associate Fellow of the Division of Education, University of Sheffield, and an OFSTED Inspector. He contributes to teaching and research programmes in Educational Management, and is former Principal of Barnsley Sixth Form College.

John Gray is Director of Research, Homerton College, Cambridge and was previously Professor of Education in the Division of Education, University of Sheffield. His research and publications in the field of school effectiveness have been widely influential.

Jenny Henderson lectures in the Division of Education, University of Sheffield; her research interests and publications include studies of Personal, Social and Health Education, and Curriculum Development (Sciences).

Colin Higgins worked as research assistant for the Enquiry into *Self-Determining Managers* (Harrison, Dobell and Higgins, 1994), Division of Education, University of Sheffield. He is now engaged on a European Management Programme.

Gillian Ireson is Deputy Head of Tranmoor Lane Infant School, Armthorpe, near Doncaster. She has completed a study (1994) on the management of curriculum innovation in a primary school setting.

John Isaac was Head of Education and Dean of Arts and Education in Oxford Polytechnic, and is now Coordinator for Educational Management at the College of St. Mark and St. John. His publications include works on teacher education and management in education. He is a member of the BEMAS Management Development Committee.

David Jesson is a mathematician and statistician. As a senior lecturer in Education at the University of Sheffield, he worked with John Gray and Harvey Goldstein, to develop their Value-added Approach to School Effectiveness. Their Report was the first 'official' recognition of the role of value-added criteria in making fair assessments of school performance.

Stephen Knutton lectures in Education at the University of Sheffield, where he is Director of Distance Learning Programmes (UK and abroad). His research and publications include studies of science education and teacher education.

Ian McNay is Professor and Head of the Centre for Higher Education Management at the Anglia Polytechnic University. His main research interest – in a wide spectrum – is the response of institutional strategies and structures to changes in the policy environment.

Jon Nixon is Professor of Education at Christchurch College, Canterbury, following research and lecturing in the Division of Education, University of Sheffield. His books include *Evaluating the Whole Curriculum* (1992) and (as co-author) *Encouraging Learning* (1995).

Peter Ribbins is Professor of Education, Deputy Dean and Director of the Centre for Education Management and Policy Studies, School of Education, University of Birmingham. He edits the BEMAS journal *Educational Management and Administration*. His books include *Greenfield on Educational Administration: Towards a Humane Science* (with Greenfield, 1993) and (with Michael Marland, 1994) *Headship Matters: Conversations with Seven Secondary School Headteachers*.

John West-Burnham is Professor of Educational Administration at Humberside University, having worked as Director of the Educational Management Development Unit, University of Leicester. His books include *Managing Quality in Schools* (1992) and an *Appraisal Training Resource* (1993).

Brian Wilcox is a Professorial Fellow in the Division of Education, University of Sheffield, and was formerly Chief Advisor for Sheffield LEA. His publications include *Time Constrained Evaluation* (1992) and, with John Gray, *Good School – Bad School* (1995).

Acknowledgements

We have been helped throughout the preparation of this book by the interest of colleagues and friends who uncomplainingly responded to our numerous queries and requests for assistance. We should particularly like to thank Rachel Willans, Shafeeq Ulhaq and members of the University of Sheffield Distance Learning Office for their tolerance and their skill in resolving problems which at times seemed insurmountable.

To you all, our grateful thanks.

J.B. and B.T.H.

Preface

Each of the three parts of our book contains chapters which present views and research findings, that contribute to the debate concerning what Trethowan (1991) calls 'talking the vision down to earth'. Contributors to Part One are concerned, focally, with the principles of educative management that support clear thinking. This part contains chapters which discuss procedures involved in planning, and issues that need to be considered in developing a strategy. Part Two addresses the most important resource in any organisation – the human resource. Much of the literature on managing change stresses the importance of leadership, and this part reports on ways in which team building and consultative leadership styles can influence the nature of educational provision in different settings. Part Three concentrates on ways in which institutions (and central government) have taken steps to improve effectiveness and efficiency – and the authors draw conclusions about the success or otherwise of various approaches.

The message which is presented throughout the book is that, while vision and values are at the core of good educative management, they mean nothing unless they can be translated into ways and means by which they can be achieved. On the other hand, plans made without vision can do little but resolve immediate problems. The one is dependent on the other, and there is no simple book of rules that everyone should follow. The way the planning is carried out will depend on context, on institutional strengths and weaknesses, on culture and values – and, of course, on vision building.

Judith Bell
Bernard T. Harrison
August 1995

Five Ricochets

A Diagnosis

(On the Roman Empire, 1000 years after its foundation):

The last 300 years had been consumed in apparent prosperity and internal decline.... The form was still the same, but the animating health and vigour were fled. The industry of the people was discouraged and exhausted by a long series of oppression.

(Edward Gibbon (1776) *The Decline and Fall of the Roman Empire,* Chapter 7)

A Remedy

We need versatile and flexible learners as well as analysts.... We need managers who love their work and their organisation and care deeply about people whose lives they affect. We need leaders and managers who combine hard-headed realism with a deep commitment to values and purposes larger than themselves.

(Bolman and Deal, 1991: xiv)

On Principles

Vision without action is merely a dream. Action without vision just passes the time. Vision with action can change the world.

Barker, J.A. (1990) *The Power of Vision.* Minnesota: Charthouse International (video)

(Quoted in Murgatroyd and Morgan, 1992: 79)

On People

It all boils down to one thing: people, people, people, people, people. I don't care what country, or what organisation, or what team you are in – it is the people and whether you can organise those people to achieve an end result that counts.

(Morgan, G. (1988: 46–52) *Riding the Waves of Change,* San Francisco: Jossey Bass)

On Improvement

Change is only anchored firmly when individuals have changed their perceptions and values, and it is important to be realistic about the time that this may take.... The essence of change is to make sure that each change that is made is anchored firmly in position before you move on from there.

(Harvey-Jones, J. (1988: 114), *Making it Happen*)

Part One: Founding Principles in the Management of Education

CHAPTER ONE

Finding a Practical Theory for Managing Education: Why Vision? Whose Values?

Judith Bell and Bernard T. Harrison

Management, as we are so frequently reminded, is about getting things done. What Duignan and Macpherson (1992: 4–5) describe as 'educative management' is about getting things done in the right way for individual institutions. By that, they mean management which takes account of context, culture and the values which inform educational aims – and which protects them. They believe educative leadership 'communicates a sense of excitement, originality and freshness in an organisation', through achieving aims that go far beyond merely 'managing for efficiency'.

No one would deny the importance of administrative and managerial efficiency. Without it, organisations can quickly become out of control, but it is only part of the picture.

The task of a book such as this may be seen, then, in terms of working out what 'educative' might mean, and providing down-to-earth accounts of how educative values actually work in practice. In a sense, we take it for granted that all leaders and managers in education will have a vision for education, and will work towards this through their own guiding values. This would be philosophy-in-action, as defined by Greenfield (1991) and Hodgkinson (1983, 1991), is echoed by Duignan and Macpherson (1992) and many others. Yet, in another sense managers need to remember that vision and values can only become worth something when they are enacted. Philosophers may (if they are lucky) be paid to think, but educational leaders are paid to fulfil their 'educative' goals.

Talking the vision down to earth

Most managers, we have surmised, may claim to have a 'vision' of the way in which their organisation might develop. Applicants for senior management positions in schools, colleges and universities will, invariably, be asked how they see the department or institution developing in the next 5 or 10 years; and woe betide them if they have no views, are unaware of likely political and economic imperatives and are unable to make a reasoned case for improvement, expansion and greater prosperity. Successful applicants may well have a personal vision of what the future might be, but they will quickly find that it counts for little if it is not shared with all, or the majority, of those who are required to make it happen – the deliverers. Many a new manager has arrived full of good ideas and plans for restructuring and has found an unresponsive or even hostile staff who have been quickly branded as behind the times, not quite up to the job or lacking in commitment. New managers may quickly be discouraged from their initially enthusiastic 'pro-active' approach and be tempted to withdraw from the fray, to retire to a study (or even a penthouse suite in these days of corporate management) and to communicate by means of memos. Their vision remains a dream – what the *Concise Oxford Dictionary* defines as 'a thing of imagination'. They are left merely reacting to their own resentful feelings about being misunderstood. If only the staff had had the sense to see what was proposed was in the best interests of the institution. If only ...

Managers quickly learn that it will never be sufficient for the vision, the dream, to remain at the level of personal belief, without shared commitment and workable structures to enable it to be achieved. It has to be 'talked down to earth, in discussions which relate it to time and place' (Trethowan, 1991: 6). Educative managers must lead the thinking about ways in which their organisation might be *at its best.* They must identify long-term targets, from which agreed, realistic short-term targets can be extrapolated (that is, what is visualised becomes achievable). They must draw up plans and cost these; all of these actions require tenacious, as well as enlightened leadership. Trethowan believes that 'no good school has ever been created without such a vision, and no school continues to be good once the vision of those who lead it has been lost' (1991: 3).

Woodcock (1979: 143) suggested that high-performing teams have a number of key characteristics, chief amongst which is a shared sense of purpose and vision where

team members are equally aware and committed to the work of the team in terms of its mission and values. They have a common understanding of what is expected, both in terms of outcomes and in terms of the values that will inform the processes used by the team to achieve these outcomes. The team is focused and energised by this common understanding.

The problem is that members of organisations are individuals who almost certainly will have their own notion of values, and schools themselves develop their own qualities which, as Hoyle (1986: 3) pointed out, can transcend their structures. These structures are

> variously termed *cultures* or *climates*. Central to the concept of *culture* is the idea of value, that which is regarded as worthwhile by the members of some group. These values are manifest in the norms which govern behaviour and the symbols – language, actions, artefacts – which express these values. Thus, in a school with an academic culture there will be norms which emphasise academic endeavour perhaps symbolised through dress, honours boards, staff qualifications, etc. However, we have a part-whole problem here since distinctive sub-cultures develop amongst pupils which can have values quite opposed to the dominant culture of the school.

Any teacher will recognise the way in which these sub-cultures can develop – and not only amongst pupils. Hoyle suggests that it is the ways in which all members of the school respond to the development of sub-cultures, that will influence the climate of the institution. He comments that this climate is 'essentially concerned with the quality of relationships between pupils, between pupils and teachers, between teachers and between the head and teachers ...' (1986: 3).

The climate, culture, ethos and personal identity of a school or college, and the values which prevail there will necessarily have an influence on making the vision a reality, yet as Trethowan (1991: 12) suggested:

> These values are long term and not easy to change. They deeply influence a school because they are the touchstone by which people decide what is right, good and correct or bad, wrong and incorrect within an organisation.

and

> Every organisation, has this value-base or ethos. Its ethos is either planned and managed or it has developed under the influence of chance factors, serendipitous incidents and random personalities.... Any planned change within a school which does not take account of the existing ethos runs the risk of failure.

Paradigm shifts

The change in the 1960s and 1970s from grammar to comprehensive schools in many cases required teachers to carry out a fundamental review of their deeply held values, and some felt betrayed by the change. They felt they were being asked to lower their standards, to abandon their view of what quality education meant and to put on one side their former beliefs and practices.

During the 1990s, teachers have faced further important changes in the curriculum, and other changes that resulted from the Education Reform

Act. Staff in further education have had to implement radical changes caused by college incorporation. And now, higher education is confronting comparable challenges, where various claims on behalf of quality in teaching and in research seem to be in increasing conflict with each other (*see*, for example, Nixon *et al.*, 1995).

The leaders – heads, principals, vice-chancellors and their senior staff – who may well share many reservations about imposed changes expressed by other staff, find themselves in the position of having to review their own values, and of having to make what Johnson (1992: 35) described as a *paradigm shift*. He defines the paradigm as 'a set of core beliefs which are specific and relevant to the organisation in which they (the managers) work and which are learned over time' (pp. 29–30). Yet he cautions that 'it would be a mistake to conceive of the paradigm as merely a set of beliefs removed from organisational action ... it is ... continually, if gradually, evolving.' The danger of the paradigm, Johnson believes, is that

> faced with pressures for change, managers are likely to deal with the situation in ways which are in line with the paradigm and the cultural, social and political norms of organisational life. This raises difficulties when managing strategic change, for it may be that the action required is outside the scope of the paradigm and ... members of the organisation would be required to change their core beliefs or 'the way we do things around here'.
>
> (p.33)

This is easier said than done. Change is threatening. Challenges to core beliefs can be regarded as a betrayal of values, while strong and continuing resistance to such challenges can result in what has come to be known as *strategic drift*. If the drift is to be halted, then it is likely that *paradigm shifts* will be necessary, and these are never easy to achieve. They may first of all require members of the organisation to question 'the way we do things around here', and require them to examine taken-for-granted assumptions.

Johnson feels there is little chance of achieving fundamental strategic change unless the *climate* for change exists. Moreover, the 'acceptance of such change is likely to depend upon 'a widely accepted perceived need for it, or a significant trigger for change such as crisis or major threat ... or the intervention of "outsiders"'.

Finding a strategic focus

Major threats and the intervention of 'outsiders' have forced change on every educational institution in the UK in recent years. Department for Education (DFE) and Funding Council circulars have regularly carried veiled (or in some case, plainly stated) threats, on the lines of 'conform and improve, or perish'. Central government intervention has forced paradigm shifts, since stakeholders have no choice but to review their practices, and we know of no sector of education in the UK which has escaped. Heads of institutions have had to develop new skills and to develop new structures which not only take account of institutional culture but which also enable action to be taken quickly in order to implement new regulations.

The fact that changes have been imposed on institutions in no way reduces the need for vision because, without it, planning becomes haphazard or disappears under the weight of day-to-day burdens. The need to examine and analyse core beliefs does not mean that all that is good must be thrown away. Trethowan (1991:13) urges educationists to:

> select from the traditions of the past those values and beliefs which help or at least do not hinder the implementation of the change. Identify them, praise them as being part of the previous tradition that will be retained. In destroying what was previously valued by a school, even if those values were not laudable, be careful not to leave the school without perceived values.

Murgatroyd and Morgan (1992: 31) place the responsibility for leading the institution into the next stage of its development squarely on the shoulders of managers, whose task it is 'to determine the strategic frame from within which the school wishes to operate and to be relentlessly successful in achieving the promise of this strategy. Strategies do not "just happen" or "emerge", they are managed. It takes vision, commitment, culture-building leadership, trust, empowerment and communication, to build a successful strategically focused organisation.'

An institution's vision of the future can be, and often is expressed in its mission statement, yet the processes in devising such statements are anything but straightforward. The easy way out is to provide what Stott and Walker (1992: 50) describe as 'endless and confusing lists of worthy aims, ideals and optimistic intentions, all based on a set of rather spurious educational aspirations', which are of little use in planning.

In their survey of the nature and use of mission statements in Singaporean schools, they reported 'the constant reference by respondents to worthy intentions, usually expressed in ambiguous terms, such as 'to inculcate moral values', 'the development of the mind', and 'to develop more self-stamina, a healthy self-image and self-responsibility for attainment' (p. 54). They question what purpose these statements could possibly serve in management terms, and comment particularly on the fact that many of the mission statements examined during the course of their survey appeared to have remained static for some years. They found this surprising, in view of the fact that substantial changes have been made in Singaporean education at primary and secondary level, which made 'the relevance of mission statements in these schools ... so low as to be an untenable claim' (p. 55).

Similar substantial changes have taken place in all sectors of UK education, yet it is likely that many mission statements will consist of vague, worthy but often ambiguous statements which in no way inform the strategic management of institutions. Peake (1994: 9) feels confident that:

> The clarification of mission is an important part of strategic analysis, and where strategic management is practised effectively within an organisation, it can be expected that the mission will become influential in guiding organisational action through the process of strategy implementation. It is likely, however, that strategic management is not yet widely practised within British further education at least, and that the mission statements of most colleges have failed to impact strongly on organisational processes.

DFE and Funding Council demands for more effective planning in schools, colleges, adult centres and universities appear now to be having an effect on the way mission statements express institutional vision and are linked to strategic management and analysis, though it is likely that there is some way to go. It is, in our view, a journey worth taking. Peake, in his review of the literature relating to institutional mission and its application to the management of further and higher education, concludes that:

> The mission process may be viewed … as a process which promotes planning, aids decision-making and communication, and also facilitates marketing and evaluation strategies. In short, the process may be viewed as a powerful method of promoting organisational change.

This view of a mission statement refutes empty rhetoric. It requires, right from the outset, a clearly disciplined approach to visualising and planning, which must take into direct account all the specific opportunities and constraints that a particular school or college faces, so that the statement becomes, itself, a framework for planning and a vehicle for action. Yet, Peake asks, does the notion of mission in practice live up to its aims?

> Maybe not. For example, if an institution's mission is conceived and written by a small group of senior mangers and never communicated to the rest of the employees, it is highly unlikely that the act of mission establishment will facilitate communication within the organisation, or contribute to the development of more open management.

Clearly, good communication involves much more than the efficient transmission of information from the centre. While good systems of this kind are commendable – they help to ensure that everyone knows, at least, what is expected of them – communication in the full sense is a multifaceted process of listening, consulting, empathising, negotiating, clarifying, modifying, re-directing, and many other things. The art of doing all this effectively may be elusive – but for a complex organisation, such as a modern school or college, it is essential for survival.

Peake makes a final point, that those who write mission statements must mean what they say:

> If the ideas and practices enshrined in a mission statement are not evidenced in the actions of management, it is unlikely that the statement will have much influence on decision-making processes. And if the statement is so bland as to be applicable to almost any organisation, it is not likely to assist the organisation very effectively in its marketing strategy.

To prepare a genuinely disciplined, clearly visualised mission statement (with a vision informed by values, and in the clear context of the here-and-now) is, in fact, the way to reclaim responsibility for the direction of a school or college. It will help to restore a sense of ownership to staff and all others, who may have been feeling (with varying degrees of justification) that their institution has been hi-jacked by political decrees. While educative leaders may feel, initially, that they cannot always act as they would wish, there is no such barrier to clear thinking and planning; these can, in turn, lead the way to self-determined action. The importance of the process cannot be over-estimated since, without it, the chance of ensuring that actions and priorities are directed to the achievement of the vision will recede.

CHAPTER TWO

Revaluing Leadership and Service in Educational Management

Bernard T. Harrison

This chapter works from a long debated question – about the relationship between individuals, their organisations, and their community – in order to examine some key terms such as 'power', 'teamwork' and 'quality'. I shall seek to apply these to good practice in modern educational management.

'The self cannot escape organisations'

– Thomas Greenfield (Greenfield and Ribbins, 1993: 54)

Managers live in a practical world. They are valued for the good things that they achieve and are criticised, rightly, for what they may fail to achieve. They work in a 'real' world – of turbulent flux in economic conditions, of continuing shifts in social policies, of unpredictable directions in moral and cultural patterns – in short, a world of irresistible change. While this will be readily acknowledged by educational managers as a fact of life, it is not to deny that vital educational *principles* are at stake in their work. School and college leaders need to be wise in many ways – social, psychological, historical, theoretical, professional, political and ethical, as well as 'streetwise' – if change in education is to be achieved with integrity and coherence. The force of this requirement to be variously wise will be seen in many of the chapters that follow – and, especially, perhaps, in Peter Ribbins' final chapter (20), on the experiences of headteachers, in enacting their lives in schools.

In order to identify *'what'* must be done in a school or college, and then to decide *'how'* achieving valued things must be done, managers need, through critical reflection, to examine regularly the *'why?'* of their actions. This will include, crucially, reflection on the values that underpin their efforts to achieve (Harrison; in Simkins, Ellison and Garrett, 1992: 273).

Greenfield and Ribbins ask us to remember (1993: 78) that schools and colleges are (like all social organisations) abstractions. Their buildings and fittings and people are material enough; yet schools themselves are not objective realities, but 'an ideological social order'. Greenfield would not, however, have agreed with a British Prime Minister of the 1980s who claimed that there is no such thing as society. On the contrary, he was deeply preoccupied by tensions between individual and organisational interests, and sought to redefine educational administration as a 'unified humane science' (Lakomski and Evers, 1994: 268; also Ribbins, 1994a: 218–22).

Greenfield's point about the nature of schools and colleges is fundamentally important for their managers. It reminds them that the values which govern their organisations are, like the organisations themselves, 'only an idea', and that ideas can be changed. Through individual ideas and actions, and through teamwork, managers can reshape their organisations, for better or worse. Their ideas, or vision, for the organisation can never be taken for granted as the 'right' ideas.

Since this is so, can management studies ever attain the status of a 'unified humane science'? Are they, after all, just one more political arena, at the mercy of the latest governmental or parental/communal pressures? Many leaders and researchers have made great efforts during the 1980s and 1990s, to develop educational management as a coherent discipline within educational studies, through drawing on a wide range of management theory and practice beyond education itself. Bottery (1994: 128–29), for example, notes the optimistic arguments of management experts – such as Peters and Waterman (1982), Drucker (1988b) and Handy (1990) – that an 'institutional isomorphism' has developed, between the management codes of commercial/industrial and of non profit-making organisations. Just as the non-profit sector accepts financial and market disciplines, so do commerce and industry promote collaboration, professionalism and equal opportunities in their management policies.

However, Bottery urges caution, in pointing to fundamental differences of aims that remain between profit-making companies, and those of other organisations. As far as educational organisations are concerned, Bottery challenges, in particular, the assumption that, in the interests of efficiency, the meanings of management should be imposed, without question, on their staff. He poses five questions:

• Is leadership really about the imposition of values?

• Does an organisation have the right to manipulate individuals through imposed visions, to achieve its goals?

- To what extent should management writers present the side of management uncritically?

- Has the management literature sold its soul by so frequently writing from the management perspective?

- What damage would school management do to schools, if they uncritically disseminate standard writing on management as 'good practice' for schools?

Commercial companies flourish on good profits, and fail if there are none. For other organisations, 'wealth creation' is more elusive to define. It might be argued – as Socrates, for example, argued – that education provides distinctive richness, through developing a critical consciousness in all individuals. Writing on the ethics of human action, Bradley (1962: 189) argued that those who have social duties (such as managing a school or college) cannot rely on a 'fixed code or rule of right'. They must develop their own moral sense, for '*unless* morals varied, there can be no morality'. Teacher–managers must therefore carry both a personal and team responsibility for their organisations, since 'personal morality and social institutions cannot exist apart and (in general) the better the one, the better the other' (p. 188). This implies a benign circle of individual/ social/moral links, where 'it would be ruinous to separate' the welfare of the organisation from the welfare of its individuals.

If this were to be applied to all organisations, national policy-makers who build economic policies, for example, on a market-led belief in the importance of 'real jobs' would need to remember that 'real people' in the community will be affected by their policies. Where education is concerned, Jon Nixon argues (*see* Chapter 18) that managers of schools and colleges who plan to provide a 'high-quality curriculum' need to take a great deal more into account than merely following government legislation on the curriculum. In all organisations, policy-makers and managers must work above all through a sense of all the people in the organisation, in order to create what Heifetz defines (in *Leadership Without Easy Answers*, 1994) as a 'holding environment', where people can gain confidence in handling change. This, I suggest, is the essential *service* that all good managers and leaders should aim to provide for their organisations.

The moral arts of judgement making

I have outlined, above, some reasons why leaders in education require a special blend of qualities, if they are to achieve change in education with integrity and coherence. Arguing on similar lines, Macpherson (1992: 290) examines what he calls the 'meta-values' of educational management. He identifies six 'distinctively different forms of leadership service': wise philosophical guidance; sophisticated strategic analysis; responsible political action; proactive cultural agency; responsive managerial services; and responsible evaluative activity. These may, of course, not be easy to apply – certainly, not all at the same time. Yet these are the high standards that should guide the thoughts of leaders and researchers in the field – and that includes contributors to this present book. To take just one example, Wilcox and Gray (in Chapter 14) provide a thoughtful overview of inspection processes in schools. They examine, through field research, the experience of teachers who have been involved with inspection visits by the English Office for Standards in Education (OFSTED); and they make important points about the need to scrutinise the values and practices of the inspectors. The 'responsible evaluative activity' on which that chapter is based demonstrates the importance of critical vigilance in educational management studies – which has special force, it may be argued, where powerful bodies such as OFSTED are concerned. Macpherson (1992), indeed, suggests (p. 290) that

> coherence can only come through power-sharing and a pragmatic holism ... we need to nurture new learning about the moral arts of judgement-making.

These 'moral arts' are practised through a critical–ethical approach to the actual world of actual management.

But what are critical ethics? Writing on 'the importance of critical ethics for the social sciences', Neumann (1982) sought to integrate a post-Kantian tradition of respect for the moral law (what one 'ought' to do) with a concern of the social sciences to understand human behaviour, and the 'everyday' morality that governs actual living (what one is actually found to be doing). This ancient problem confronts us all in our daily lives.

Neumann examined Kant's categorical imperative (that we should be able to justify all our actions in the name of universal law). He found Kant's formula to be irrefutable; yet it is too far removed from the cut-and-thrust of daily business to be much more than an 'empty formula' (p. 17), which can only find meaning through being applied to everyday actions. Neumann cites Fries, who sought to develop Kant's ideas by introducing principles of personal equality and dignity, on which to build a practical social code. Developing further this concern for workable laws, Neumann then suggests (p. 17) that Nelson's work (1949) on Socratic method addressed 'in more detail than Fries the problem of collision and conflict', in constructing 'situational ethics'.

However, Nelson, too, was detached from the everyday work of organisations, and emphasised individual rather than communal (or collegiate) integrity. He argued that values, no matter how universal they may seem, cannot be imposed without being changed; they can only be understood (this applies most obviously to views concerning personal and political freedom, whether 'liberal', 'socialist' or 'capitalist'). Following the critical–ethical method of Socrates, Nelson found that morality (laws), unlike facts, cannot be understood by observation, only by insight: 'Any command imposed by outside will is entirely beyond the range of our insights ... one ought because another wills it is a contradiction in terms' (1949: 68).

For Nelson, doing what we personally hold to be right overrides doing what we are told to do. It is an empowerment, strong enough to dislodge the absolute authority of enclosed systems of thought, such as ritualised religion, or logical positivism, or doctrinaire Marxism, or freemarket economics. This moral independence is, moreover, 'bound up with moral accountability' (p. 78), since critical ethics should provide the essential self-criticism that guards against self-pride (or taking yourself too seriously).

For Nelson, the moral life of an organisation – the state, a company, or a school – will flourish 'only when the independence of the ethical task is recognised' (p. 62). This robust view of the just individual confronting the unjust society may have had a clear appeal to an earlier generation of leader–managers, trade union bosses, or headteachers, who were expected to act as 'great people', and whose uncompromising individuality was taken to be an indicator of their great authority. Yet, following Nelson's (or Socrates') line of thought, what happens when the just individual meets another just individual or – even more difficult – a just group, who disagrees with her/him?

When the question is put this way it suggests that the Socratic version of critical ethics must lead to an inevitable confrontation of simply opposed views. This is of little use to a modern educational organisation, dedicated to a real (not contrived) collegiality and to developing synergism through teamwork. A more useful way of examining complex patterns of diverse viewpoints would be through the influential conceptual framework of *communicative action*, as proposed by Habermas (1984). In identifying the pitfalls of choosing only between an individual, encapsulated 'subjectivism' on the one hand, and socially prescribed 'obligation of consensus' (p. 341) on the other, Habermas argued for the use of 'communicative' (as opposed to 'instrumental') reason (p. 398). He claimed: 'A subjectivity that is characterised by communicative reason resists the denaturing of itself for the sake of self-preservation'. This version of a proper subjectivity refers neither to a self-preserving individual self, nor to a self-maintaining social system, 'but to a symbolically structured life world that is constituted in the interpretative accomplishments of its members and only reproduced through communication' (p. 398).

This statement could lead, of course, to a further important (if not fashionable) question: who constructs, changes and demolishes the basic symbols of that life-world, if communication only 'reproduces' these? Is there still a place here, perhaps, for the 'great' innovative scientist/ artist/philosopher who works, alone, at frontiers of meaning? For present purposes, however, it is enough to acknowledge the emphasis placed by Habermas on communicative reason and action, where schools and colleges are concerned. To return to Neumann: while recognising the strength of Nelson's ethics, Neumann recognised, too, that 'it does not do justice to the fact that individual social action is embedded in society as a whole' (p. 23). Nelson's position needed to be tempered with an infusion of sociological role theory, and Neumann proposed his own amendment to the moral law: 'do not impose on anybody roles which you could not also accept if they were your own'. This precept, further modified for practical purposes, might help to bridge the 'ought' – 'is' gap, between moral law and actual codes of living. In conclusion, Neumann applied his proposal for a sociology of ethics to a critical interrogation of the free market economy, and the 'axiom of self-interest' which he discerned at the heart of its values.

We may see more clearly, now, that Neumann's version of a socially infused critical ethics provided a means to challenge narrow market forces policies that have been imposed on education in the 1980s and 1990s. If British academic and professional leaders in education had argued more robustly against these, then the disproportionate influence on education of, for example, the government-backed Centre for Policy Studies might have been averted. Courage, tenacity and skill – both individual and communal – are needed, in any struggle to accomplish revaluations in the management of education. While educational leaders can never be certain that they are right, they cannot avoid the risk of conflict. Writing on hermeneutics, Ricoeur (1991: 98) declared:

> It is because absolute knowledge is impossible that the conflict of interpretation is insurmountable and inescapable. Between absolute knowledge and hermeneutics, it is necessary to choose.

It is we who confer meaning on things. Those who would see knowledge as 'objective' and who hold that events 'exist and have their character independently of human thought, will face a problem with scientific study of meaning' (Tiles, 1987: 45). This was made clear in Bartlett's seminal work on *Remembering* (1932), which demonstrated the processes of understanding, whereby a living being *organises* all its past experiences into meaning. Bartlett's aphoristic summary of this – 'effort after meaning' – underlined how meaning is not given, but it is made. Each of Bartlett's terms have their Greek counterpart – *nisus* (effort) and *telos* (meaning) – which evoke Socratic modes of critical investigation as a crucial process of discovery.

Writing on the heuristic philosophy of Polanyi, Gelwick (1977: 151) suggested that, in a world where nothing can be final, humanity must seek satisfaction through facing 'its responsibility to seek the truth even when the enterprise seems to be one that is impossible or mistaken'. Educational leaders in the 1990s may find some bleak comfort in this view, given the often conflicting pressures on them to 'deliver' high-quality education to disparate interest groups (*see* Mike Bottery's discussion of this, in Chapter 4). Humanity's problem – and the problem, in turn, of educational organisations – is, suggests Gelwick (p.152), essentially one of 'historical consciousness and authority', where a belief in scientific certainties has led to a fear of intellectual venture in the face of risk. Thus it is that tyranny of fixed ideas, imposed by government or other power groups, can reduce human enterprise to the calculus of mechanics and a one-level ontology.

Revaluing educational leadership

In a critical study of values in educational management, Greenfield (1991: 201) examined the 'moral complexity that flows inevitably through administrative action'. Greenfield invoked Hodgkinson (1978: 5) – 'the intrusion of values into the decision-making process is not only inevitable, it is the very substance of decision' – to support his attack (p. 212) on the 'devalued and technocratic science called "managerialism"'. Following Scott (1985) he identified the need for educational leaders to be concerned with *fair opportunities* (against material poverty), *essential equality* (against divisions of class, gender or race), *a climate of creativity* (against cultural poverty), and *a respect for intellectual honesty* (against the corruption of ideas in academic and professional life). Finally, in proposing the school as a 'crux of value', he declared – echoing Hodgkinson (1991) – that the administration of education is a 'moral art', which involves 'will and power; of bending others to one's will and of being bent in turn by others' (p. 214). Although he endorsed a principle of hierarchy in leadership, Greenfield also acknowledged the impermanence of all values, with their flux of 'complexities, their dilemmas and their unrelenting challenge' (p. 215). He allows, then, as did Neumann (1982), that educational leaders need to exercise some form of principled flexibility, decisions and take 'right' actions. In short, they cannot simply 'act by the book'; their work is too important for that and, in any case, there is no reliable 'book' to direct them.

Just how difficult their actual work is, in practice, may be highlighted by looking at three familiar management terms: *power, teamwork* and *quality*. While one might, for example, agree with Shotter (1984: 167), that 'the world of everyday life is a moral world, which works in terms of people's rights and duties', such principles are easier to declare than to apply. In the heat of the management kitchen, it is through direct dealings with people and with critical issues, that thinking managers are forced to acknowledge gaps between principles (what they ought to do) and practice (what they are found to do).

Even definitions for the three selected management terms (above) can be tantalisingly elusive. Where 'power', for example, is concerned, an interview with a headteacher (reported in Chapter 15 of this book) revealed her suspicions about 'open management'. She thought there was a danger that this could involve an abdication of her powers of leadership; yet subsequent observations of her in action with her senior management team revealed her full commitment in practice to consultative management. Recognising a familiar problem here, linguists propose a useful distinction between *denotations* (meanings) and *connotations* (associations and values) that speakers attach to words. If we wish to open up critical enquiry, it may be that, rather than insisting on fixed and final definitions, we should be sensitive to the many denotations and connotations that terms such as 'power', teamwork' or 'quality' may accumulate in a range of disciplinary, social, gender, professional or cultural contexts. To illustrate, I offer a brief and highly selective note on each of them.

Power as 'enabling'

'Power' is, perhaps, the most emotive and elusive of management terms. For present purposes I wish to link a value-statement about power (the Promethean view, that power should be about empowerment), with the actual experience of women staff in primary schools (where most teachers are female, even though the ratio of female to male headteachers is far smaller).

Compare these two examples of staffroom talk in different primary schools:

(a) This is a very, very happy school and you feel you can make a mistake without being jumped on. There is a lot of support and if something goes wrong they will help you sort it out.

(b) We are guarded, you have to watch what you say. We all know the Head's failings and we worry what gets reported back. We said we would all support each other in staff meetings. There was an INSET day about 3 years ago, which was supposed to be a role play to let us talk about the problems in the school. It was a catastrophe, I think it was supposed to bring out the character of the staff but it was terrible, it all went wrong and there was no debriefing.
  – quoted in the Report *Effective Management in Schools*, commissioned by the United Kingdom Department for Education (Bolam *et al.*, 1993: 66–67).

How can these contrasting staffroom views be explained? In one case a teacher expresses unqualified approval of a successful management team; in the other, a teacher discloses her anxieties about being 'guarded' in the staffroom, and condemns the head's ineffective attempts to improve staff relations. Writing on the specific concerns of women in management, Natasha Josefowitz (1980) proposed an alternative version of 'power' which had wide impact on management studies in the 1980s. Against traditional, patriarchal notions of power as masterfulness, she emphasised that the powerful manager is one who enables others to be effective in organisations. Furthermore, it 'included the idea of granting more autonomy to those with less power' (p.4). Her accounts of women in management provided a comprehensive rejection of the 'great man' (or, indeed, 'great woman') view of leadership.

The gender-aware insights of Josefowitz into the nature of power were shared, among others, by Beth Kanter (1983, 1989) and Don Mixon (1989), whose study of power and obedience concluded with a rejection of the tyranny of the 'Divine King'. To contrast authoritarian with consultative management is not simply a matter of interchangeable management 'styles', but to identify two fundamentally opposed views of human society, and of social power. Put in its most simple form, each individual, each organisation and each community must choose between an autocratic, or democratic course. The conditions for successful democracy will depend on whether organisations can operate an effective *critical ethics* and a *principled flexibility*, in developing all the talents of all the members of an organisation.

The two contrasting glimpses of primary school staffroom experiences (above) may suggest that some schools are doing this, while others are failing. The National Commission on Education (1993: 340) suggested that a well-designed educational system 'will encourage professional teachers and trainers, and also educationalists, to contribute to the running of the system'. It found, however, that:

> We are struck by the extent to which German and French education systems place responsibility on the shoulders of professional teachers. It contrasts sharply with the mood of distrust of the professionals that has grown in this country in recent years, not without government encouragement.

To sum up: enlightened leadership aims to exercise power, through releasing the creative powers of all who are in the organisation. Where education is concerned, professional effectiveness depends on the empowerment of professional teachers.

Realising through teamwork

Critical ethics involve an understanding of how things are, a vision of how they should be, and a dialectic among all those involved, on how to achieve the vision. These processes are familiar throughout modern studies of management and leadership. They are examined, for example, through Kanter's robust views on collaborative modes of interaction

(1983, 1989); in Bottery's (1992, 1994) accounts of professional, as opposed to bureaucratic processes in educational and other organisations; in the work of Wallace and Hall (1994a; 1994b) on consultative management, at both school and interschool/college levels; and in later chapters of this present book (*see*, especially, 5 and 15).

The vast amount of writing on teamwork in management (and such allied terms as communication, negotiation, interpersonal processes, staff/work relations, collaboration and so on) reveals comparably huge variations of views and approaches. All human progress depends on teamwork, yet students of its processes have to admit that, when one person talks to another, 'the process is so complicated that it is a wonder that anyone understands or is understood' (Cohen *et al.*, 1976: 169).

Yet teamwork in management must justify itself through clear decisions and delivery of programmes. It depends on both a strong individual and also communal purpose. As Pfeffer (1992: 7) emphasised, 'problems of implementation are, in many instances, problems in developing political will and expertise'. The skills needed for effective action need not, suggests Pfeffer, be exercised in an overbearing or 'charismatic' way. Indeed, it is more likely that success is achieved through submerging one's own personality through teamwork, to achieve organisational aims. While managers must complete impersonal tasks of planning, implementing and monitoring policy, they achieve these in the give-and-take of a personal world, which require their whole attention.

There was much work in earlier decades on 'conflict' management, which was derived from political and social conflict theory. Westen (1985: 241), for example, drew on Durkheim, Weber and Marx, to argue that the directly conflicting needs of self and society 'are the stuff of which moral conflict is made'. This present chapter has, however, invoked Neumann's critical ethics, and Habermas's theory of communicative reason, to propose a solution to the apparent dilemma of irreconcilable conflict between self-needs and social needs. In a spirit of communicative reason, Hogg and Abrams (1988:218) concluded their study of intergroup relations with a notion of 'social identity'. This aims to circumvent inevitable individual – social conflict:

> By avoiding the reduction of groups to individuals, it allows us to conceptualize the relationship between individual and society, and to place theoretically the group within the individual.

While it would be foolish not to expect and even to welcome conflict, critical ethics would argue that this ought not to be first purpose of teamwork. This 'ought' is based on nothing else than complete respect for working colleagues, even though conflict of viewpoint may require us to focus on what really 'is', when working with others. It takes time, of course, to integrate the 'ought' with the 'is', when making decisions. The acronym TEST MATCH might help to summarise some essential advice for teams:

TIME	to
EXAMINE	proposals
SHARE	planning
TEST	the programme
MONITOR	progress and
ACHIEVEMENTS	of the
TEAM	then
CONSULT	and prepare to
HEAD	the next programme

In this way, the well-crafted bat of teamwork, rather than cudgel of conflict, ensures that 'when we throw up an idea and give it a little knock, it might ... *travel*' (as a character suggests in Tom Stoppard's play, *The Real Thing*).

To sum up: teamwork requires a 'heterarchy' of professionals, to replace traditional 'hierarchies' in schools and colleges. This involves a relocation of authority, throughout each member of the team, and the manager's special responsibility is to ensure that this is taken through to successful conclusions.

Quality management in education

A concern for 'quality' in human activity is as old as invention itself; it is, arguably, a basic requirement that governs the evolution of all species. Yet a newcomer to management studies might be forgiven for assuming that it had just been invented, given the proliferation in the 1990s of whole books and journals devoted to issues of quality management. These concerns have spread rapidly into educational management following, for example, West-Burnham's claim (1992: v) that 'issues of quality and service are the major management concerns for all organisations in the 1990s'.

An obvious breaker to this huge new wave would be to assert that educational staff have pursued high standards in education for many years. If only for this reason, we may share West-Burnham's prediction that issues of quality will remain prominent in the future. The quest to improve quality is a prominent recurring theme in this present book, and the term is directly addressed by Mike Bottery (in Chapter 4) and Judith Bell (16).

I suggested earlier that Neumann's version of critical ethics (1982: 20) might provide an alternative view to that 'axiom of self-interest' which is at the heart of ethics of the free market economy (*see*, also, Harrison,

1992). Given the haste with which 'quality' mechanisms have been introduced by educational managers in the 1990s, the meanings that have become attached to the term 'quality' provide an especially appropriate focus for critical–ethical scrutiny.

In his chapter (4), and also in his book *Lessons for Schools?* (1994) Bottery examines how, in enterprise terms, quality is concerned with customer orientation. To simplify, this may be seen in manufacturing terms of 'fit for the purpose', or in public sector terms of 'meeting and exceeding customer requirements'. Yet Bottery's chapter explores some problematic aspects of 'quality' control (which are illustrated most blatantly in, for example, crude 'league tables', that compare unweighted examination performances) and, at another extreme, an over-complex 'bureaucratic process of compliance to a system' (Ryan, 1992: 10). Jenkins (1991: 101), an enthusiast for 'stressing quality', also warned:

> There is a distinct danger that the more extensive and intricate the method of quality management, the more teachers are involved in activities which are draining their energies away from the key tasks of teaching and developing their learning.

Yes, as Judith Bell argues in Chapter 16, quality is an inescapable management issue; we must all be able to show that we *'are* self-critical and *do* consider procedures that are appropriate for the maintenance of quality.'

Once we accept that quality is a management issue, we can proceed to set up a sensible and disciplined framework to monitor quality. Here, the recent history of quality management provides useful lessons. West-Burnham (1992a), for example, traced the 50-year-old history of the Total Quality Management (TQM) movement, stemming from the post-war reconstruction of Japan, and influencing the remarkable success of Japanese enterprise since then. Jenkins (1991: 105) proposed the 'three MU's' – *Muda* (waste), *Muri* (strain) and *Mura* (discrepancy) – 'as criteria for examining situations within a school in terms of their complexity'. This return to Japanese origins of quality management is taken further by Bottery (1992), in a thoughtful chapter on 'What can we learn from the Japanese?'. He examined the attractions of their *ringi* system of consensus-based, 'bottom-up' decision-making, and of their 'quality-circle' mechanism. This involves regular meetings of small teams, which aim to 'increase efficiency, improve product quality and improve communication' (p.138). Bottery accepts that there are things that might be learned here, by Western education; he also counsels caution, though, since Japanese systems, whose roots are intertwined with its own unique culture, 'would almost certainly not respond to simple transportation' (p. 146). Even so, this cannot be an excuse for failing to try.

To sum up: issues of value are at the heart of quality issues. In the search for good frameworks of quality assurance and control, managers need to avoid either simplistic 'quick-fix' approaches, or over-complex bureaucratic procedures.

To conclude

In a world of profound social change, those who work in educational management must work out their values and build their own frameworks for successful schools and colleges. This is achieved through the distinctive leadership and the distinctive service that educational managers provide. To support them in their work, they have much to learn from other cultures. Yet they cannot simply 'lift' ideas from commerce, or Japan, or elsewhere. A critical ethical approach will help us to develop, inspect and, when needed, dismantle values and frameworks for our schools and colleges – for, while we cannot work without values and frameworks, we need to remember that these, too, are only provisional and are always in flux.

(This chapter is an extensively revised version of a paper that was first published in *Educational Management and Administration* (Harrison, 1994). Thanks and acknowledgements are due to the editor and to the British Educational Management and Administration Society (BEMAS), for kind permission to draw from copyright material in the journal.)

CHAPTER THREE

Constructing the Vision: Changing the Culture

Ian McNay

In this chapter I want to develop several models to stimulate and structure reflections on the nature of an organisation: its values and operating norms; its strategies and structures; its cultures and leadership; and its commitment to changing and learning as an organisation. I shall also point to dangers of diversion from, or even corruption of, the ideal, and ask why it isn't how it 'should' be. Most of the models have been developed in my research and organisation development work in further and higher education, but I also use examples from other sectors to illustrate their applicability.

Basic values

Clark (1983) identified four basic values which can underpin systems of higher education: liberty, social justice, loyalty, and competence:

- *Liberty* he sees as linking concepts such as 'choice, initiative, innovation, criticism and variety' with democratic values raising expectations of individuality within a society and an emphasis on self-expression – the peak of Maslow's hierarchy of needs (Maslow, 1954). There are strong echoes of the arguments on academic freedom within institutions and on institutional autonomy within national systems (Russell, 1993). Freire's (1972) concept of adult education as emancipatory also fits here.
- *Social justice* involves equality and equity for students, staff, and sectors of systems. If liberty implies variety, here we find 'equal but different', at least in the best forms. There is fairness, even handedness, and, perhaps, positive action to redress previous lack of fairness. These values underpin the access movement in Britain.
- *Loyalty* aligns with Freire's concept of education for domestication. It ties

education closely to the state, its survival and development on terms defined often without reference to education, which is seen as a servant of the polity and the economy (HMSO, 1987).

● *Competence*, too, will be tied to stated aims by government in relation to the supply of qualified personnel in relevant fields, though Clark also linked it to academic competence and a meritocratic élite setting standards of excellence.

Organisational forms

Clark was writing about systems of provision, and I have given a truncated version of his arguments. I wish to link his four values to organisational forms and cultures, using Weick's (1976) concept of loosely-coupled structures as a starting point. Weick was writing about schools, and described an organisation which had considerable local self-determination with few, if any, lateral linkages among units and even less interdependency; controls from the 'centre' were general and lightly exercised. My work has used concepts of tightness/looseness to develop four organisational types as in Figure 3.1.

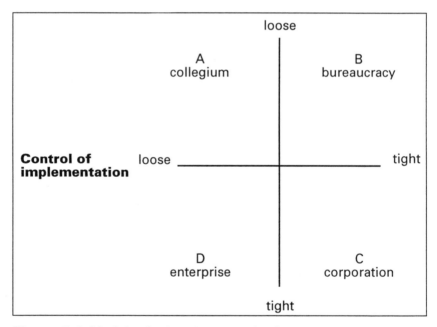

Figure 3.1 Models of education organisations

The alignment with Clark's values is as follows:

A	liberty	collegial academy
B	social justice/equality	bureaucracy
C	loyalty	corporation
D	competence	enterprise

There is not a total congruence. Clark puts excellence within D; I see a need for rigour and relevance and so put it as an AD combination.

I have developed aspects of the model elsewhere (McNay, 1995a,b). Let me try to encapsulate the essence of my four labels before moving to my prime concern, which is to examine the way they condition implicit or explicit values, set cultural norms for behaviours and procedures and therefore influence the way the institutional vision is formed. Later I shall link them to a model of change:

- *The collegial academy* is the classic concept of a university, with autonomous academics operating in 'secret gardens'. Departments had a strong discipline base, professors were powerful (and not necessarily democratic). Individual networking was strong, with linkages outside the institution to an invisible college of peer scholars often being more important than internal loyalty.

- *The bureaucracy* (with hints of hierarchy) is not necessarily an unconditional evil, which is the image it has collected. Having a constitution and rules of procedure can be efficient, in avoiding the need to treat every situation as novel. Regulations can set standards of behaviour required now by institutional audit and underlie quality standards. Committees are arenas for dealing with the exceptions, for resolving conflict and for setting precedents for future reference.

- *The corporate model* provides strong leadership from the top: the senior management team supported by advisory working parties controls policy development, and by financial and other devices controls the delivery of activities and services. The development of pro-vice chancellor roles can be seen as academics recapturing control lost to the administrators (Fielden, 1975), though when those appointed to such posts lack professional training, they may become bureaucratic and managerialist, especially when they operate as *de facto* heads of functional areas in a fragmented administrative support service.

- *In the enterprise*, within a defined policy, operations are delegated to project teams (such as research, teaching, consultancy, recruitment, continuing education) along agency lines equivalent to government quangos. They are there to exploit market opportunities in a flexible, cost-conscious way. This box can also be seen in curricular terms, as giving customer consciousness to the collegial academy, since it develops student-centred learning or partnerships in learning with other entities.

These four forms within institutions mirror externalities. The collegial academy has already been identified with the invisible college – controls are via external examiners or peer review. At school level in the UK there used to be *local* decisions about appropriate English texts, balance of subjects offered and so on. Those in Box B within institutions would relate most readily to regulatory bodies such as the Business and Technology Education Council (BTEC), National Council of Vocational Qualifications (NCVQ) or School Curriculum and Assessment Authority (SCAA) in curriculum terms. There is now a national, standardised school curriculum, or at least a core. There are grading controls on school-related Examination Boards, and rules on the balance of course work within assessment.

The power culture (Handy, 1993) of Box C means that ministers use 'campaign' policy-making – through announcements at conferences followed up, if necessary, by legislation. A Higher Education Funding Council for England (HEFCE) former chief executive has denied that the Council had a policy role, or even a steering function; yet each institution had closely prescribed recruitment targets – Maximum Aggregate Student Numbers (MASNs) – which, inevitably, defined policy on growth, access and balance of provision, especially when accompanied by financial sanctions for over- or under-recruiting. Institutions were in a lose-lose situation, because policy *and* implementation were both tightly controlled, despite claims by ministers and senior civil servants (Holland, 1993) to have 'rolled back the frontiers of the state' and given freedom of decision making to the lowest possible level. Although grants to universities and colleges are mainly general, they are derived by transparent formulae and, therefore, all funding is seen as specifically linked to particular activities. Supplementary funding has all been specific and used to re-orient provision by successive marginal changes.

The move to quadrant D, the enterprise, is seen in the corporate status given to polytechnics, further education and sixth form colleges, and grant maintained schools, who are now free to lose money and be closed down because of a 'free' competitive market. On the curriculum side, Technical and Vocational Education Initiatives (TVEI), City Technology Colleges (CTCs), Enterprise in Higher Education (EHE), General National Vocational Qualifications (GNVQs) and numerous other initiatives lend support to a competence-based conformist culture in the guise of enterprise skills.

I detect, then, a trend from AB to CB to CD, at both system and institutional level. This perception is widely shared, as work with diverse groups has shown. Other countries show different patterns: the emergent post-communist countries go from BC to AD. This shift affects the balance of contributions to decisions on institutional mission policy and strategy, as gatekeepers in different quadrants draw on different external stakeholders and environmental changes to argue their case.

Strengths and weaknesses: conflict, corruption, conditioning

Each quadrant, if dominant, has strengths and weaknesses. Handy (1993) identifies some in his four cultures which can be aligned with those already treated:

person	A	(collegium)
role	B	(bureaucracy)
power	C	(corporation)
task	D	(enterprise)

The *person culture* can be innovative, committed, dynamic, but lacks focus and organisation. It is dependent on key people but, as long as they are content in their work context, their intrinsic motivation and personal professional standards will ensure the quality of what they do. It may not, however, easily 'fit' with institutional and system levels (Becher and Kogan, 1992), and it is wrong to base government policy on a belief that a fit can be forced in a Procrustean way by bribes, threats or penalties.

The role culture is secure. There is a place for everything and a procedure to put things in their place. It is fine in a stable environment and in a 'batch-process' mode, where successive cohorts of pupils/students are processed through a well-regulated routine. It is not a quality system: performance beyond prescribed role levels can be disruptive of the 'normal' and threatening to the average, satisfactory masses. It is also slow to change because due process takes time.

The power culture, by contrast, is made for crisis, and the charismatic leader. It can effect radical change but is dependent on the quality of leadership as to whether the change is the right one. It can function well in small paternalistic organisations with strong employee loyalty, but is less good with large, diverse organisations. Here the leader moves from the kind of shepherd who leads and whose sheep follow, confident in his voice, to the British model which drives from behind and needs a staff with a crook on it and two dogs to help.

The task culture is team based and adaptable but unstable. It may be good at initiating projects but commitment to maintenance can be poor as many academic course teams have experienced. Creativity and novelty are the drives; this may then neglect quality and durability. That is fine for products with short life cycles, such as bespoke short courses but, for these, the planning/delivery ratio is uneconomic. The competitive nature of the team in a market can also turn inward when resources are tight and lead to conflict, not co-operation.

The four cultures may be appropriate to different activities in a diverse organisation such as a college or university. I have already identified B (bureaucracy) with standard award courses, and D (enterprise) with continuing education; A (collegium) is a research culture, C (corporation) is transformational – but will not be tolerated for long without alienation and anomie.

Each also contains the seeds of corruption. The autonomy of the *collegial academy* can degenerate to anarchy, unchecked freedom, licence. The restricted reference group can lead to comfortable conservatism in curriculum and research domains reinforced by cronyism within procedures for assessment. Certain cliques can capture resources for research and resist new approaches which challenge them. Staff in B (*bureaucracy*) can project their own values and knowledge on to the rest of the world, assuming in their judgements – on students for instance – that all are familiar with the small print of regulations. Regulation becomes rigidity, and a commitment to common standards becomes a defence of standardisation. For those in C, (*corporation*), political manoeuvring can become pervasive, where image is more important than reality. There is also, again, a restricted reference group to outside opinion formers. The membership of corporation boards of governors defines this and leads to values being inappropriately imported from foreign domains of business and commerce, when the 'real worlds' to be served are much wider. There is little accountability beyond governors, which can lead to disastrous results. The 'buzz' from crisis management may lead to the need for a creation of constant (false) crises to allow senior staff their regular 'fix'.

In the *enterprise* quadrant the importance of students and the income they bring can lead to grade inflation; to ghettos for overseas students following second-rate courses, yet paying top-rate fees. The commitment to relevance can lead to instrumentalism and the discarding of underlying hard theory in favour of short term rote learning of procedures. Or, as has happened in some parts of the world, a combination of B and D puts professors into paddy fields to keep them in touch with 'reality'.

There can be conflict between the cultures, too, especially those in opposite quadrants. The flexible quick response in negotiating with clients in D cannot be regulated from B, yet many universities try to do exactly that, setting three levels of approval as requirements before a contract can be concluded, or requiring the committee cycle to roll inexorably on until it can consider an urgent proposal. Often, too, staff in A want to pursue work not supported by senior staff in C: in one survey conducted by my Centre, on international activity, over 30% of staff said that what they did was in conflict with institutional policy (most said their institution had no clear policy!).

The best balance may be to operate differentially for different activities, and to condition behaviour in one quadrant by its neighbours. So academic activities in A should benefit from the relevance and customer consciousness of D, and should accept the need for corporate concern expressed through the procedures of B. Correspondingly those in B should not lose sight of their reason for existence – to support and serve activities in A. Equally, the tendency to cut all budgets either shows a lack of judgement or a cowardly failure to exercise it in determining priorities which come from C. The power exercised in the political frame of C needs to be informed by professional administrators from B to avoid illegality. Part-time amateurs as clerks to governing bodies are a recipe for a crisis that even this culture cannot control. The need for delegation to D means some acceptance of different interpretations of mission. Those in D should recognise the collective mission on which they operate, and their accountabilities internally, as well as their proactivity externally. They also need the quality renewal of their service products from A to ensure continuing customer satisfaction. Currently, there is a widespread problem of over-concentration on a C culture, where senior managers are separated from those active in A, subordinate those in B, and give too little supervision and support to D, where the dangers of 'mission drift' (and vision drift) are, perhaps, greatest. Under pressure, and with the isolation of the institution from previous influences, a bunker mentality can develop in the Senior Management Team.

Planning for change

If agreement on values determines *why* managers do things, and the recognition of norms shows *how* they behave – severally and collectively – within an organisation, the question still arises: *what* do you do? What *should* you do? Here another kind of vision is required: an imaginative vision with a capacity, like a helicopter, to rise above the daily mundanity and see the organisation in the context of the flow of events; indeed, to see those events as they unroll and to predict (not project – there are too many discontinuities) what might happen. Leaders develop scenarios, and appropriate responses to be called on when the need arises.

The process of change

Planning is often focused on *products*, and others in this collection look at some approaches. Here I want to look at some models of the change process, some key factors to consider for success, and at reasons for failure.

The first question is *how much* change? My colleague, John Davies, has developed a useful model (Davies, 1992), on to which I superimpose one drawn from Becher and Kogan (1992) to give labels to the four boxes (Figure 3.2). Davies asks how far the change permeates the institution and how systematic is the support given to it; that's an *internal* model. Becher and Kogan plot responses to *external* pressures and have four categorisations. Both of these sit fairly comfortably on top of my four 'cultures' developed earlier. The stimulus for change in A and D is likely to be internal; in B and C the impact of external factors is likely to be more dominant, or be given more prominence.

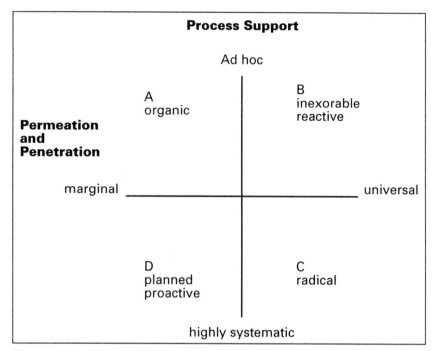

Figure 3.2 Change: scope and process (Adapted from Davies (1992) and Becher and Kogan (1992).)

Each of the four boxes has, then, different process characteristics. The first, A, is informal, individually based with few procedures. Personal networks may develop to spread ideas by 'infection', but there are few incentives offered by the corporate institution and market intelligence is likely to be weak: personal commitments/ideologies, or 'hunches', or small-scale experience drive innovations at a local, constrained level.

Under B, change has a higher profile: there is high opportunity and general encouragement to adapt, with freedom as to the mode of response – a recognition of academic autonomy. There is still an unsystematised information system, a failure to explore links with core mission, a benign framework for change with confused structures, uneven support – often decisions are 'no' after development rather than 'yes' before the effort is dedicated to it.

Radical change is led from the centre (or top depending on your images; Wilson, 1994). There may well be specialist central offices and officers. Mission links will be strong; there will be search, too, for synergy between activities. Strong incentives will be based on rigorous monitoring of emergent markets which, in turn, will demand good management information systems (MIS) for investment and, later, evaluation decisions.

That corporatist approach cannot be developed instantly: quadrant D may be a more attractive location for those seeking for some focus and clarity. Here, selected developments, tested against the mission, and linked to core business will be sponsored, to move the organisation's perceived profile and develop unique selling points. One might be music as a curriculum strength in a secondary school; in higher education it might be a former polytechnic developing a small number of research nodes to develop a research culture in certain areas. That is certainly true in my own university, whereas on other issues we are in other boxes: on modularisation in C, on open learning A (with hints of B), on internationalisation in B (with hints of C).

One issue in B was highlighted by work done recently on internationalisation (McNay, 1994). In surveying staff in institutions I was amazed to find that many institutions had a policy with hardly any definition and in over 30% the work being done by activitists was in conflict with the wishes of senior management, and in most of the rest there was consent of an instrumental, calculative kind rather than full-hearted collective commitment. There was no congruence between policies, plans and practices. This reinforces the point I made earlier about the SMT becoming separated from the rest of the organisation in the corporation.

To explore the need for integrated processes, I suggest four models, each of which has four points. The first model links four S factors – *strategy, systems support, staff support*, and *structures*. Its main message is that all four have to develop together: progress is at the rate of the slowest and neglect of one can make the whole project collapse. Too often, strategists may race ahead without exploring the consequences at the implementation stage.

As an example, some years ago a university vice-chancellor decided to devolve budgets to departments; in the next 2 years there was an accrued deficit of over £4 million. The MIS systems did not give heads of department good data to monitor commitments and cash flow; staff had not been trained sufficiently to handle new responsibilities, and, I believe, the department was the wrong structural unit for such an exercise in relation to other support systems.

The second model was developed during work for the Further Education Unit (McNay, 1988), which revealed discontinuties in development planning. In many colleges there was no connection between curriculum development, staff development, management development, and policy development, so that the first and last might well not match, and the competences for either of them were not developed in the middle two. Nobody seemed to identify the need for linkage or ask questions about congruence, coherence or consistency.

The third model was developed by Davies and Morgan (1983). It identifies four phases in policy-making to introduce change:

1. *The 'garbage can'* – There is lack of problem definition; there are

people with pet solutions, others who protect their own interests with closed minds, and a lack of an agreed language to reinforce poor communication.

2. *Negotiative/political* – Where a few key figures accept ownership, put shape to the issues, discuss, consult, bargain, and compromise.

3. *Legitimation* – When the outcome of the previous stage comes out in to the open to a superficially democratic collegiality; guidelines for action and implementation are agreed; and agents to do this are identified.

4. *Bureaucratisation* – Executive action in an agreed framework; minor adjustments in the light of experience.

The point here is that, normally, all four stages need to be completed. Any attempt to rush from (1) to (4) meets strong resistance; the issue bounces back to phase 1, and progression past that the second time round is made more difficult. In general, time spent on phases 1 and 2 can mean not only a quicker resolution in the end, but a better solution, and one with greater acceptance and ownership.

That is reflected at the individual level, too. Change is threatening to people's security; it often means giving up things which are familiar and comfortable. Managers, therefore, need to be bereavement counsellors in helping other staff to work through four stages of mourning: denial of reality, resistance to change, exploration of a new way of being and commitment to the future. Again, the process cannot be rushed.

Why doesn't it work? Learning to change

In education, we are bad at learning to change. In a collection edited by Susan Weil (1994) one head of an institution after another recounts their experience of introducing change from the top. They show that after 3 years or more of effort and painful experience they have learned some of the lessons that this chapter sketches. Robin Middlehurst (1993) identifies the anti-learning cults in the culture of education, where professional development programmes are for everybody but us:

1. The cult of the gifted amateur (any intelligent, educated individual can undertake the task – in our case, leadership – without training).

2. The cult of heredity (those with natural talent will emerge since they are born to the task; leadership is an art and therefore unteachable).

3. The cult of deficiency (training is essentially remedial or for those who are personally ineffective; 'training is for the second eleven' as one pro-vice chancellor put it).

4. The cult of inadequacy (once qualified, loss of face is involved by admitting gaps in one's knowledge or competence).

5. The cult of the implicit (development takes place by gradual induction into the norms and operations of academe; learning by osmosis is the hallmark of success).

6. The cult of selection (the selection of good staff will ensure good performance and will obviate the need for – and the cost of – development).

7. The cult of the intellectual (there is no scientific basis to 'management' – therefore it does not deserve to be taken seriously).

There are other reasons for failure to change:

- change overload and fatigue;

- lack of status or power for change agents who are given responsibility without resources;

- poor follow-through, where initiating change is more exciting, and probably more rewarding, than implementing it, so that impetus is lost;

- lack of ownership which reinforces that, and flows from failure in the partnership at the planning stage.

Leaders make change *wanted*; managers make it *happen*; other staff make it *work*. The links between these three make it a joint operation and all are equally important. That is a lesson still to be learned in one modern university with which I have worked, where it was claimed that 'all new ideas come from here' – the corridor with the offices of the senior management team. The team could not understand, then, why such excellent policies were failing at the implementation stage. They blamed others: I suggested that they look at 'the beam in their own eye'.

There are more general reasons, relating to the culture of the institution where things may go wrong, or decline from a previous satisfactory level. If personal values/norms and professional practices do not match, one or other will be dominant (Becher and Kogan, 1992); if institutional values favour practices which conflict with personal values, professional workers may fall in line and do their best to work within a framework, to modify or even undermine it (Taylor, 1995). That is a position many of us have been in. In some cases the espoused values of the institution are contradicted by its 'policy-in-action' (Argyris and Schon, 1974).

Pedler *et al.* (1991) suggest that breakdown can occur when communication, feedback and what they call 'energy-flow' are broken between four aspects of an organisation, namely policy, operations, ideas and action. This again emphasises the holistic nature of the organisation and the internal interdependence of its various activities. Policy needs renewal by ideas; it needs testing against operational feasibility. Individual actions need to be set within an operational frame and feed back to it for refinement; individuals' action-based learning can spark ideas to feed to policy, and so on. The four areas need constantly to learn from one another; that is a learning organisation.

There needs to be commitment to learning by both individuals and the institution as a collective. How else do we set a positive role model for our students? Figure 3.3 suggests the odds are 3:1 against this:

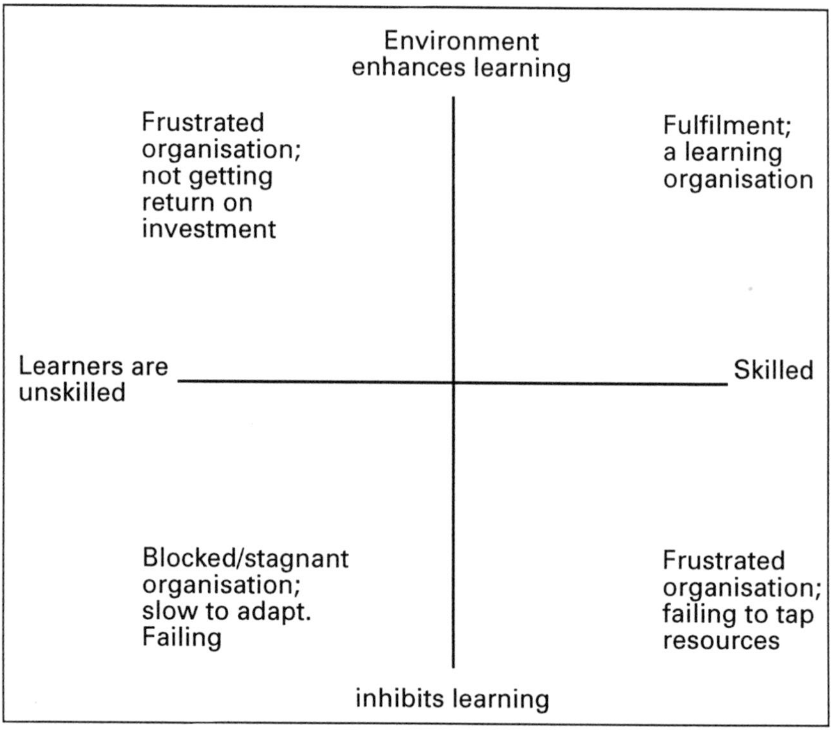

Environment
enhances learning

Frustrated organisation; not getting return on investment	Fulfilment; a learning organisation

Learners are unskilled _____|_____ Skilled

Blocked/stagnant organisation; slow to adapt. Failing	Frustrated organisation; failing to tap resources

inhibits learning

Figure 3.3 Learning and learners in an organisation (adapted from Roderick, 1993)

Too often, under pressure of resource constraint, training budgets are easy targets for cuts. This has been a national failing in the UK for 150 years (Barnett, 1986). Surely, in education, we should recognise the need for renewal of our human resources as we do, for instance, for physical resources in, say, computing? Yet investment in learning must be a specific budget, supplementary to day-to-day running costs. Promoting change needs supplementary funding, otherwise support to on-going services is robbed. The calculation of work load for a job needs to take account of the learning needed to do it, and to do it better, but there is increasing reluctance in education to provide time for training.

When will we ever *learn*? *When* will we *ever* learn?

CHAPTER FOUR

Education and Quality: Is a 'Business Perspective' Enough?

Mike Bottery

The meanings of 'quality'

Questions of international competitiveness in an economic era of static or decreasing budgets, allied to political philosophies of customer satisfaction, and tied in with educational issues of professional performance, have all combined to make 'quality' one of the keywords of the 1990s. Yet its meaning can be unclear. Many dictionary definitions of the word suggest little more than something to do with excellence or superiority: that better quality is attained by buying a more expensive product. Yet the term needs to be more carefully conceptualised, because, along with other terms like 'empowerment', 'decentralisation', 'responsibility' and 'freedom', it runs to the heart of educational management. (Judith Bell shows this in her study of 'quality' issues across various educational sectors in Chapter 16 of this book.)

Tse (1985) suggested that there were four possible concepts of quality:

- *Quality control*, where the comparison of a product with a standard leads to action to correct any deviation from the standard;

- *Quality assurance*, where attempts at the eradication of defects are dealt with early in the production process, rather than, as with quality control, waiting until the product is completed;

- *Total quality control*, where a commitment to quality is seen in all departments; the final, logical stage;

- *company-wide quality control*, a commitment by all employee levels in all areas of the company to the continued improvement in quality.

Yet even within these distinctions (derived from a business perspective), it is possible to see differences of origin. Thus Davis (1990) points out that business analogies derive from two distinct camps. One is that of manufacturing industry, where standardisation and similarity of product are hallmarks of quality. Quality control and quality assurance fall most easily within this camp. The other camp, however, is that of commerce, where satisfaction of customers is accomplished by personal service, where quality is achieved precisely by individualisation and non-standardisation. Education, through the use of total quality control and company-wide quality control, seems to fit much more comfortably into this conception.

Murgatroyd and Morgan (1992), and Morgan and Murgatroyd (1994) have argued that a revolution in quality – Total Quality Management(TQM) – is occurring in the public sector through the movement from *Quality Assurance* (quality as defined by external experts), via *Quality Conformance* (quality defined locally by practitioners) to *Customer-Driven Quality* (quality as defined by those on the receiving end). This is a revolution, they argue, because such movement suggests that those nearest to the customer/client are best able to make process improvements, and that therefore there needs to be an 'inverted pyramid' of decision-making, whereby those at the the bottom of the organisational pyramid, and therefore closest to the customer, are given the freedom to make decisions appropriate to that customer.

TQM is a broad church and has a number of tenets to it (well described by West-Burnham, 1992), but one in particular worth drawing out here is that, whilst there are 'external' customers, there are 'internal' customers as well – anybody, in fact, who receives a 'service'. So a 'chain' of customers, internal and external, is being described, as well as a system of management which 'empowers' those nearest the 'customer' to decide on the most appropriate manner of their satisfaction. TQM then is a continuous process of improvement at all levels, and by everyone within the organisation, with responsibility and empowerment devolved to them. In theory at least, this makes not only for inverted pyramids, but fairly flat ones as well.

Issues of quality

Definitions do not, however, dispense with questions. The educationalist, whilst benefiting from business ideas, must also be conscious of an uncritical transfer of notions such as TQM to education. Some questions which might be asked with respect to issues of quality are:

- Who is the customer?

- Whose quality is it anyway?

- Do customers want to be customers?
- Is the customer always right?
- Is quality measurable?
- What does a quality practitioner look like?

Who is the customer?

If TQM extends the notion of customer to develop notions of internal and external customers, translation of the term from a business to an educational context raises other issues. Is this customer the child, the parent, other teachers, government, business and industry, or society in general? And if each has different demands, how is one to decide which one – or several – is to be satisfied first? This must depend upon the particular set of values one holds, which suggests a contestability as to their prioritisation. Quality defined as customer satisfaction is not then as simple as it might at first appear. Quality control and quality assurance may still have their part to play.

Whose quality is it anyway?

This follows from asking who is the customer. If there are a number of different customers, they may have conflicting demands – the child, for instance, may not want what the parent wants, who may not want what business and industry want. Now quality, as understood within TQM, does not inhere in the product or service itself, but rather in the customer's appreciation of it. Not only will its standard be variable, but it will be defined differently by different customers. This explains Murgatroyd and Morgan's (1992: 23) remark that 'quality is a function of strategy ... until you have defined the strategy your school is pursuing, quality is secondary'.

The need for such a statement will be clear, for unless customers and their desires are defined, then how can quality be defined? Yet who is to decide which definition of quality – and the values behind this definition – is to stand as the important one? Where financial resources and teacher time are limited and there are contesting social, political and educational visions, all definitions will not be satisfied. In such circumstances, quality – or rather, definitions of quality – become objects of contestability.

Do customers want to be customers?

Much current quality literature – because of its business derivations – defines those people receiving a 'service' in a quality relationship as 'customers'. Yet even to say this is to concede an important conceptual point. Bridges (1994: 65) describes one group within the educational relationship – parents – who may be cast within very different roles. They may, he suggests, be: puzzled bystanders; supporters; partners; governors; co-educators; or, finally, customers. They may wish to see themselves as co-educators or partners, and rather less as customers. Thus, the use of business language such as 'customers' may restrict personal and organisational possibilities within education, and by so doing impoverish them. If this is the case, then when Murgatroyd and Morgan say (p.xi) that 'many people do not like the wholesale importation of the language of business ... into the practice of schooling' it will simply not do for them to argue (p.2) that

> We are not concerned with such matters; this book is not intended to discuss the ideology of schooling, but to sensitize and help those now leading ... schools to understand and respond to new contexts that governments have legislated.

Whilst there can be no quibble with helping individuals to understand and respond to government legislation, there must be questions raised over whether this is possible without addressing the ideology of schooling. If the use of the term 'customers', and similar business terms, can limit one's appreciation of educational possibilities by focusing purely upon these business analogies, then *that* is an 'ideology of schooling' which must be discussed. So if 'customers' don't want to be customers, it might be because they suspect that there is more to education than the analogies – and the possible straitjacket – of business.

Is the customer always right?

In the late 1980s, BP Chemicals drew upon the work of the management writer Philip Crosby(1979) to help them push forward a major initiative in developing quality systems within the company. There were within Crosby's conception some startling notions for education, such as the stress on 'zero defects', and 'the price of non-conformance' (*see* Bottery, 1994: Chapter 2 on these). Perhaps the bottom line, though, was that quality was to be defined (Crosby, 1979:15) as 'conformance to requirements'. So, on this conception, a Rolls Royce is not a better car than a Lada: if a customer wants a Lada, and gets it, they are being sold a quality product. Similarly, if a BP customer buys the chemical they want, they are being sold a quality product.

However, what happens, it might be asked, when a customer wants chemical X, but a BP employee knows that chemical Y is far more appropriate? When, as part of my research on BP (Bottery, 1994) I enquired about this, I got the answer expected: the client is educated as to the better suitability of chemical Y. But then, what happens if a new product is discovered, which customers don't even realise they had a need for, but the provider feels would be of benefit to them? The answer, is, of course, that a requirement is *generated*, by means of advertising, personal contact, education, or other routes.

It is clear that neither is the customer always 'right', nor is quality 'conformance to requirements', in some simplistic sense. There will always be situations where ignorance of the facts plays a part, where lack of expertise is important, where to leave a decision to the customer would be dangerous and unprofessional.

Now this is *not* an attempt to denigrate attempts at satisfying 'customer requirements': educational 'producers' have perhaps been too effective in the past at concealing their secret curriculum garden (*see* Nixon, in Chapter 18 of this book). However, I suggest that customer satisfaction on its own will not do; other forms of quality, such as quality assurance and contract conformance are, almost inevitably, going to have a part to play. Getting the balance between them right will be a problem – and a practical as much as an intellectual problem.

Is quality measurable?

An old story, originally a telling criticism of radical behaviourist psychology, may also help to illustrate the shortcomings of some approaches to educational quality. A man is walking home one night, and sees a stranger searching for something under the street light. He offers to help, and is told by the stranger that he is looking for his watch. After an exhaustive search, there is still no sign of it. He asks the stranger if he is sure he has dropped it under the street lamp, only to be told 'no, but the light is better here'.

This story seems to apply to educational quality in at least two ways at present. The first is in the sense that those who work beyond the school setting, precisely because they do not and cannot understand the individualities of school contexts, may attempt to derive data which are easy for them to measure but which may be of little validity – indeed may be positively misleading – because of their over-generalisability. This to some extent explains the increasing disillusion which Hopkins(1994) describes in the findings of top-down school effectiveness studies of the 1970s and 1980s. These, by attempting to pinpoint general features applicable to all schools, have increasingly been questioned by findings which suggest that culture and context are crucially important. Useful generalisation is therefore exceptionally difficult. There is an increasing interest instead in school improvement studies, which focus on initiatives developed at the school level, and use a more bottom-up qualitative appreciation to explain and improve the individual school's effectiveness.

The second sense in which the story applies is with respect to current measurements of quality through performance indicators. Thus we must be aware that what we (or our political directors) choose to measure, can reveal a great deal about that which is most valued, and that which is given the most attention. So, if a system of assessment is developed which focuses on certification, it is not likely to be sensitive to problems of diagnosis, precisely because the latter asks the student to be open about his or her problems, whilst the former suggests precisely the opposite. Moreover, performance indicators can be very damaging in their consequences. For example, with regard to the performance indicator of percentage passes, Fitz-Gibbon argues (1984: 142):

> Logically, percentage pass rates should be expected to encourage teachers to push out of their classes students who are likely to fail ... (and) ... should encourage teachers to concentrate their teaching on the borderline students

– thus depriving some students of an education from which they personally might benefit, and leaving many of the higher-achieving students to fend for themselves, whilst the teacher concentrates her energies elsewhere. Fitz-Gibbon goes on to argue (p.144) that of four kinds of data – raw, comparative, residual, and experimental – only the last two can be fairly used in an assessement of performance, and yet so often the first two, more accessible kinds of data are utilised instead. The result may be an apparent rather than a real causality. As Fitz-Gibbon points out, delinquency rates vary from school to school: but so does the incidence of leukaemia, and it is doubtful whether we would wish to assign a simple causality to the school here.

What does a quality practitioner look like?

Two trends seem to be occurring in business management which suggest a useful marriage. The first is the distinction being made between 'hard' and 'soft' approaches to TQM. The original 'hard' approach placed its emphasis upon systematic measurement and work control via statistical processes. More recently, however, a 'softer' version places its emphasis on qualititative aspects of the work process, and thus tends to highlight the necessity of hiring and developing the right people, and providing an enabling management framework. Of course, this topic is not new. Back in 1954 Gouldner wrote about the problems produced by extra layers of supervision stemming from a desire for increased managerial control, resulting in the creation of 'punishment-centred bureaucracies', with the consequent demotivation, antipathy and subversion of such structures by employees. Curiously, government departments differ on their appreciation of this. The Department for Education (DFE) still seems wedded to inspection: the Department for Trade and Industry (DTI), on the other hand, has suggested that

> ... to believe that traditional quality control techniques ... will result in quality is wrong. Employing more inspectors, tightening up standards ... does not promise quality.

Instead, they suggest, one needs to change 'the focus of control from outside the individual to within' (quoted in Burridge and Ribbins, 1994:193). There is a lesson for the DFE to learn here – that the needs of education cannot be met through outmoded ideas from the business sector.

A second trend is the realisation that because people are people, they individualise institutions to create cultures which mould the way an organisation does things, and they 'customise' the jobs they are given. Rather than seeing these as detrimental to an educational system, they can be seen as liberating, anti-Procrustean, and personally and organisationally healthy. In the business arena, Ricardo Semler's (1993) description of his company's phenomenal growth and commercial success is underpinned by both the development of a culture and of individual customising. In the educational arena, the work of Hopkins (1994) on school culture, and the rich, qualitative work of Peter Ribbins (1994a) further suggests the strength of such an approach.

If this is the case, then how *do* we specify what quality practitioners look like? They will not be isolated, but collaborative; they will not be developed but developing; they will not be determined, but determining. This does not cohere with recent reforms in the UK which attempt to specify teacher quality through the articulation of a set of measurable competences as the outcomes of teacher education courses. MacNamara (1992), for instance, suggests that there is a radical difference between being *competent* (which describes the judgement of an individual's ability to do the job in circumstances beyond those in which we have observed him/her as being competent), and having *competences* (where we assert that they are competent in certain (measurable) behavioural areas). The problem lies in that competences are necessary but not sufficient for competence: for when we judge in terms of competences, we judge a limited, observable public performance. So, firstly, two 'experts' may differ over the excellence of that performance; whilst, secondly, we cannot be certain that such behavioural competencies will transfer to other reasonably similar situations, and will become increasingly less likely the more one situation differs from another. Further, it is extremely doubtful that such behavioural competences will help in any way when a practitioner is faced by the unexpected situation. One may be forgiven for thinking that those who concentrate on the measurement of competences with such zeal are in danger of behaving like the stranger looking for his watch in the wrong place, but with the best light.

Yet one can move from Peters and Waterman's (1982) seminal book, through Kanter (1989), Peters (1992) and Handy (1994) and see that a key theme running through contemporary management literature is the need to be able to manage change in an age of the rapidly changing. Suggestions that western society is moving into a post-industrial, post-modern age are beginning to influence the literature of the public services (Burrows and Loader, 1994), as well as that of education (Hargreaves, 1994; Smyth, 1993). If this is the case, it has to be asked: does training someone in a fixed set of competences provide them with the attributes which allow them to cope with this?

The management and development of those who deal with the ever-changing and the unpredictable suggests the need for a general competence, which a list of competences could never fulfil. If this is the case, then quality will not be generated by a narrow competences training, but rather through the development of an overall competence in individuals, most probably in a collegial context, which indicates a greater emphasis upon the initial selection of competent people, their continued development and training, and the sensitive and empowering management of the organisation within which they work.

Such individuals will thus bear strong resemblances to Schon's (1983) 'reflective practitioners'. They as professionals will face a rapidly changing world, where knowledge bases and skills will never be stable, where situations will need to be defined and conceptualised *as problems* before they can be tackled. Such practitioners will need the willingness and ability to listen to others – including their 'customers' – in order for the framing and re-framing of problems to be possible. In a striking metaphor, Schon (1983:43) describes two kinds of professionals:

> There are those who choose the swampy lowlands. They deliberately involve themselves in messy but crucially important problems, and when asked to describe their methods of inquiry, they speak of experience, trial and error, intuition and muddling through.

> Other professionals opt for the high ground. Hungry for technical rigour, devoted to an image of solid professional competence, or fearful of entering a world in which they feel they do not know what they are doing, they choose to confine themselves to a narrowly technical practice.

Increasingly, it would seem that the professionals of the high ground need to experience and complement their skills with an understanding and appreciation of the realities of the swampy lowlands of practice.

Empowerment, quality and democracy

Such movements in the conceptions of 'professionalism' and 'quality' – in the move to reflective practice, and in a focus on general competence rather than behavioural competences – suggest a different orientation to the treatment not only of quality but also to that of the professional. If competences training, because of its pre-specification of behaviours, suggests a lack of trust and an emphasis on control, then competence training suggests a greater belief in the individual and an emphasis upon empowerment and participation.

Now both 'empowerment' and 'participation' are key words in the Total Quality Management lexicon, and ones which at first sight have great promise for education. Nevertheless, one needs to be aware that this is a vision derived from industry, and that the terms may come with a restricted view of their possible meanings and application. Murgatroyd and Morgan (1992: 121) suggested that

> Basic empowerment begins when the vision and goals have already been set by the school leaders. What a team or an individual is empowered to do is to turn the vision and strategy into reality through achieving those challenging goals set for them by the leadership of the school.
>
> *Individuals are being empowered in terms of how they can achieve the goals set, not in terms of what the goals might be.* (my italics)

Two things need to be said about this. Firstly, no organisation can afford the luxury of a decision-making free-for-all: schools have management appointed to envisage the future, to chart courses, and to effect change. Nevertheless there is, it seems to me, a too-clear distinction drawn in the quotation above regarding staff participation in the 'how' of implementation, and their non-participation in the 'why'. For some, as TQM comes from a business background, this may not be too surprising. Thus, Hollway (1991) argues persuasively that a close analysis of the change in managerial styles and philosophies throughout the twentieth century indicates *not* so much a change in underlying philosophy as a more pragmatic concern with the best way to get the same result – to implement management decisions. Further, Leat (1993) suggests that current participative, empowering conceptions of business management will survive only so long as they deliver commercial and economic success. Actual research on this aspect of TQM in the business arena tends to bear out such pessimistic conclusions (*see* Wilkinson and Willmott, 1995). From such origins, then, it is perhaps not too surprising that 'empowerment' should be so constrained in its possibilities.

Yet one might argue that it is precisely in this area that schools and colleges differ from business, for if one of their key features is the need for them to develop the citizens of the future, then part of this development must be in precisely the development of empowerment – where empowerment means the nurturing and encouragement of ideas and visions which come from within, not simply the implementation of others' visions (Bottery, 1992). And all the stakeholders in a community – teachers, parents, local community, not just the pupils – have a need for this, which suggests that the limited empowerment of the business perspective is insufficient for educational institutions. In any case, it is highly unlikely that those who seek to limit empowerment to implementation would be successful. The difference between implementation and vision is less of a distinction in kind than different ends of a continuum: and those who are encouraged to be implementationally empowered are going to be drawn to the issues of strategy and vision at the other end. If the idea of TQM is to invert the pyramid of decision-making, then this becomes almost inevitable. If quality is truly meant to be a bottom-up phenomenon, and if education is genuinely concerned with citizenship education, then words like participation and democracy must become part of the quality lexicon.

One further point: it is very easy for 'empowerment' to become a weasel word: for it to become the excuse for nothing more than the delegation of extra responsibility and work. Just as bad, it may be genuinely intended to free creative thinking, but then not be supported by the time and resources necessary for concepts to be assimilated, modified, and implemented. When writers like Morgan and Murgatroyd (1994: 17) suggest that 'What a team or an individual is empowered to do is to turn the vision and strategy into reality through achieving the challenging overarching goals set for them by the leaders or senior management', managers have to be very careful that they do not – and are not seen to – leave it simply to those lower down to sort out someone else's brainchild. Finally, in an era of massive legislative as well as organisational change, when initiatives have a tendency to follow on each other's heels, the development of empowerment may come to be seen as nothing more than one more initiative in a death by a thousand initiatives. It is all too easy for those doing the empowering to fail to recognise the implementational problems involved in personal and organisational change (*see* Fullan, 1991, on this). If any of these occur, quality is the casualty rather than the product.

Conclusion

Educational managers need to be clear about their visions, and about how to achieve those visions. With the concept of quality, one needs to be clear what quality means, and how it will be achieved. If we use the three concepts suggested at the beginning – expert-defined, local contract defined, and customer defined – there will be a place for all of these within an educational framework. The accountability of public money can only be ultimately answered by rigorous, external inspections (although, as Wilcox and Gray show in Chapter 14 of this book, inspectors too need to be scrutinised). At the same time, the informal agreements between parents and school, teachers and children, will continue to provide the mediation vital to sensitive application. Finally, market rhetoric is not the only reason for the increased interest in, and of, the school's customers: the realisation of the value of others' visions, of their contributions to the framing and re-framing of problems can only be good for their solution, as well as for the general consultative, and ultimately participative framework it can engender.

At the nodal point of educational quality, though, are the practitioners: their selection, training, continued development, and care; and the kind of practitioners desired and nurtured will determine the kind of quality achieved. A vision of practitioners, already predefined in terms of certain competences, stretched to a pre-set limit, constantly monitored and inspected, ultimately does education and society little good, for they will not have the capacity to adapt to new situations, to learn how to learn, to welcome the framing of problems with others' help, and in so doing further the education and understanding of all concerned. True quality is derived from the valuing and nurturance of the adaptable professional. Such a professional will be a key player in the complex, changing society of tomorrow, and in the development of a truly participative citizenry within it.

Part Two: Leading People in Educational Organisations

CHAPTER FIVE

Managing to Make Things Happen: Critical Issues in Team Management

Bernard T. Harrison, with Tony Dobell and Colin Higgins

This chapter discusses a study of critical reflections by middle and senior managers in education (mainly secondary schools), and in public and private sector organisations. The discussion includes six main issues: training and development needs in management; age profiles; responsibility posts; consultative leadership; equal opportunities issues; and communications in organisations. Each of these is examined, under two main headings: *issues of staffing* and *interpersonal issues*.

One prominent general issue that emerged from the study concerns pressures on teacher–managers to accept disciplines of commercial/industrial management, in educational organisations. Such pressures need not mean the 'de-professionalisation' of teachers, as long as the profession responds inventively to demands for change. Through critical reflection, and through well-directed teamwork, new versions of professional teacher-management can emerge. In particular, traditional hierarchical structures of management can be replaced by more streamlined, flexible forms of consultative management.

Introductory Note: Investing in people

Fashions change in the rhetoric of management, as in all human affairs. From time to time, 'hard' notions – such as strong top-down leadership, centralised power, delivery, and strict line management – are challenged by 'soft' notions – such as collaboration, empowerment, teamwork and collegiality. In recent years, the field of educational management has been exposed to varying pressures from both 'hard' and 'soft' sources. Notions behind such 1970s slogans as 'your caring neighbourhood comprehensive school' were found to be soft-headed. They had to give way in the 1980s to sterner, 'real world' versions of schools and colleges as 'businesses'.

Following the Government's drive to 'raise standards' through the Education Reform Act of 1988, pressures grew on teachers to conform to national decree, rather than to assert their (much criticised) professional autonomy. In the face of such pressures Bottery (1992: 177) predicted, with understandable pessimism, that 'teacher participation in management decisions is not likely to increase, given current ideological impulses behind legislation and training'. There was, it seemed, too much to do – in adjusting to new modes of management and to new versions of the curriculum – for them to reclaim their lost sense of professional autonomy. 'For the time being at least', Bottery surmised, 'teachers will probably continue to be seen as lower-grade functionaries in a greater economic scheme of things'. Or, as one despairing teacher put it:

> I feel I'm being de-skilled. Maybe I should think of premature retirement or doing things outside education.
> (quoted in Imeson, 1994: 37)

Yet these 'de-professionalising' pressures have in turn been challenged in the 1990s – not least, by enlightened approaches from the business world and from Government itself – to develop new versions of professional management in education that can meet today's needs. As Imeson pointed out, the challenge that came, for example, through the 'Investors in People' initiative, was a joint enterprise between private business and the Employment Department – not the Department for Education – which aimed to involve educational and training organisations. In the interests of sheer organisational efficiency the Investors in People movement asked: what is it that makes one organisation more effective or successful than another, especially, in the way that it uses *people*? This initiative identified the need for organisations to make a systematic analysis of training needs – both of the organisation and of individual staff – and also to involve staff fully, in the task of identifying training needs.

The Investors in People programme required *commitment* from senior management to develop all employees; systematic *planning* of staff training and development needs; *action* on development programmes; and *evaluation* of their effectiveness, in order to improve future effectiveness (Imeson, 1994: 12).

In this emphasis on investing in people, the classic requirement that all managers should make things happen, does not change. The exercise of power itself may be seen as the *accomplishing* of plans for innovatory change. As far as consultative/collaborative management is concerned, this should be about ensuring that collaboration must lead to *delivery*. Pfeffer, in *Managing with Power* (1992: 7) declares:

problems of implementation are, in many instances, problems in developing political will and expertise ... the desire to accomplish something, even against opposition and the knowledge and skills that make it possible to do so. Today, more than ever, it is necessary to study power and to learn to use it skilfully ...

These essential political skills need not be exercised in an overbearing or 'charismatic' way. Moreover, power is not the exclusive possession of established management. Pfeffer suggests, indeed, that it may often be better to submerge one's own personality (through, for example, teamwork), in order to achieve what is needed. This view, when applied to a school/college context, suggests that the ultimate aim of good management does not stop at the well-being of individual teachers or teams as such, even though any programme of investment in people must give 'well-being' a high priority. Even more crucially, managers and all staff must use their power to ensure that the school/college is successful in meeting its aims (which ought, we would argue, to include the 'well-being' of all individuals in the organisation).

Following Pfeffer's points concerning power: to be effective in the use of power, all those who manage need both personal and social–political maturity. It is difficult to see how the maturity needed for successful management can grow, in organisations where there are rigid hierarchies. Hierarchies thrive on power at the top, and submission from below; in that hive, there is room for only one mature queen bee at a time. If (as we believe) all teachers should see themselves as managers, it follows that all teachers require opportunities to make a mature contribution. They need space to develop *creative and critical thinking*; to sharpen their *consultative and political skills*; and to develop necessary qualities of *willpower*, to ensure that management tasks are accomplished. In this way, suggests West-Burnham (in Davies *et al.*, 1990: 67), good human resources management can ensure that

> Staff become an asset in which to invest, to be developed so as to help the organisation achieve its objectives. The cultural shift, is, therefore, from control to enabling: to providing people with the resources, targets and opportunities to contribute to the growth of the organisation whilst enhancing themselves.

This 'flexible culture' will be achieved, suggests Lawrence (1994:72), when organisations have 'systems with informal structures, informal human relations and multiple channels of communication, in which great emphasis is placed on cooperation, flexibility, sharing, pooling and rapport'.

Identifying key issues from the study

In our study of attitudes by middle and senior managers towards their organisations (reported in Harrison, Dobell and Higgins, 1995), we worked with 12 secondary schools and four other organisations in South Yorkshire. The non-school organisations included two in the public service sector (administration of health and of higher education) and two private businesses (food and drinks industries – one large and one smaller company). We consulted three secondary headteachers with established national/international reputations for their work in the management of education. Teacher–managers who were engaged on University of Sheffield Management in Education programmes were also involved. In the initial phase of the study, a total of 152 initial questionnaires were completed and returned to us. These provided the information that we required, to select suitable interviewees from the 76 respondents who indicated that they were willing to be interviewed, and we conducted 30 follow-up interviews. The interviews were designed to draw on a range of the experiences and views, amongst a variety of managers (taking gender and age especially into account) and of managerial responsibilities (from middle to senior, in a number of different fields). While our study was concentrated on secondary schools, the additional focus on the four other organisations provided useful evidence for critical comparison of management attitudes in different contexts.

What impressed us most, perhaps, during the interviews that we conducted on this programme, was the high level of commitment, among all interviewees, to the success of their organisation. As far as the schools were concerned, in the light of numerous reports during the 1980s and 1990s about stress among teachers, we would not, initially have been surprised to find some loss of morale, even apathy – especially, perhaps, among middle managers. Yet the reverse was true; simple, but clear evidence of this was provided in responses to the initial questionnaire to teacher–managers, where all respondents agreed or 'strongly' agreed, that they enjoyed management tasks and responsibilities. Compared to this, less than two-thirds thought that they would enjoy their management tasks more if they were paid more. Responses from both public sector organisations were almost identical with those from teachers. Private sector replies were also virtually unanimous about enjoying their management tasks, and very few of these thought that enjoyment was linked to pay (except for one irascible reply: 'stupid question. Of course your job is related to your pay').

This strength of commitment might, of course, be explained by the fact that we were 'outsiders', and that those whom we contacted and interviewed would be unlikely to betray cynicism or other 'unprofessional' reactions. Yet we collected a weight of evidence, from various kinds of teacher–managers and other managers in a range of different settings, which showed their willingness to speak candidly about their experiences as managers in their organisations. This reflects well-grounded evidence, summed up by Riley (1994: 17), that managers 'are flesh and blood and their critical incidents have established a variety of moral dimension'. Their roles reflect a 'dynamic, complex and often tense relationship between the free and rational actor on the one hand and the formal structure of role expectations of the other' (Best *et al.*, 1983: 54).

On the sensitive issue of stress, for example, questionnaire returns showed an almost unanimous view, across all organisations, that they would be in more assured control of their management tasks, if only they had more *time* to fulfil their management tasks well. They were only too aware of advice such as Bell's (1992: 36), that 'above all ... middle managers must be able to manage their personal time'. Yet they knew, too, that when there *is* no time to plan, and barely time, even, to react to the 'crisis of the day', then stress will quickly lead to distress. Replies from the private sector, however, were more inclined to be self-critical, stressing that it is the responsibility of all managers to manage their own time effectively, in order to set a good example to their teams.

Other evidence, from the initial questionnaires, showed that teacher–managers:

- agreed, almost without exception, that they *enjoyed working on task teams*, to work out specific policy/planning issues;

- agreed overwhelmingly (with only four disagreeing) that their own school needed a more effective management system – in particular, that *more open lines of management* were required;

- were unanimous in their view that teacher–managers *do not receive adequate provision for staff development and training that they require*;

- believed (with only three disagreeing) that their own *management skills as teachers were transferable to commerce or industry*.

Initial responses revealed, then, strong views and a sense of clear confidence, among these teacher–managers, in what they have to offer to their organisations. This willingness to criticise their organisations was shared to the same degree by respondents in public sector administration, who asserted even more robustly their urgent training/development needs in management. Private sector responses were more cautious, however, about offering direct criticism of their companies; they preferred to offer 'no opinion' to questions in this area. (Interestingly, in several cases where private sector respondents 'agreed' or 'strongly agreed' that the management of their company was effective and did not need improvement, they also supported a view that management should be more open.)

Among the teachers, it was clear that some of those interviewed felt confident, too, that their views and criticisms were valued by their senior colleagues. Mike, who is Head of a large Science Faculty, declared:

I'm quite happy about senior management taking up my own ideas, or anyone else's, even when they sometimes forget who gave them the idea in the first place. When our team was working on the new school Record of Achievement profiles, we were building on each other's ideas all the time. In my last job, the Head took any suggestion, or advice or criticism as a personal offence. He moaned, once, because I'd gone ahead of myself to make a link – quite a big one – with the local library service .... We wanted to get Years 9 and 10 reading a lot of books. But I'd already asked him, twice, to set this up for us, and he'd done nothing.... But here, they'd be only too glad to let me do something like that, and you're likely to get some real support. To be fair, I think they'd give me credit for it, as well.

In other cases, interviewees expressed constructive frustration about their own lack of opportunities to contribute to policy-making and planning. Their views were, again, shared almost identically by the public service managers (one of whom complained, 'For all the rhetoric about enterprise, we're in a state of total bureaucracy here'). Compared with this, private sector respondents were less critical of 'line management' structures in their organisations; yet they also indicated that they enjoyed being empowered through being engaged on a task team for a specific project, and that this happened in fact quite regularly.

Among the teacher interviewees, Anne, a curriculum co-ordinator, criticised the hierarchical 'pyramid' structure of management in her medium-sized school where, as well as a small senior team of a Head, two deputies and three senior teachers, there were 10 holders of Grade D allowances, virtually all of which were held by male colleagues, aged 50-plus. This was (we were glad to note) an unusual example (although there were other cases where the age of staff was, one way or another, a critical issue). Anne commented that, while she enjoyed the challenge of her management tasks, she resented not being fully recognised or paid for what she regarded as an important contribution. Her curriculum expertise was not fully used, partly because the school was reluctant to recognise important work with appropriate rewards.

She pointed out that the senior management team was more inclined to set up old-style working parties (in one extreme instance, a curriculum working party had looked for a whole year at 'general' curriculum issues, and its report had contained nothing that required implementation). Anne divined the direction that the interviewer's questions was taking, when she declared that new-style task teams, with a schedule of specific tasks and targetted completion dates, would suit the needs of the school much better:

They're nearly all nice people here, you know. That makes it worse, really, if I dare to tell them that what we all need around here is good kick up you know where ... or, at least, a really good programme of staff development – above all, a programme for management training. But how else will we 'change the culture', as you call it, of this school?

The interview with Anne left an impression of a talented, industrious colleague, whose abilities were being insufficiently used by the school. Clearly, she felt some irritation about her position, although this was expressed almost entirely in terms of the advantages that would accrue to the school, rather than to herself, if only it would adopt a more task-oriented approach to management planning.

Through the 30 interviews (with 18 secondary school, 6 public and 6 private sector managers) we identified six key issues, which may be conveniently located under two main headings of *staffing* and *interpersonal issues* (though, as will be shown, many of these issues interrelate, and cannot be easily separated from each other).

(A) Issues of staffing

(1) Training and development needs in management

As responses to the questionnaires promised, all school and public sector interviewees had strong views on the need for better provision of staff development. To quote from just one among many eloquent statements:

> *David* (Head of senior school): Take this city now. A steel city? Not so much, these days. I'd like to bet that education stands a chance of being one of the biggest businesses in the city now, along with health services – two universities, the biggest FE college in Europe, all these schools ... But where's *our* staff college? Where are *our* school leadership and promotion courses?

David saw himself as ambitious to take on further leadership/management responsibilities. He liked organising people and resources, and encouraged his own team to take initiatives: 'I get irritated by people who can't think ahead, who can't imagine next week's, next term's, next year's problems ... they always end up looking to me for a lead'. He found satisfaction in following a task through to completion. There was no point in having ideas unless there was the will to carry them through. Yet, although he admitted to being 'a bit of a perfectionist', he did not want to end up as a 'spent-out work-aholic':

> I have a young family, and I like my time with them. Recently, though, I kept a log of work-related activities in just one week. I counted 25 hours when I was actually teaching, and 45 when I was planning, marking, organising my area, or otherwise wholly engaged on school business. Would the private sector exploit anyone like this – and not even realise they're doing it?

On this evidence, David is heading for what the Japanese call '*Karoshi*', or death by overwork. His views reflect Lawrence's complaint (1994:79) that teacher–managers are over-burdened by routine administrative tasks, which impose 'a senseless waste of professional expertise'. They also, however, reflected the views of all our private sector interviewees, who complained just as strongly about having to work too long hours, in order to fulfil their duties. The solution, for education, David thought, lay partly in more effective school organisation, partly in improved financial investment in schools, and mainly providing *real* opportunities for management training, right through the school:

> We need to learn about more open lines of management, about quality circles. What did you quote earlier, about 'thinking smarter'?
>
> *Interviewer*: You mean, in a speech by Bill Taylor: 'It's not a matter of working longer hours, or even of working harder, but acting smarter ...'?
>
> *David*: That's it. We need to know all about time management, delegating, negotiating with people ... and stress management, too – though can't you think of a better name for it than that? But if all this doesn't lead to making good things happen, it doesn't add up to much, does it?

David was also, in his spare time, working his way through a Master's course in Educational Management (which he regarded as 'extra' to all his school-related duties). He welcomed contact and exchange of expertise with other organisations, even though he insisted that educational management must develop its own distinctive patterns and principles: 'It's fair enough to expect us to be business-like, but any organisation must decide what it really is there *for*, and act accordingly. We're in the business of teaching and learning, and we'd better not forget it'.

Other teacher interviewees expressed similarly strong views on the urgent need for staff development. Some thought that the needs of middle managers should be given special priority: 'I'm coming towards the end of my second year in this post,' said Ben, who is Head of a large languages faculty, 'And I'm just feeling relieved that I've survived so far. Believe it or not – and I hope for the sake of others that this is unusual – I've never had even one day's training in management or leadership.'

Others thought that priority should be given to their senior management team, especially, for both initial and regular refresher courses, to ensure that they were competent in all the areas they had to manage. Helen, who had responsibilities for learning support in a large inner city comprehensive school, compared the 'naive' policies of her senior managers – especially their financial dealings – with private commerce, where she had gained extensive experience before entering teaching:

> They really could benefit from a placement in industry, you know. I'm sure they might teach industry a thing or two, as well, but the main lesson they might learn is not to be so *timid about money*. It's hard to believe how much time I have to waste, to arrange purchase of some minor pieces of equipment – say, a hundred pounds or so, which may be urgently needed for learning support. And while the SMT may dither for weeks about whether to grant this,

the education of dozens of kids grinds to a halt. They only have one chance at school, don't they? I'm not suggesting that all teacher–managers have to be financial experts, though – a good administrator could surely handle finances. But we *do* need to be more confident about making informed financial *decisions*.

Mind you, my old firm had just the same kinds of problems as this school, when it came to the wrong people in the wrong positions promoting the wrong people ....

Her view on wrong promotions was endorsed by interviewees in both of the private sector companies. 'You'd certainly get sacked on the spot for any kind of dishonesty', said one, 'but there's no doubt that some people round here work really hard, while some others know how to take it easy. And no amount of staff training will change that. It's the same everywhere, I suppose ...'.

The need for sound policies of staff development was perhaps the single most important issue that emerged from our interviews, and was seen as one on which solutions to other critical issues most depended. This should come as no surprise to those who have studied Japanese modes of management. Lorriman and Takashi Kenjo (1994), for example, urge that the prime role of management is to develop all staff – a lesson that still needs to be learned in British education.

(2) Age profiles

In this sensitive area, interviewees agreed that it is important to avoid charges of 'ageism', which would create resentment amongst older staff (nobody can help advancing years). Even so, a number of interviewees – across all the organisations – had serious concerns about imbalanced age profiles on their staff. Rigidities in this area created barriers to restructuring that may be needed in the organisation, and caused lack of opportunity for younger staff to make significant management contributions.

Some older interviewees were, themselves, critical of inflexible staff structures that offered little choice between 'soldiering on' in a position they no longer enjoyed, or accepting redundancy/premature retirement, even though they felt they still had much to contribute. Could they not be allowed to move into positions where they might feel both more comfortable and more valued? It is important, of course, to acknowledge that the issue of 'age' is quite separate from issues of *effectiveness* of staff. Yet, having realised that, it is still important to aim at a good range and balance in the age profile of a staff. Flexible systems of reward and promotion, at all levels, will clearly be of benefit here. It was interesting to note a consensus of experience and of viewpoint on this issue, across school and public/private sector interviewees. The need for effective policies to take longer life expectancy into account extends beyond individual organisations; it requires action at national and international levels, to support more flexible policies throughout all organisations.

(3) Problems concerning responsibility posts

While problems in this area may relate to both of the areas already discussed above, there are other aspects that interviewees raised. For example, Christine, a school curriculum manager, complained that she had to make 'sometimes supreme efforts' to compensate for the poor work of her (younger) Head of Faculty. Although he was a member of the senior management team of the school, this Faculty Head was a 'weak link' who had 'little experience and even less interest in policy and planning'. Yet, she declared, he was a successful classroom teacher, who retained his enthusiasm and effectiveness in areas where he was directly involved with pupils. Christine thought that there was often a need for women in her position to assert their claims against existing hierarchies: 'I know they sometimes see me as a pushy feminist round here, but you'd be surprised at the number of my women friends and colleagues who say the same thing as me ... that they would just like to get recognition for what they actually do in their place'. (Our interviews with other women-managers often confirmed Christine's experience, and ensured that we were not surprised by her account.) An area that concerned several – though not most – teacher interviewees, was a sense that their schools tended to over-reward holders of pastoral posts (such as Head of Year), at the expense of emerging planning and management needs in the school. Jane, a Deputy Head with curriculum responsibilities, criticised 'one or two people I know here who have organised comfortable dens for themselves, they've worked out easy ways of expanding their work to fill their hours. Meanwhile, there are just not enough hours in the day for others ...'

Her view was matched by a public sector interviewee, Jo, who described one of her senior colleagues as 'something of a genius at passing all real work on. He acts the part of looking busy to perfection ...'. Mike, though, described how his private sector company had decided to slim down drastically the personnel department of his organisation. 'They must have saved many tens of thousands of pounds a year – and frankly, I don't think anyone has noticed any difference in the way the place is run'.

As a way of avoiding hierarchies – or, even better – as a way of replacing hierarchies altogether, most interviewees supported the use of management task teams. These could enable the organisation to draw on specific skills, such as financial expertise, which can sometimes be found among staff who have, until then, not been involved in 'whole organisation' management operations. In this way, the task team can provide genuine 'on the job' training.

Many interviewees insisted, however, that, to be effective, task teams must be properly established. Their members should be given a clear mandate to deliver in a particular area; rewards for completed work should be clearly defined and promptly paid; and, as one teacher–manager said, 'they must get the backing of the SMT when the flak is flying'. It was the SMT's duty to declare that 'this is a problem', and the task team's duty to report that 'here is a solution'. This kind of interaction will, inevitably, involve comment and criticism from both sides. While this should be constructive where possible, and always well mannered, it must above all be candid, since 'the whole purpose of criticism is to make sure it leads to insights on how to do something, to work out best ways of doing it' (David).

One point of interest in these reflections on entrenched hierarchies versus fresh management approaches, involved contradictory views of how private business handled 'dead-on-the-job' staff. Arthur, a Head of Humanities with responsibility for a number of outside agencies in the school, expressed strong feelings about having more responsibility than power in his management tasks, especially where deployment of staff was involved. However, he questioned whether commercial organisations were any more effective in handling incompetent staff: 'My wife, who works as a manager for a local company, has just the same problems as me, even though you might think she's just there to work for the company to make a cash profit'. By way of contrast Penny (a Deputy Head) reported that her partner in the private sector 'has much more freedom to act than I do, when push has to come to shove, with people who just won't do the work they're paid for'. Our own interviewees in the private sector were mainly agreed that dismissal was, in fact, a rarely used option. John, a progress manager, said:

> Put it like this: there are other ways of easing someone out. I usually opt for some kind of 'restructuring', which will mean that I'll just have to let someone go... and you can guess who that will be, if the choice is between a good and a poor worker.

(B) Interpersonal issues

(4) Consultative leadership

Important aspects of consultative leadership have already been touched on, in the discussion of hierarchies (above). Understandably, interviewees revealed how they were much preoccupied with finding successful patterns of consultation and teamwork in their own areas of responsibility.

Similarly, a number of interviewees commented critically about their own involvement with inadequate or insincere versions of consultation. When Rowland (1993: 42) drew attention to a 'dilemma of negotiation', he suggested that 'deception and manipulation occur when an appearance of negotiation is offered merely to seduce the participants into a sense of ownership'. Ian, a teacher–manager whose responsibilities for GNVQ and TVEI development involved him in regular meetings with the senior management team of his school, identified the sometimes bland response that he encountered, when offering constructive criticisms or proposals to the team, as the 'we all work very hard' reaction. Senior managers had established and encouraged this culture as a means of fending off uncomfortable ideas:

> At first, I was simply pleased when they went to great lengths to thank me or other colleagues for tasks that we had carried out for them, but this 'we all work very hard culture' can put a fire blanket over any real enquiry into how we should improve systems and quality in the school.

In settings where active consultative management flourished, several teacher interviewees (who were all female) declared that the least pleasant aspect of handling and negotiating with teams was the experience of conflict, especially with male colleagues. Barbara, a Deputy Head with special pastoral responsibilities, expressed some unease about the ways in which some task teams in her school had sometimes become 'over-enthusiastic' about their own field of work, and had 'tried to impose their views on the rest of the staff'. However, she thought that the answer to this problem lay in even more open systems of management, where all staff become skilful in handling differences of viewpoint and policy, without giving or taking personal offence. She disclosed, at the end of the interview, that she had not looked forward to talking to the (male) interviewer, because she had recently become involved with a clash of views with a male colleague, that had become 'personal'. This point relates to important equal opportunities issues that were raised in the interviews (see below).

Judith, Head of a large school technology faculty, also commented on her negative experiences of conflict, when trying to implement change through teamwork:

> Our school is not yet really launched into 'task teams', although we've had quite good experience of them, whenever the Head has finally come round to setting them up. One of the most satisfying things I've been asked to do was to lead a task team to develop a new policy for Information Technology in the school. We involved outside agencies, and had good support from the LEA. I think that we did a really good job of it – at least, the Head was pleased, and agreed to implement everything we recommend.
>
> We didn't get paid for it, but that didn't matter.... The only thing that spoiled

a really good experience was the resentment that a group of older staff showed to everything that we did. They hated the idea of any change, and they were determined to let everyone know their views. The memory of their unpleasantness is as strong as the pleasure of doing a good job. Still, we did win the day ....

This experience of being encouraged to complete her task was also evident in responses from private sector managers, none of whom had encountered the kind of resistance that Judith reported from other colleagues ('No-one would dare to challenge a commercially good idea that had senior management backing', said one). The public sector interviewees were, however, critical of frequent hierarchical or bureaucratic restraints on such initiatives: 'By the time any proposal from me has gone through all the committees that have to review it, time has often moved on too long for it to be useful'. As these and the teacher–manager interviews revealed, consultative management is no soft option, and initiatives from individuals or teams can be resisted by hierarchical interests. It requires tenacity and courage, as well as sensitivity and flexibility, to ensure that managers overcome these.

(5) *Equal opportunities issues*

Three of the school interviewees (two female, one male) and one female manager in the public sector held specific responsibilities for equal opportunities, either individually or as a committee member. In our limited enquiry into the private sector, we were not able to identify any female managers for interview. Most responses from all sectors suggested that publicly expressed patriarchal attitudes were a thing of the past in their organisation. However, as indicated above, improvements in rhetoric do not always lead to improvements in reality. An extreme example of an equal opportunities problem was provided by Sheila, who was Head of a large faculty in a rural comprehensive school:

There is a senior management team of five – all males – in the school. When one of them retired recently I applied for the vacant senior teacher post, of course. I'm regarded as the 'senior woman' in the school, by experience as well as status, and I really thought I'd get it. But no – it went to a male rival. Yet the Head must know he'll get some severe criticism from OFSTED, at the very least, and that if only I was more assertive, I'd surely have a case for complaint, I think.

This was an exceptional case among our interviewees, many of whom reported that their organisations honestly tried, in their view, to follow good practice in equal opportunities (although women managers 'are thin on the ground here', said a private sector interviewee). Yet we found several other cases, where women managers felt that they were being passed over for reasons other than competence. These reflect evidence cited, for example, by Davidson and Cooper (1992), about the disproportionately low representation of women managers in all areas of employment. This is also the case for secondary school teaching. Coleman (in Bush and West-Burnham, 1994: 178–89) drew on striking evidence from DFE statistics for 1993, to show that discrepancies become notably more gross, as seniority rises. Moreover, Coleman cites evidence from the Management and Organisation in Secondary Schools (MOSS) Project, which indicates that 'women are also working harder than men to qualify for these positions'. The Project found that, although women had far fewer actual posts of responsibility, they tended to have 'two specific posts of responsibility at the same grade as men who only had one of the jobs' (Weightman, 1989: 119). Even worse patterns of unfairness are evident in primary schools where, although women teachers outnumber men by a ratio of four to one, 'women are only appointed to half the headships' (O'Brien, in Lawrence, 1994: 53).

Such problems may be seen to have a direct bearing, of course, on the health of consultative management and on the effectiveness of task teams in educational and other organisations. Barbara reflected on her work as a Deputy Head on the senior management team of her school:

> I'm sure that not all women in management feel a sense of sometimes being 'put down' by male colleagues, but I know I do. And other women have admitted things like that to me, you know.

> *Interviewer:* Could you provide an example ...?

> *Barbara:* Well ... I wonder if your women colleagues experience any of my frustration, in just trying to get some males to *listen*? You find yourself first getting irritated, then making a superhuman effort to be nice, then wondering whether just to ignore them.... It's up to me to do something about it, I know – and assert myself against the hierarchy. But when people can't or won't listen, it's hard to get good teamwork going, isn't it?

Barbara eloquently points out, here, a crucial link between achieving conditions of genuine equality and respect, and developing effective teamwork in management – where good practice can hardly help but grow, when there are fair conditions and opportunities for all.

(6) Issues of communication in organisations

Leaders, suggests Brighouse (1991: 15), ought to ensure that all the people they meet should be able to believe 'themselves to be the most important in the world at that time'. When consultative management set up task teams they expect things to be done. However, as virtually all our interviewees pointed out, teamwork is a *process*, which depends entirely on the quality of communication within an organisation. Communication essentially involves, as Brighouse declared, giving one's full attention to the other, whether speaking or listening. This includes a willingness to accept the 'otherness' of the other person, not only in terms of their point of view, but also their whole person. As Riley (1994: 35) suggested, 'Realistically, staff should be able to exhibit negative emotions such as guilt, anxiety and anger as well as being able to admit publicly to failure; a quality unheard of in some schools'.

This is a vital, yet not easily measured aspect of communication, on which all teamwork must rely. There is however, one aspect that *is* measurable, and of great importance in the day-to-day running of an organisation. This concerns what should be a fairly straightforward matter of ensuring that information is efficiently transmitted to all who require it. Both the public and private sector managers reported no special difficulties in this respect: 'We've all got E-Mail, faxes, and mobile phones,' said John (private sector). 'You can usually get through – at least, to anyone who's willing to listen.' Yet a number of teacher–managers revealed that they could not always rely on this in their schools. Cliff, a Deputy Head, admitted:

> We're quite good, I think, at the human interaction side, but we have some real problems here, with three different school sites. Just locating somebody can be difficult, with the result that people often just don't bother to try to contact, unless it's a life-or-death thing. Messages can get picked up days after they were sent ... we also have too much of a sense of rush here – no time allocated for the kind of informal meetings where you might really start exchanging new ideas. It's a good job we're not running a hospital.

This shows, in part, a need for school leaders simply to manage the administration of routine communication more effectively. A large organisation such as theirs might, for example, consider: a daily bulletin, which all staff are expected to read and on which they should act, where indicated; use of IT, including electronic mail; possible use of fax machines and mobile phones for select staff, as well as a number of other well-known devices for improving communication systems. The interviewer asked Cliff whether he could, in fact, genuinely claim that his school is 'quite good ... at the human interaction side', when mechanical systems seemed to be failing so badly? He replied:

> Well, we do take our teamwork seriously, you know. The SMT, for example, and the teams that I run, work out meeting dates for up to two terms ahead. It's the emergency meetings we're not good at handling, where we have to meet – or at least exchange messages – at short notice. At my last school we had an almost opposite situation – self-contained site, a Tannoy system in every room, the head briefing the staff every morning. It was just like Orwell's *1984* – lots of messages telling you what to do, but no-one was listening. Perhaps we need to use the systems from that place, combined with the good teamwork that we get at this school ....

All communication and interaction depends, of course, on people being prepared to listen, and to make sure that their own response is communicated in return. That, as so many of our respondents recognised, lies at the heart of effective teamwork in management. It provides essential ways and means of ensuring that all members of the organisation should have their opportunity to contribute as fully and creatively as possible to its well being and further development.

Concluding note

Staff at London's Ritz Hotel will receive training today on flatter structure communication   (News Item, Radio Four, 25th November 1994).

Drawing discussion from the six main headings together, it emerges that our interviewees, who were all hard-working, feet-on-the-ground middle and senior managers, shared a view that old pyramid-structures of authority were inefficient, and should be consigned to history. However, many of them felt that they were still working in such rigid hierarchies.

Old patterns of stepping slowly upwards into 'dead men's shoes', or of shuffling through 'tiny, step-by-step increments' (Lawrence, 1994: 71) are irrelevant to modern organisations. Instead of that, modern organisations need to raise levels of commitment and performance, through fostering what the Japanese term '*Ringi-Ko*', or consultative design-making (Hales, 1994), and through valuing genuine achievement. Fairness of opportunity must, in the future, depend on the willingness of an organisation to give speedy rewards to talent and teams to achieve best performances. In this way, an organisation can help to release what Handy (1993: 40–41) calls the 'E-factor' (involving effort, energy, excitement, enthusiasm and emotion) among all its individual members and teams, to achieve the crucial E-factor of *effectiveness*. Some of the issues raised in this chapter will be examined further, in Chapter 15 (on the work of school senior management teams).

CHAPTER SIX

Leading the Team – Managing Staff Development in the Primary School

Stephen Knutton and Gillian Ireson

'Staff development does not take place in a vacuum'
(Oldroyd and Hall, 1991: 15)

Following a rapidly changing curriculum and increasing controls upon teachers in Britain, their needs for staff development are ever increasing. Specific staff needs will, of course, reflect particular work contexts. The study reported here concerns a primary school which had recently been formed by the merger of junior and infant schools on the same site. Therefore, beyond the needs of primary teachers who were coping with immense curriculum change and an associated administrative burden, there was a new need to promote the development of common understandings and good relationships.

Staff development and school leadership

Staff development has often been used as an umbrella term to cover a wide range of activities, from visits to other schools and traditional INSET courses, to the sort of personal professional development that leads to a qualification. In recent times, changes to the funding of INSET, and the burgeoning demand for help to cope with change have placed new stresses upon the system. To some extent, the introduction of an appraisal system for teachers, although broadly welcomed by the profession, has complicated matters by raising issues of accountability and effectiveness in potentially threatening ways. In the light of this flux in teachers' careers, this study explores the role of management in meeting the widely differing demands of the school community, and the individuals employed within it. What is it that teachers perceive that they need? How can the management team match the interests and personal needs of a diverse staff, whilst ensuring that whole school requirements are met? What is the role of appraisal within this framework?

The increasing complexity of schools, new curricular arrangements and the community responsibilities of schools have served to focus minds on the need to develop alternative styles of leadership. Helen McMullen (1991: 167) claims that schools which make a positive contribution to an individual teacher's development are characterised by certain features, such as open discussion of issues, ownership by teachers of both problems and solutions, an effective evaluation system, and a school management with a directed vision for the future. Therefore, rather than relying upon traditional, hierarchical models of managerial leadership there has been a determined exploration of alternative styles, which seek to engage others in a commitment to change, to involve others in decision-making, rather than being the recipients of handed-down decisions. These alternative styles draw on cultural and symbolic, as well as technological sources (Caldwell and Spinks, 1992). Leaders and senior managers relocate their 'power', and are then freed to guide new developments. Teachers are given *ownership* in some significant parts of their own working environment and are consequently *empowered* to act. This constitutes *consultative management* (*see* Chapter 5) in which staff, given the opportunity to develop their skills and talents to help their school to progress, become more self-confident, more willing to take the initiative, solve problems, take decisions and develop policies. In such circumstances staff become responsible for their work. They are more likely to become motivated, creative and receptive to change.

Staff development has a crucial role to play in the creation of such a consultative culture within a school. It is, however, only one part of the process since, if staff are to become truly receptive to change, they must adapt to consultative management, with its delegation, team building and empowerment of staff. This is initially achieved through the school's leadership, but will also require the energies of all staff. The required shift in management style can be summarised as :

From:	To:
fixed roles	flexible roles
individual responsibility	shared responsibility
autocratic	collaborative
control	release
power	empowerment

Hargreaves (1994: 103) adapted notions from the anthropologist Edward Hall (1984), of how different teachers perceive time. He identified *monochronic* and *polychronic* conceptions of time, the former being more 'masculine' and the latter more associated with 'female' socialisation. With polychronic time people engage in several things at the same time, regard completion of transactions, as opposed to schedules, as vital, are highly sensitive to context and are strongly oriented towards people. This is typical of the primary school, where there is a predominantly female teaching force. The distinctive contribution that women can make to management was well documented by Shakeshaft (1987), and is also discussed by Esmeralda Brodeth in Chapter 11 of this book. Several aspects of the shift in management style represented above, such as collaboration and shared responsibility, could be seen as moving in a direction more suited to non-patriarchal strengths. Primary schools, with their smaller staffs, provide opportunities for rapid changes in patterns of leadership.

Effective leadership therefore involves not only getting things done, but also supporting those who are doing it. In the context of staff development Bradley *et al.* (1983) identified a number of issues that need to be addressed by headteachers if they are to facilitate the development of individuals:

- fostering a collaborative and participative approach;

- making maximum use of the talents of each member of staff, by creating an efficient structure of responsibilities within the school and then delegating effectively;

- encouraging staff to take responsibility for their own development.

One danger in this approach to leadership lies in the kind of headteacher who clings to proprietorial attitudes (Hargreaves, 1994: 250). As Hargreaves observes,

> With *visions* as singular as this, teachers soon learn to suppress their *voice.* Management becomes manipulation. Collaboration becomes co-optation. Worst of all, having teachers conform to the principal's vision minimizes the opportunities for principals to learn that parts of their own vision may be flawed; that some teachers' visions may be as valid or more valid than theirs.

Fullan (1992) noted, too, that when educational visions are grounded in the leader's personal and prior vision, they can become visions that blind rather than visions that illuminate. Another example of restricted vision can arise from an over-emphasis upon school-based INSET, where there is a danger of introversion and a loss of critical perspective. Just as private organisations recognise the value of high quality external consultancy, so do colleges and schools need outside expertise for full staff development (Lally *et al.*, 1992: 113).

To sum up, school managers are shifting from being supervisors to being planners, who rely on the ideas and actions of the staff as a whole team. The head leads this team – as facilitator, organiser, listener, communicator and resource person. Teamwork enables expertise, experience, instinct and knowledge to be put to use and gives staff a real chance to be involved in the management of the school. Such involvement is itself a potentially rich source of professional development for individual teachers. This is summed up by Handy (1990: 93), who comments on the sharing of power among 'a variety of individual groups, allied together under a common flag, with some shared identity'; where 'the initiative, drive and energy come mostly from the bits'. The harnessing of that energy for the benefit of the pupils, the school and the community must surely be the key role of the head teacher. Central to achieving a successful outcome is a well-planned staff development programme to meet the needs of both staff and school. This is identified by Joyce (1990: xv), in *Changing School Culture through Staff Development*:

> ... the future culture of the school will be fashioned largely by how staff development systems evolve. How good schools will be as educational institutions – how humane and vital they will be as places of work – will be functions of the energy and quality of investment in their personnel. Whether better-designed curriculums will be implemented, the promise of new technologies realized, or visions of a genuine teaching profession take form, all depend to a large extent on the strength of the growing staff development programs.

The context: Millheath School

Millheath School was created in September 1993 by the merger of established separate infant and junior schools, under the leadership of the existing headteacher of the infant school. The merged schools occupied the same site in attractive modern buildings, at the edge of a coal mining community. The new school staff of 16, including the headteacher, also included three new teachers. The staff of both the previous schools had experienced around 18 months of uncertainty awaiting the decision on amalgamation. Initially, therefore, the priorities determined for the new school were concerned with whole school needs such as:

● the development of staff relationships

● the building of team spirit and

● beginning the processes of monitoring and evaluation of the curriculum.

The views of teachers at Millheath School

The views of staff at Millheath School were gathered by the deputy head (who was also staff development co-ordinator), through interviews and a short questionnaire.

Despite frequent reports of low morale in the teaching profession the responses of the staff at Millheath reflected an eagerness to extend their skills and knowledge. One teacher saw it as 'developing personal qualities, conquering new ground and contributing to a *whole* – the school and the wider community'. As Rudduck (1991) noted, despite the enormous pressures facing teachers they still want to learn and move forward. At Millheath the teachers felt strongly that staff development should be a two-way process, whereby the development of the individual would, in turn, lead to the development of the institution and eventually benefit the pupils themselves.

The teachers at Millheath covered a wide range of experience, from two newly qualified teachers (NQTs) to two teachers, each with 27 years of teaching experience (in one case all in the same school). Thus the staff were at different stages of their careers so that their professional needs differed considerably. The two NQTs were in a 'survival and discovery' phase (Huberman, 1989), where their needs for basic support were uppermost. By way of contrast, another teacher saw her own future through a deputy headship; she thought that staff development should extend her beyond the classroom, and provide experience appropriate to a future management role. Another teacher, with 18 years experience, wanted staff development to 'make me into a better primary teacher' and provide 'more confidence in the classroom'.

Needs identification and prioritisation

Usually, the Millheath teachers felt able to identify their own individual needs and were also keenly aware of whole school needs. Interestingly this awareness was mainly fostered through staff meetings, working parties and staffroom talk; not, as might have been expected, by the formal routes of the GRIDS (Guidelines for Review and Internal Development in Schools) system, or the School Development Plan. One teacher observed that her 'world revolves around my classroom' and that 'staff meetings tell us what to do'. For such teachers the importance of 'talking to each other' and of staff meetings (as opposed to written means of communication) should not be underestimated by school managers.

Balance of needs

Interestingly the staff at Millheath felt that their individual needs would be met by current staff development provision. Staff felt that both their long-term professional needs and their personal career development were covered. This is interesting, given the present climate of in-service provision, where there is evidence of a shift, from developing the individual towards developing the institution (Day and Gilroy, 1993). How did the school achieve this? The school is certainly no better off financially than other schools in an urban environment, and therefore the funding available is no more generous than for similar institutions.

The answer may lie in the confidence that the staff had that their needs would be met. What is the basis of this confidence? As far as individual and long-term professional development needs were concerned, the reasons staff gave for feeling that individual and long-term professional development needs would be met, included support from colleagues and management, the opportunity to raise issues for development, and a feeling that they were always 'listened to'. As far as whole school needs were concerned they felt that trust in the management, and the fact that management cared about everyone being involved, were the main reasons for believing that these needs would be met. Stress was placed upon the opportunity to be involved, for matters to be discussed openly and the chance to be heard. When it came to deciding upon INSET courses, neither personal nor whole school needs predominated. In fact areas of weakness, roles of responsibility, personal needs and school needs were all taken into consideration. Almost all staff agreed that it was possible to separate individual and whole school needs, but invariably they drew attention to the desirability of a linkage. As one teacher wrote,

> Yes, it's healthier ... otherwise you have a very narrow view/field. Individual needs widen horizons, refresh – but there still needs to be a link.

The role of quality leadership in creating a supportive climate in the school was confirmed as crucial, if teacher development (and school development) is to be successful.

Interestingly, however, the general level of satisfaction with the balance of individual, whole school and national needs did not extend to the opportunities provided in school, for meeting the needs of small teams through staff development. Here, dissatisfaction was expressed by every member of staff, who identified the need for team developments as potentially crucial.

Why had such a gap developed? Was it a result of lack of time or planning, or had the importance of teamwork not occurred to staff before they were confronted with its possibility, through the interviews?

Staff views on future staff development activities

Clark (1992) portrays primary teachers as largely active, knowledgeable and innovative, with a visionary view of professional development and who see self-development and self-understanding as keys to professional growth. The responses of these teachers certainly supports the view of teachers as thinking reflective professionals, who are prepared to meet innovative challenges in staff development, as envisaged by Barber

(1992), Day (1991) and Fullan (1993). Most staff were willing to be committed to the setting up of staff portfolios, and of a staff development committee, provided that appropriate guidelines could be agreed. Whilst several saw staff portfolios as highly personal and private, and expressed concerns about confidentiality, there were others who saw that 'openness would be essential'. Many indicated a willingness to participate in weekend residential sessions and evening seminars. Some had already taken courses which they had funded themselves.

Staff development or INSET?

One curious aspect of this study concerned the staff's apparent perceptions of staff development and INSET. Views of staff development came through the interviews, whilst the questionnaires had sought data on INSET. Interviewees ignored mention of INSET, but referred to staff meetings, working groups and parties, discussions with colleagues and training days. The questionnaire responses perceived INSET as merely concerned with courses and formal training. This may be attributing an instrumental perspective to INSET, seeing it as being concerned with acquiring specific knowledge or skills (tips-for-teachers), whereas the interviews signalled a belief that 'real' staff development is about developing relationships and working teams. The disparity of viewpoint between the interviews and the questionnaire suggests that managers should value the 'whole needs' of teachers, and not seek 'quick fix' versions of INSET, to solve complex problems.

Appraisal and staff development

Professional development should serve a number of interrelated purposes, including those of the individual, community, the school and pupils (Day, 1991). Neglect of individual staff development needs can lead to neglect of pupils, the school and community. On the other hand, where whole school priority needs take precedence, then it could be argued that pupils and community needs are being met. In these circumstances, is it right for the professional development needs of the teacher to be restricted to those areas prioritised by the school? It is in this context that we should consider appraisal (*see also* Chapter 10). The aims of the School Teacher Appraisal Circular (DES Circular 12/91) included:

i)   recognising the achievements of school teachers and identifying ways of improving their skills and performance;

ii) helping to determine whether a change of duties would aid the professional development of teachers and improve their professional prospects;

iii) identifying the potential of teachers for career development and, wherever possible, assisting with appropriate in-service training;

iv) helping teachers who have difficulties with their performance – through appropriate guidance, counselling and training.

In addition, the circular also sought to provide information for those responsible for writing references for teachers in relation to appointments. Appraisal, then, can be viewed *either* as a means of identifying individual needs and providing opportunities for staff, *or* as part of an accountability-driven response to sort out the problems or deficiencies of either individuals, groups or of the institution. Eraut (1986) argued that the real purpose of appraisal is determined by the intended product. Where the product is an action plan for development then the appraisal interview, to all intents and purposes, becomes a staff development interview. If, however, the intended product is an agreed appraisal of the teacher's performance, to be put on file, then staff development purposes will be pushed into the background. It then becomes primarily retrospective in its judgement. As a professional development, strategy appraisal has the potential to bring together both the demands of individual and institutional development (Jones, 1993). As such, appraisal could be seen as an essential component of a school's staff development strategy and to bear close links to the school development plan. Appraisal requires vision and sensitivity on the part of managers, and there must be transparency in the stated objectives of the exercise. Without this, appraisal can threaten the self-esteem of teachers. If appraisal is too closely linked to the school development plan, then the temptation for it to be used as a management tool to aid the meeting of institutional needs will all too easily become emphasised, to the possible detriment of individual needs.

Appraisal at Millheath School

Teachers at Millheath were fairly divided in their views of the relationship between appraisal and the staff development programme. There was a tendency for less experienced teachers to approve of some linkage between the appraisal process and the staff development programme. More experienced teachers saw difficulties because, 'while ... it's separate it's not threatening. It could (however) be used as a basis for future staff development'. Many of the staff reactions to questions about appraisal referred to the outcomes of the process, in the form of targets agreed with the appraiser. Most clearly saw a connection between their individually agreed targets, their own possible needs for development assistance in the areas concerned, and the potential for all or most such targets being brought together in the staff development programme. There was, however, some reluctance to fully accept this. One stressed the need to prioritise individual targets for future staff development, but also to maintain anonymity, whilst another talked of going 'slowly and with permission'. Others saw the need for a more regular update, a rolling programme of appraisal with structured follow-up.

The reactions of staff in this newly formed school underlined the potentially threatening nature of appraisal, and the need on the part of management for sensitivity in their approach. Interestingly, about three-quarters of the teachers regarded appraisal as a unique opportunity for discussion, thinking and reflection – something of a 'special time' just for them. This accords with findings by Turner and Clift (1988), who reported that teachers invariably 'express satisfaction with the time of exclusive and uninterrupted discussion with their headteacher afforded by the appraisal interview'. The teachers' view of appraisal as a special time also resonated with that of the headteacher, who found it 'a real privilege to be able to go into somebody's class and appraise them, and be able to share that experience with them'. For the teachers at Millheath, there is obviously confidence in the processes being undertaken. Would full implementation of Circular 12/91 (DES, 1991a), with its reference to linking appraisal to the school's objectives, put this perceived benefit in jeopardy? Whilst the majority felt positively towards appraisal, a significant minority did not. Their doubts should not be ignored; there is still a need to make appraisal a less threatening and anxious experience than it currently is for some teachers. Perhaps some rethinking of the role of management acting as appraisers is needed. This was certainly an acceptable possibility to the head, who saw great potential for teachers appraising each other as peers. Genuine consultations on, for example, classroom observation, could lead to significant staff development. On the other hand, if appraisal were to find itself closely linked to performance-related pay schemes, then teachers at Millheath School may lose their 'special time' altogether, with potentially damaging consequences for their morale.

Consequences for management

Headteachers and Senior Management Teams have to satisfy several different audiences at the same time. They have to carry out a balancing act in which, first and foremost, they must ensure that the individual and educational needs of pupils are met. This is the most crucial criterion for a successful school. However, as Oldroyd and Hall (1991:63) point out

> it is important not to lose sight of the intimate link between staff development and school improvement – so inextricably bound together that one cannot happen without the other.

The task of the head, together with the Staff Development Co-ordinator, is to attempt to achieve a balance between the needs of the school as an institution and the differing personal needs of individual members of staff. This is a considerable challenge for any school and involves finding ways of dealing with the tensions between the needs of individuals, teams, whole school and the LEA in planning staff development.

Oldroyd, Smith and Lee (1984) found that schools which had good staff development programmes were characterised by a collegial, participative style of leadership where senior staff were ready to consult, delegate, encourage staff ownership, make use of staff talents in INSET, encourage networking, lead by example by themselves engaging in their own professional development and, above all, contributing towards a positive climate by offering professional support to staff.

To conclude

Following amalgamation, Millheath School has experienced a remarkable degree of success in a short period of time, and achieved an impressive degree of mutual understanding of the institution's direction and goals. The headteacher paid tribute to a perceptive, talented and dedicated staff, in coming to terms with the realities of the new school. It is evident, however, that her own policy of involving all the staff in decision-making is crucial. This leads to staff experiencing a degree of autonomy about the development of the school, its curriculum and their own role in the school, with 'everyone feeling a part of the process'.

CHAPTER SEVEN

Leading the Team: Managing Pastoral Care in a Secondary Setting

Michael Calvert and Jenny Henderson

Introductory note

This book is concerned with issues of value, vision and changing cultures, in managing education. Arguably, nowhere in the curriculum are these issues more important and potentially problematic than in the area of pastoral care. It places special demands on managers to provide a supportive framework, which will equip pupils to cope with the ever-increasing pressures of life. Often under-valued and misunderstood, inadequately resourced and prepared for, pastoral provision can be patchy. A lack of commitment and consensus can lead to problems, where management may lose its way, unable to reconcile conflicting demands and pressures.

This chapter will examine some challenges that the pastoral domain poses on management, and show, through case studies, how these were handled in three schools. The studies reveal some pitfalls that poorly managed change can bring about, and also show examples of good practice.

Before we examine the challenges we must first establish what is meant by pastoral care. We have followed a widely accepted definition, that pastoral care is concerned with the welfare of pupils, and the help which they need, to develop personal and social skills and understanding that will be of use to them in later life.

In its widest sense, all teacher–managers are involved in pastoral care, which permeates every aspect of school life. This chapter, however, will concentrate on two main facets of pastoral care which are a normal feature of secondary schools in the UK, namely the role of the form tutor and the teaching of Personal and Social Education (PSE). The form tutor has responsibilities for administration, discipline and the welfare of pupils. The teacher of PSE, who may often be the form tutor, is responsible for teaching a set syllabus, which covers a range of issues with a personal, social, vocational and moral dimension. There are great differences between the roles of the form tutor, ranging from schools where the form tutor has an almost exclusively administrative role and PSE is taught by 'experts', to schools where PSE teaching is seen as an integral part of the form tutor's work. These descriptions recognise the dangers of compartmentalising pastoral roles (Calvert and Henderson, 1994), but should help the reader to differentiate between the two main functions of administration and teaching.

Pastoral issues for management

The above description of the pastoral domain may seem straightforward. It does, however, disguise complexities and conflicts that can arise. These may include:

- *a lack of shared understanding and agreement* as to the purposes and nature of pastoral provision;

- the existence of an *academic/pastoral divide* – misunderstanding about the importance of the complementary nature of the two and a lack of recognition of the importance of the contribution of the pastoral (Marland, 1989);

- a resulting *inferior position of the pastoral curriculum* (and lower status for staff involved) with an over-emphasis on academic results (Ketteringham, 1987);

- pressures of an *overcrowded curriculum* and reduced funding (Shaw, 1994);

- *teacher overload* – an increase in workload and expectations (Fullan and Hargreaves, 1992; Hargreaves, 1994);

- the difficulty of encouraging teachers to take on an enhanced pastoral role in a climate in which increased demands are being made on teachers generally and *high levels of stress* reported;

- *a lack of pastoral care for staff* under such circumstances (Mc Guiness, 1989);

- *a lack of commitment and confidence* in the pastoral domain on the part of many teachers (HMI, 1988a);

- *a lack of consensus as to the aims, nature, content, skills and processes* of PSE work (Shaw, 1994);

- *a lack of appreciation as to the value of PSE* on the part of teachers and pupils (Lang, 1983);

- *a lack of suitable materials* and *ineffective use of available resources* (Blackburn, 1983);

- *a lack of a clear role for management* (Hamblin, 1989) and insufficient regard to the training needs of management, as well as of form teachers and teachers of PSE;

- *inappropriate management structures* for developing pastoral care;

- *difficulties in providing adequate preparation for Newly Qualified Teachers* in initial teacher education and induction (Calvert and Henderson, 1994);

- *difficulties of monitoring and evaluating pastoral work* and measuring success (Blackburn, 1975) and inadequate evaluation of courses and assessment of pupils (HMI, 1988b);

- *lack of support* for pastoral care at national levels.

The above list presents a daunting task for management. Clearly, we should not want to paint an exclusively negative picture of pastoral care provision nationally, and the work of NAPCE (National Association of Teachers of Pastoral Care) and others shows that valuable work is done in schools. Yet practice is variable, and it is difficult to find a school with consistently high standards of care running throughout the institution.

Our case studies offer a glimpse of three schools facing some of the challenges, and looking to improve their provision during times of considerable upheaval, involving a changing intake and/or a reduction of the number of sites on which they are working. All the schools happen to be split site, but they were selected because they each offered a different type of pastoral provision and were located in three different areas. Interviews were carried out with heads, pastoral managers, teachers and a cross-section of pupils in each of the three schools.

School A

School A is an 11–16 city comprehensive school of 900 pupils situated on a split site. It resulted from the amalgamation of two schools in 1986. The school population is largely drawn from two large council estates and one lower middle class estate. In 1994, following closure of two local schools, it received an increased Year 7 intake and 16 new members of staff. Year 10 was also substantially increased, while Year 8 and Year 9 were only marginally affected. In the same year it moved from a 20 to a 25 period (1 hour) week and a longer working day. Until 1994 pastoral care had been administered in three vertical pupil divisions, managed by three dedicated senior staff. Owing to the increase in size of the school, decisions were made to move to a pastoral system divided into five year groups. The pastoral co-ordinator is a deputy head. There had, up to this point, been a 35 minute tutorial lesson 'tagged on to a form tutor slot' one day a week, PSE being taught by form tutors. With the new day, form tutor time was reduced to 10 minutes in the morning and 5 minutes in the afternoon, only long enough to cope with administration.

Instead of PSE being taught as a discrete subject, the content was shared by the English and Science departments, both of whom were allocated extra curricular time. Topics associated with health and environmental education are taught within Science. Other areas including study skills, aspects of equal opportunities, law and politics are covered by the English department. One member of the Science department is responsible for the science element of the PSE programme. Together with an enthusiastic team from within the science department they have produced components for a PSE course, largely in their own time, which is up and running. The English department, with a newly appointed head of department, is in the process of producing its own PSE materials. PSE at Key Stage 4, with an emphasis on careers and Records of Achievement (the school was one of the first in the country to introduce Records of Achievement) continues to be taught mainly by form tutors 1 hour each week, with input from the careers department.

It is worth noting that the influx of so many pupils this academic year has placed an added strain on the pastoral resources of the school.

School B

School B is a comprehensive school with 1200 pupils on roll. The school population is drawn mainly from the more affluent suburbs of a market town, with a fair degree of parental support. The school originated in 1991 from the amalgamation of three schools, each with strong traditions and loyalties. Until 1993 the teaching was on five sites. The teaching currently (1994–95) takes place on two sites but the school has now completed an extensive building programme, bringing all the teaching together on one site.

The head of lower and upper school have the pastoral role high on their list of priorities on their staff development plan. In their words the pastoral organisation has 'chugged along' over the last 2 or 3 years, as provision has been influenced by practical considerations and compromises associated with split site schools. The school, again in their words, has spent 'a year coping, a year recovering and a year developing', to which we might add 'a year planning'.

Form time at present consists of one 30 minute period, 3 days of 20 minutes including one year assembly, and one day with a whole school assembly. There is a 5-minute registration in the afternoon. PSE is not taught by form tutors: it is delivered on a rotating basis with Information Technology, Religious Education and Careers. Years 7, 8 and 9 have a double period a fortnight. The PSE co-ordinator is responsible for the programme for each year.

There are heads of year and assistant heads of year. The year teams meet once every 6 weeks and their meetings are attended by the appropriate head of upper or lower school. The PSE co-ordinator chairs meetings of all those involved in the delivery of PSE. At present these teachers may include those with light timetables and some would not see themselves as strong teachers of PSE, or with particular gifts or commitment towards PSE teaching.

The school management sees the 1995–96 academic year as the opportunity to put wide-ranging policies in place. It is anxious not to rush these changes, but to 'get it right'. They want the school to have a 'corporate image', with a clear statement as to what the school stands for and they are looking for standardisation in policies, practices, presentation and documentation. They see the pastoral domain as an important aspect of their whole school development plan. Enhancing the role and raising the profile of the form tutor is central to these plans and they hope that the teaching of PSE can be understood to be part of the role of the form tutor.

Development plans were overshadowed at the time of writing by the announcement of the need to lose 12 staff at the end of the 1994–95 academic year.

School C

School C is a 13–18 city comprehensive school on a split site, with 1000 pupils on roll. The school is divided into years, each with a year head who is responsible to a deputy head. There is a PSE co-ordinator and two experienced teachers responsible for Health Education and Careers. Each head of year is responsible for the PSE programme for that year and has a deputy, who is described as a pastoral assistant. The school is in an area which includes two large council estates, with incidence of economic and social disadvantage and high unemployment. While holding the view that pastoral care is important for all schools, the staff here recognise the importance of its particular contribution at their school in helping to raise pupils' self-esteem, build their confidence and enrich their cultural background.

The pastoral organisation for Year 9 is different from that of the other years. The form tutor plays an important role, spending 10–15 minutes each day plus extra tutor time 1 day each week with their form. They are also responsible for teaching PSE for 1 hour a week. Year 9 tutors are more involved with communicating with parents than in Years 10 and 11.

Staffing is generous for PSE, in that some specialist staff 'float' to support staff with topics such as health and sex education. All Year 9 tutors volunteer to undertake the role, in the full knowledge that it involves commitment to teach PSE, and such an arrangement is a priority when formulating timetables. At the end of each year the Year 9 tutors are asked if they would wish to continue in the following year. It is a measure of the success of the programme, that 6 out of 10 of the original staff of the team established in 1988 (when this scheme was introduced) are still in the team.

In Years 10 and 11 the form tutor is identified more as an administrator. Owing to the problems of a split-site school, pupils often do not see their tutor twice a day. At present the form tutor is not responsible for teaching the PSE element, which is covered by teams of teachers who have acquired specialist knowledge, supported by those on light timetables. There is one 70 minute period each week, and pupils follow a modular course with materials prepared for the teachers. There is a recognition that the programme is complex but, as far as the school is concerned, 'The model works for us' as a short- to medium-term model.

With local reorganisation, School C will become an 11–18 school with a lower school of 900 pupils housed on one site, which will entail substantial changes.

Perceptions, visions and values

Teachers' perceptions of pastoral care vary enormously. Many feel the pastoral side of the curriculum to be very important and that an absence 'would have severe consequences on the school'. They feel form tutor time to be an important time for getting to know the pupils. Those teachers committed to teaching PSE feel it to be an important programme which should stand in its own right as a subject. Many feel unskilled:

It's a different way of working. That worries me. I'm a bit traditional and like a bit of control. I worry we're not doing enough work, not just sitting around and talking.

and:

I was concerned because it was sex education and I was frightened I couldn't deliver it in the right way.

Pupils' perceptions vary, too. Some feel that tutor time provides an opportunity to discuss problems. A Year 11 pupil at School A stated:

PSE helps you to communicate more with people; it makes you adapt to people around you. I respect people in my class more because they've opened up.

Others have a different view. A Year 9 pupil in School B said:

It's not an important time. The form teacher is not an important person, just does the admin.

Pupils have mixed feelings about PSE. Some feel it allows them to 'get the whole class's opinion, not just the person sitting next to you', that 'it's a chance to unload your feelings'. Others do not look forward to it, find it is 'wasted in academic terms' and wonder 'why we don't come to school 10 minutes later'.

With these different views on the pastoral curriculum, management has a real problem in promoting its own vision and values, whilst at the same time recognising a range of attitudes and practices. To have a mandate for an enhanced pastoral system the head needs a measure of consensus, based on full and open consultation. One teacher commented: 'You can't "press gang" teachers into formal teaching of PSE'.

In School B the head recognises that commitment to the pastoral role is not mirrored across the school. Successful implementation of change will only occur if ideas and values are shared and communicated. A head of year with 30 years' teaching experience felt strongly about this:

> If it's on the timetable we need to know what it is and why we're doing it, or pupils will switch off and think it's a waste of time. Academic students will turn round and say, 'I'm wasting my time when I could be passing exams'.

Central to a coherent and comprehensive approach to pastoral provision must be the 'whole' vision and values of the school shared by staff, and also understood and accepted by pupils.

In the three schools it is clear that each head has a set of values and, to a greater or lesser extent, a vision of how they see the pastoral system in their school developing. School A, led by an extremely caring and approachable head who prides himself on knowing all the pupils in his school, has, for a variety of reasons been unable to bring together the different aspects of pastoral care in a coherent way. The school accepts that the PSE programme is not working. Until 1994 PSE was taught by form tutors, many of whom felt inexpert. This state of affairs led to staff resentment and, following discussion, senior management determined to make changes. The deputy head, who is also PSE co-ordinator of School A, took the view that the school was never going to win a united battle with the whole staff, so, he 'steamrollered a content-led programme'. Needless to say, dissatisfaction persists and the head is aware that much remains to be done.

The head of School B strongly believes that all teachers are pastoral teachers and, while believing that in an ideal world a pastoral system would not be necessary in school, recognises that often pupils need care and attention and a pastoral 'safety net' is required to ensure their needs are met. She has a clear vision of an enhanced role for the form teacher, which would include teaching PSE, but she is realistic enough to recognise that she will never get '100% commitment to that role'. This would only be possible 'if I could wave a magic wand and be quite sure that it would be delivered effectively and sympathetically'.

The head of School C has a strong belief in equality and pupil entitlement. He feels that, with the children in his charge, 'the school is the last free beacon of opportunity. It's the last place they can get quality'. He believes that every teacher is a pastoral leader. He is aware that this vision 'comes out in everything you do'. He feels it is necessary to have clear aims and that staff should be aware of these. His short term aim is to get heads of departments to be pastoral leaders. Eventually he would like to see every teacher delivering PSE. He recognises that for this to happen every member of staff would need the confidence and skills to handle pastoral care. His long-term aim, once all this is achieved, is to destroy the existing pastoral system, because everyone would be a pastoral teacher, but, he admits, 'I am light-years away from that'.

Climate and culture

It is, arguably, teachers who bring about change in schools. Without the support of the teachers, little meaningful and lasting change is likely to result:

> Educational change that does not involve and is not supported by the teacher usually ends up as change for the worse, or as no real change at all.
>
> (Fullan and Hargreaves, 1992:22)

It follows that the culture of schools and the climate, both nationally and locally, are likely to strongly influence teachers' attitudes towards any changes, and towards the way in which they approach collaborative working with colleagues.

As we have noted, all three schools face radical changes. Staff futures have been at stake, responsibilities and duties will change. All of this is set against a background of a further round of changes in curriculum and assessment, with the publication of the final National Curriculum Orders, and the introduction of new public examinations in the UK.

In this climate it is not surprising that there are instances of mistrust of management, and suspicions of 'hidden agendas' in some schools. A training day at School B was influenced by impending redundancies, which made discussions about an enhanced role for form tutors and the possibility of form teachers taking on the teaching of PSE very delicate. In School A there was a strong reaction from staff, at decisions reached 'behind closed doors' about future changes in PSE. Eradicating all negative feelings towards management is impossible, but it is clearly advisable to create a climate of trust and openness, which might reduce these.

Climates can change, and be subject to a number of outside factors such as those mentioned above. All schools do, however, have their unique culture, which is typically complex. To bring about any important changes it is essential to foster a culture which responds positively to change. Understandably, staff can feel threatened, under stress and often de-skilled at the prospect of change. Many have become hardened to the all too common 'initiative fatigue'. As the head of School B stated, 'The only constant here is change'.

As well as having a staff that is open to change, it is obviously helpful to have a culture which provides a supportive environment for pupils and, crucially, for staff. Few schools would appear to see the pastoral care of staff as a high priority. Teachers often feel undervalued. They do a stressful job in often poor working conditions. Many feel insecure outside the confines of their specialist subject. Little wonder that they are not always in the best state of mind to be as caring as they would like to be to others. The head of School C is adamant that staff morale is essential for good relationships:

> We are talking about adolescents who are all too often too keen to snarl and too loath to smile, and I think we have to work on it and if we all have that approach to children and are positive and happy, and we do treat their views with respect and want to listen to them ... then we're getting somewhere.

In the same school a teacher stated:

> If you have a grumpy member of staff on the PSE programme you have no chance.

Both comments underline the importance of the way in which people deal with others, and the respect they show each other. If the medium is the message, then how else might relationships in school be conducted?

Structures

It is clear that there needs to be a strong framework to co-ordinate those involved in the different aspects of pastoral care: to offer support, disseminate information, facilitate monitoring and evaluation, and provide appropriate training. The traditional pastoral structure is hierarchical with either a year or house system, the head of house or year being in charge of a team of form tutors and responsible to a deputy head. In this arrangement the heads of year often have some responsibility for the PSE curriculum for their year. Such a system, running parallel to the academic line management system, appears superficially to satisfy the pastoral needs of the school. There appears to be an accountable chain of communication and responsibilities, which facilitate close collaboration and shared commitment. In practice, however, this structure can have serious weaknesses. The most obvious effect of this parallel structure is that the pastoral is divided from the academic, as if the two were not crucially related. This carries the risk of pastoral aspects being marginalised. As the head of School C put it:

> ... in the past they (heads of year) fed into a pastoral committee, which fed into a pastoral deputy and that was that. As long as they did that they could be forgotten about.

In this school the head has disbanded the pastoral committee, and the head and deputies all have a caseload of pastoral responsibilities. Schools are such complex institutions to manage, that crude job descriptions along the lines of a 'pastoral' deputy or a 'curriculum' deputy are disappearing. Management is getting flatter and more flexible, to cope with the range of responsibilities. In School B there are no deputies with an overall pastoral responsibility, and the heads of lower and upper school have both a pastoral and an academic brief. In School A, however, the responsibility for pastoral care lies with a deputy head. He has found it very difficult to involve others and would like to write a 'teacher-proof' syllabus for Years 10 and 11, where he sees the major weaknesses lie. His workload is such that he is unable to find time for this, and it is questionable whether staff would respond positively to such an initiative, without some significant provision of staff development in this area.

This division between the pastoral and the academic also fails to address what the head of School C would see as the *raison d'être* of pastoral care, namely as a 'support for learning'. He makes the simple, persuasive point, that enhanced care leads to better performance. This echoes Shaw (1994:37): 'if learning is to be facilitated in the most effective way, good pastoral care is essential.'

Pastoral leaders need to be good managers capable of building teams, resolving conflicts, counselling and providing support. Often these qualities are wasted, because they pick up the discipline and other problems that might (a) be better dealt with by classroom teachers and (b) stem from the nature and content of the teaching, which should be addressed by the head of department. A head of year at School C complained of being worn down by the demands of a minority of teachers who wanted the head of year to do their job for them. He claimed that:

> You cannot sit down in the staffroom without people coming up to you to talk to you about a pupil.

This begs the question as to whether heads of year are necessarily the best people to develop the pastoral work of the school. In Schools A and B there are examples of heads of year who are set in a reactive mould, and who could not be counted on to develop the pastoral care in the school. In contrast, the head of School C states that the school boasts:

> a strong tradition ... of pastoral management in terms of year leaders, quite highly paid ... very well selected ... of people doing a good job to support teachers under pressure.

Unfortunately:

they do spend a great deal of time on 'sticking plaster' jobs, far too much, and not half enough time on the positive.

An answer may well lie in establishing teams with a shared commitment. However, not all teams are successful. Poor management can lead to what Hargreaves (1994) describes as 'contrived collegiality'. Putting staff together who do not have shared values and a common purpose is a recipe for disaster. For example, at School A 'last year's PSE stuff was put together by a group who were thrown together and it's not very good'. It is interesting to look at the three schools and to see what teams have produced the best results. At the same school, a group of Biology teachers have since come together to write the Science-led components of the Key Stage 3 PSE course. With goodwill and commitment they have, almost entirely in their own time, put together an impressive package of materials. At School C the Year 9 form tutors are all volunteers. When this scheme was introduced senior management recognised the potential strength of the team, and gave them the opportunity to go on a residential course for appropriate training.

Concluding note

What is management to do, faced with such a minefield of misconceptions, conflicting interests and pressures? The answer may well lie in Hamblin's (1989:x) message, in the introduction to his book:

> A blanket solution to complex problems is a delightful thought but it is still an illusion. The book stresses not so much *what* is done but *how* it is done, and the *meaning* of that action in a context of conflicting forces.

None of the heads of the three schools would pretend to have gone as far as they would have liked, to improve the pastoral care provision in their school. Indeed, the head of School C, which arguably has advanced the most in terms of having a workable system in place, that enjoys the acceptance and support of many staff and pupils, freely admits that he finds the treatment of a minority of staff towards pupils and other staff unacceptable. He, like the other heads, retains a vision of a caring school. While he looks long-term to the abolition of the pastoral system, he aims in the mid-term to have staff working within a framework of a strong developmental, pro-active structure led by capable middle managers and backed by tutors willing to assume responsibility, and who receive appropriate training, resources and support. This, arguably, points the way to a system that meets the needs of all pupils.

CHAPTER EIGHT

Quality, Chaos and the Management of Change in Further Education

Terry Cowham

This chapter reports on the outcomes of an investigation into the process of managing change at a large further education college in England. This is sited on three campuses in the centre of a major conurbation. The college has recently been re-organised and, even more recently, incorporated. The study examines the importance of investing in people in the context of major external change, centred on the developing requirements of the Further Education Funding Council (FEFC), at a time of extreme turbulence both for the college and for the sector in general. A theoretical perspective is provided to support the analysis. This perspective draws on various sources, to develop a unified model for quality assurance and portfolio development.

Each year the college enrols over 25,000 students, which equate to over 6,000 full-time equivalent students; it employs 355 full-time teaching staff, with a similar number of support and ancillary staff. The college was formed from a major re-organisation of further education in the city, occasioned by the need to achieve massive budget cuts which coincided with the implementation of the Education Reform Act in 1990. The re-organisation was implemented in great haste and led to massive disruption of the service, destroying any former attempts that had been made at strategic planning and institutional staff development. In 1990, following the re-organisation, there were 460 full-time teaching staff. At reorganisation, over £8 million was taken from the further education budget, followed by a further estimated £3 million between 1990 and 1993. A consequence of the re-organisation and subsequent cuts during this time was that the college was burdened with an annual deficit of over £1 million, which was transferred into incorporation.

The college has a hierarchical management structure consisting of:

1. A 'principalship' of principal, deputy principal, senior vice principal and college secretary.

2. Three directors, holding functional responsibilities, who are being retitled vice principals and who, together with the principalship, form the Senior Management Team (SMT).

3. Fourteen heads of department who manage independent cost centres, which are also units of curriculum delivery.

4. Four support functions (finance, estates, personnel and management information), with developing functions of student services, learning resources, and marketing.

5. Programme teams or sections, at sub-departmental level, headed by senior lecturers.

Literature and theoretical background

During the course of this investigation, four modes for achieving change were observed. These related closely to those identified by Chin and Benne (1974):

1. *Bureaucratic*, which remains the dominant theoretical perspective on organisations, associated with the work of Max Weber. The perspective is based on a clear-cut division of labour, a hierarchical authority structure and system of rules and regulations.

2. *Collegial* or democratic, which recognises that educational institutions differ from many organisations, in that they have large numbers of professional staff, who have substantial discretion in how they perform their teaching role. In its pure form all members of the collegium have an equal opportunity to influence policies, with decisions emerging through a process of discussion, leading to consensus.

3. *Political* modes, which stress conflict as being endemic in organisations, rather than the consensus of the collegial model, with decisions being the product of a process of bargaining and negotiation, and where issues are resolved according to the relative power of participants.

4. *Ambiguity* modes, which stress the turbulence and complexity of organisational life. They suggest that institutional goals are unclear; the decision-making process is characterised by fluid participation and problematic technology. Cohen and March (1986) described a process in which participants dump problems and solutions into a 'garbage can'. Thus many decisions may be taken with no reference to, or indeed in conflict with, stated organisational plans and priorities, due to the sheer complexity of an organisation and its environment, and inadequate communication. There is a clear

relationship here with chaos theory.

Bolman and Deal (1984) use the term 'conceptual pluralism' to describe how different modes can have a role in explaining behaviours and events in educational institutions.

The operation of these models is considered both within the college and in its external interactions with the FEFC. A hypothesis is developed, that the FEFC, through attempting to impose a systematic and bureaucratic planning structure too rapidly to a highly varied sector, which was subject to a considerable degree of ambiguity when under the former LEA control, is in fact in danger of increasing the ambiguity and 'wildness' of the sector. Carlson (1975:191) drew a distinction between 'wild' and 'domesticated' organisations. Wild organisations

> struggle for survival. Their existence is not guaranteed, and they do cease to exist. Support for them is closely tied to quality of performance.... Wild organisations are not protected at vulnerable points as are domesticated organisations.

By contrast domesticated organisations 'are fed and cared for. Existence is guaranteed'. It can be argued that central control and the use of rational procedures, which may be following political imperatives at the national level, is an attempt to standardise and 'tame" a sector that is generally noted for its 'wildness'. However, the pace of change introduced for domestication appears to have the potential for driving it out of control, and increasing its wildness.

In such a climate, tensions will inevitably develop between managers seeking to effect change, by employing whatever styles and strategies are most likely to succeed. In the present investigation, many different approaches were observed, including those identified by Chin and Benne (1974) as:

- *Empirical–rational*: attempting to convince people by rational means, appealing to reason and logic.

- *Normative–re-educative*: attempting to affect the norms, habits, and values of people and groups through education and training.

- *Power–coercive*: attempting to bring about change by political, economic, or other sanctions.

The external context

The Further and Higher Education Act of 1992 removed further education institutions from local government control and funding with effect from 1993; they became incorporated charitable institutions funded by a Further Education Funding Council, directly accountable to government through the Department for Education (DFE). The first circular from the

FEFC (1992a) required colleges to draw up strategic plans, using a rational planning structure (*see* Appendix 1). A prescribed framework requires colleges to draw up 3- or 5-year strategic plans, structured around a minimum of five defined elements, and supported by detailed annual operating statements, which are subject to an annual review and evaluation. Since 1992 colleges have become accustomed to receiving over 30 FEFC circulars each year, many of which require a great deal of complex statistical and/or financial information. Inevitably, the pressures on colleges to take on total responsibility for their budgets and all their own affairs, which came within an extremely tight timescale with incorporation in 1993, have been immense.

Of particular significance in the developing policies of the FEFC is the requirement for colleges to grow, in terms of increasing participation in further education, by approximately 8% a year (25% over 3 years). The growth targets explicitly support the government's National Targets for Education and Training (NTETs – *see* Appendix 2). A natural consequence of this growth is an increase in efficiency, in that any increase in resources to individual colleges will be at a significantly lower rate than the growth in student participation. This policy of growth links with policy to converge unit costs between colleges over 3 years, from a wide range of differential historical costs. These different costs reflect a highly complex sector, in a wide variety of institutions with different profiles and traditions. To support these policies, *Funding Learning* (FEFC, 1992b) introduced a complex recurrent funding methodology, where colleges must bid for their annual funding, based on their strategic plans, success in meeting previous targets, and level of unit cost. Inevitably colleges were forced into an extremely competitive environment, in order to survive.

Combined with FEFC's priorities of promoting growth, increasing efficiency and standardising costs is a concern for the quality of educational provision made by colleges. *Assessing Achievement* (FEFC, 1993a), describes a framework for the inspection of colleges in the further education sector, where colleges are to be inspected at least once every 4 years. This circular provides an additional approach to quality in a burgeoning quality industry, where various badges and charter marks proliferate. Among these are the long-established BS5750 (now known as ISO 9000), Investors in People (IiP), the Training and Enterprise Councils' (TECs) Quality Assurance procedures for their suppliers, and the alleged 'holy grail' of Total Quality Management (TQM).

The role of the TECs in the changing external context for colleges approaches that of the FEFC in its significance. Various commentators have noted a recurrent power battle between the DFE and the Employment Department, which is responsible for the TECs, in the arena of vocational education and training. Colleges must consult TECs on their strategic plans and, with the introduction of Youth Credits, it is TECs, not the FEFC, which fund part-time education for 16–18 year olds, as well as for many adults. TECs have a particular responsibility for ensuring that the NTETs are met, and also assessing organisations for the IiP standard.

The internal context

In many ways, college incorporation presented less of a trauma for the college than many others in the sector, in that it had enjoyed a high level of devolution of powers from its local authority from its inception; it had also become accustomed to being entrepreneurial, in order to obtain resources when they were reduced, as a result of local authority budget crises. However, dealings with the local authority had tended to be highly politicised, focusing on local issues and priorities. There had been little pretence at planning and a high degree of opportunism, which was reflected in the internal culture of the college and which was compounded by the consequences of a chaotic reorganisation.

The principal has long experience of a political style of operation, and admits to being primarily power-coercive in his approach to managing change, but also claims to be essentially pragmatic. He was faced with culture shock when encountering the bureaucratic strictures of the FEFC. It seemed that the FEFC was adopting a highly rational approach to organising a complex, diverse and disorderly sector. However, the pace at which new bureaucratic systems with an apparently rational intention were being introduced, and the over-simplistic assumptions that were being made, presented great dangers to the college, which in its range and variety of provision form a microcosm of the sector, as a whole.

Interestingly, the governing body, when examining their role and function at the beginning of 1992, had decided that they required a business plan for the college. A residential weekend was organised where the governing body would work with the Senior Management Team in preparing a plan. Coincidentally Circular 92/01 (FEFC, 1992a) was received just in advance of the weekend, providing a framework for what was to become the strategic plan. The preparation of the plan became the responsibility of the senior vice principal, who holds responsibility for Quality and Curriculum Planning. He claims to hold a rational perspective, and believes in promoting collegiality as means of assuring quality of provision, and in using a normative re-educative strategy to achieve the effective management of change. Although the Governing Body and the SMT were pleased with the resulting plan, this was less well received by line managers, who felt that they were excluded from the process. This mismatch between the SMT plan and the perceptions of line managers which Hoyle (1986) called 'organisation pathos' and which Becher (1989) termed the 'implementation gap' required a speedy revision. The problem of generating ownership of the plan can be

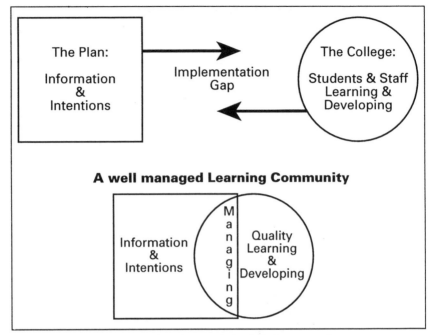

Figure 8.1 The strategic plan and the implementation gap

represented diagrammatically, as is shown in Figure 8.1.

As will be seen later, the square and circle symbols in this figure can be generalised, so that squares with their hard edges are used to represent systems, plans and procedures, while soft-edged circles can be used to represent the processes that are required to develop and implement plans and procedures effectively. Of course, in Figure 8.1 the reality of the college would be more accurately represented as a web of small linked and overlapping circles, corresponding in many cases to the activities of staff operating in programme teams.

Bridging the implementation gap

From the above analysis, it can be argued that a prime function of management is to bridge implementation gaps, and to ensure that there is a harmony between new systems and the processes that are employed. Furthermore collegial processes are likely to be more effective than political processes, implying a need for either empirical–rational or normative–re-educative strategies, rather than power–coercive ones. In the case in point, it was essential that the line managers and their staff came to own the strategic plan. In order to effect this a further residential conference was organised, which involved the line managers and SMT along with only the Chair of Governors and Chair of the Personnel Committee. Outcomes from the conference were to form a second version of the strategic plan, which was to be submitted to the FEFC, with a set of annual operating statements that would indicate to the FEFC how the plan was to be implemented in its first year of operation.

The senior vice principal organised the programme, so that three groups were formed, each with a director from the SMT and four line managers. These worked as a team, unpicking two out of six elements or themes from the plan, and working on draft operating statements that had been prepared, relating to the six planning elements. The groups addressed:

- curriculum and human resources

- finance and physical resources

- marketing and quality.

The principalship and two governors formed a separate 'strategic group'. There were two feedback sessions, where each group reported, in turn, their proposals for amending the plan and then for the operating statements. The participation of all concerned was impressive; probably the most successful outcome was the agreement that each department would prepare a set of operating statements, using a common framework which mirrored the college's statements, and cross-referenced to the strategic plan. This provided a structure for action planning and review throughout the college, as well as a means for the strategic plan to be embedded in the operation of the college. A further significant outcome from the planning conference was the decision that the college should commit itself to pursuing the Investors in People (IiP) standard.

IiP is concerned with promoting the development of staff, implying a need for structured training. The reasons behind the decision to pursue the standard for the college included:

- the college's self-interest in encouraging employers to provide training for their employees, and the need to 'practise what it preaches';

- the attraction of obtaining a 'badge' for promotional purposes;

- using the standard for promoting good practice within the college, in terms of human resource development, industrial relations and quality management;

- contributing to the college's work in strategic planning and quality assurance.

The deputy principal, in common with the principal, tends towards a political perspective of events. Believing in firm management and admitting to being often a Stalinist, his approach to managing change is primarily power–coercive. However his responsibility for Industrial Relations and Human Resources make him particularly interested in the IiP standard. The college secretary's perspective is primarily bureaucratic, and his approach to effecting change is essentially empirical–rational. The differing perspectives of the principalship are replicated in different managers throughout the college. However, the decision to pursue the IiP standard was universally accepted, albeit for different reasons. It can be argued that the response to external change in the approach adopted for strategic planning, and the decision to pursue the IiP standard, indicated a shift from the political to the collegial perspective in the management of the college.

Changes in the external context

As the FEFC continues to pursue its policy objectives of a radical change in methods of recurrent funding, and a convergence of costs between colleges, the pressures of change on institutions continue to grow. At a conference organised by the FEFC on methods of funding and second-phase strategic plans, college managers expressed grave concern over simplistic, bureaucratic approaches in a highly complex sector. One Principal of a large college spoke for many when he voiced his frustration to FEFC officers:

> Do you realise that between us we are engaged in the highly structured planning of chaos ...?

Pressures are further compounded by budget holdbacks on colleges, requiring them to demonstrate that new contracts are being introduced for staff, which will ensure greater efficiency of operation. The College Employers Forum (CEF), which represents most college employers, has engaged in a highly confrontational approach to lecturers' Unions, which has led to wide-scale disruptions of industrial relations in the sector. In short, it can be argued that an over-simplistic, over-hasty bureaucratic approach has introduced high levels of ambiguity in the sector.

Quality and assessment

Factors affecting the preparation for IiP assessment relate to other quality developments in the college, including its placement on the schedule for FEFC inspection, and its industrial relations. With respect to industrial relations, the college did not join the CEF, and was able to negotiate an agreement with its recognised trade unions on the introduction of new contracts of employment for all its staff. This approach harmonised the different management perspectives represented in the principalship. Politically expedient in avoiding disruption, it also helped promote collegiality and was rational. The negotiated agreement includes procedures for appraising all staff in the college. However, introduction of the appraisal system had to wait until final agreement had been reached on staff contracts.

As for quality developments, building on earlier experiences of BS5750

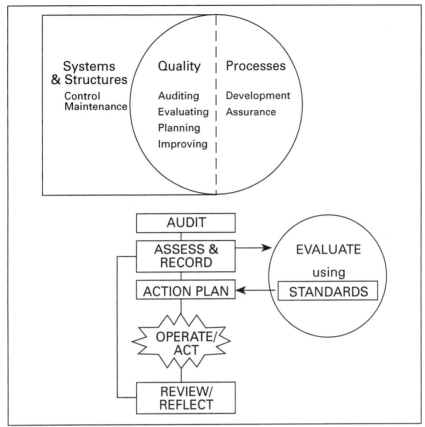

Figure 8.2 Quality, systems and processes

registration in five departments, the college became involved in a development project concerned with a unified approach to quality assurance. This addressed the requirements of six quality standards, which included BS5750 (ISO 9000), IiP and FEFC inspection. As part of its work on this project, the college devised a generic model for quality development, which is shown in Figure 8.2, and which builds on the experience gained with strategic planning and shown in Figure 8.1.

The quality cycle that should underpin all quality processes is shown as a flowchart, underpinning the overlap of the square and circle. In fact the processes involved in auditing the present position, which are necessary for the preparation and implementation and evaluating of a plan, are cyclical. This is consistent with the use of a circle symbol, except that a third dimension is required, which shows the process of applying the quality, resulting in an evolutionary spiral. Systems and standards should be subject to adaptation, development and improvement with each cycle in the spiral. It is argued that the model provides a generic approach to quality which, in the case of an educational institution, should permeate all levels of operation, from strategic management, to operational management, to staff development and training, through to the prime function of supporting students' learning. Applying quality management in this way can be used to promote a learning culture for the whole institution, which should guarantee constant institutional improvement.

Portfolio development

Using the conceptual model described above, the college has devised a comprehensive scheme for portfolio development, which covers the whole institution and which should provide a structure for organising the evidence of quality control systems and quality assurance processes, required for a quality audit. The portfolio structure is diagrammatically represented in Figure 8.3. The scheme assumes that all students should build a portfolio of their attainments, which should be mirrored by staff holding a portfolio of their own personal and professional development. Students' learning requires them to record and evaluate their learning as a pre-requisite for action planning, and the collection of evidence to demonstrate their achievements. Similarly the college's appraisal system is based on staff completing a self-assessment leading to an action plan, prepared as a result of the appraisal interview, which in turn requires the collection of evidence. The programme team is the key unit in managing curriculum delivery, and had been the focus of the college's developmental work in quality assurance. A portfolio structure had been developed for programme team manuals, to be compiled by all programme teams in the college. This arose from work undertaken in departments that achieved the BS5750 (ISO 9002) registration. A portfolio should hold policies or statements of intention, plans for achieving the intentions, procedures for carrying out the plans and evidence of achievement, which can take a number of forms. The seven headings under 'Inspection/Audit' are taken from the FEFC's inspection categories, described in *Assessing Achievement* (FEFC, 1993a). The decision to use the seven FEFC categories in the portfolio structure was taken, after an analysis of requirements of the six quality systems considered in the Mapping Quality Assurance project. This framework has the merit for the college of explicitly including curriculum issues such as teaching and learning.

In preparing for quality assessments an institutional portfolio has to be prepared for the Quality Assessors, which includes evidence that the college meets all indicators for the standard. A case in point is the IiP requirement for a storyboard to be included in the institutional portfolio, describing how the organisation has introduced one or more initiatives using IiP principles. The merit of having a generic portfolio structure, is that an institution can use the same evidence for quality audits for any quality standard, rather than falling into the trap of introducing different systems and information to meet the differing requirements of different

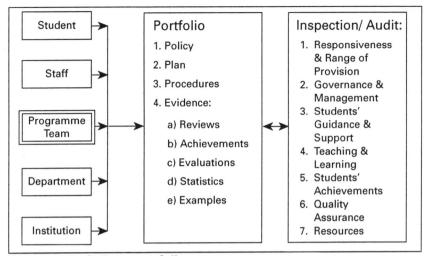

Figure 8.3 College portfolio structure

standards. This is proving to be invaluable for the college, in maintaining its BS5750 registration, preparing for FEFC inspection and for IiP.

Institutional development can be focused on the processes of auditing the quality of the portfolios across the institution, as well as in the evolution of the portfolio structure. The portfolio structure has now been further developed in Figure 8.4 to include three related components, namely Management Information Systems (MIS), Training Resources and the college strategic plan. MIS are shown as having to inform performance and costs, that is resource consumption, at the level of:

- the individual student (the FEFC now requires submission of Individual Student Records from colleges);

- individual members of staff (the FEFC also requires submission of staff; individualised records from colleges);

- programme teams;

- departments; and

- the overall institution.

The strategic plan is shown, with its five prescribed elements feeding into the seven areas of audit. Key to the building of portfolios is provision of training materials that can be developed from Guidance Notes on what is required in the form of procedures to be used, 'instruments' such as records to be used in the portfolio, and a bank of learning materials that can be used to support learning processes.

Conclusion

In developing this scheme the senior vice principal would argue that he

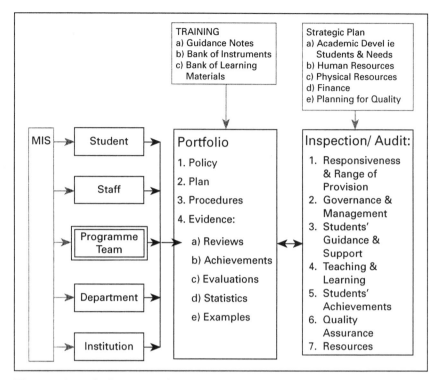

Figure 8.4 College portfolio structure version 2

has attempted to promote a collegial approach to empowering staff and students across the institution, to participate in the processes of review, evaluation and planning for improvement, and thereby promoting a learning culture that permeates the institution. By adopting college-wide transparent processes, he believes that the institution can demonstrate that it practises what it preaches, in promoting a learning culture that implicitly invests in people, whether they are staff or students and at every level in the institution. The imposition of external assessment has been taken as a window of opportunity. This is consistent with chaos theory, as applied to a '*wild organisation*' (Carlson, 1975), in effecting a change of culture in the institution. This, it can be argued, is a necessarily political strategy, achieving a greater institutional commitment to quality.

Questions remain with what I have termed the 'burgeoning quality industry' as to whether the emphasis is too heavily weighted towards bureaucratic systems, at the expense of collegial processes. The requirement for all institutions to be subject to imposed external inspection can be argued as being power-coercive, in the context of a centralisation of bureaucratic power. *Assessing Achievement* (1993a) can be interpreted as seeking to promote a partnership approach in promoting quality, particularly through the process of self-assessment, and thereby being normative–re-educative. However the net effect of publishing grades that affect funding, on the basis of inspectors armed with check-lists, who descend on a college and depart after brief visits, having made necessarily hasty summary judgements, is quite different. It remains to be seen whether the college, in responding to changes imposed by the FEFC, can counter the heavily bureaucratic approach that is generating chaos, and promote effective quality processes, supported by robust systems, which will assure quality experiences for its staff and students, and an effective evolutionary strategy to the management of change.

Appendix 1: FEFC strategic planning model

The planning model represented in Figure 8.5 first appeared in FEFC Circular 92/01 and was repeated in Circulars 92/11 and 92/18. It has also been widely referenced, in circulars relating both to funding methodology and the framework for inspection (*Assessing Achievement*).

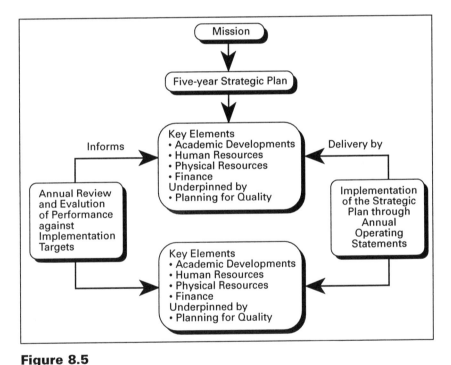

Figure 8.5

Appendix 2: National targets for education and training (NTETs)

NTETs were issued by the Confederation of British Industry (CBI) in 1991, as a major initiative designed to bring about the skills revolution that the UK needed to improve its position in an increasingly competitive world. These targets will be reviewed and updated, with an eye to 2000 AD:

Foundation learning targets

1. By 1997, 80% of young people to reach NVQ 2 (or equivalent)

2. Training and education to NVQ 3 (or equivalent) available to all young people who can benefit

3. By 2000, 50% of young people to reach NVQ 3 (or equivalent)

4. Education and training provision to develop self-reliance, flexibility and breadth

Lifetime learning targets

1. By 1996, all employees should take part in training or development activities

2. By 1996, 50% of the workforce aiming for NVQs or units towards them

3. By 2000, 50% of the workforce qualified to at least NVQ 3 (or equivalent)

4. By 1996, 50% of medium to larger organisations to be "Investors in People"

CHAPTER NINE

The Identification and Management of Teacher Stress

Marie Brown and Sue Ralph

Introduction

So far, the chapters in this section of the book have been concerned with processes of managing change. This present chapter is the first of four to consider, in various ways, the kinds of *support* that teacher–managers may require in their work.

In many countries today teaching has been identified as one of the most stressful occupations (Hunter, 1977). In the USA, inner-city high school teaching is now ranked as the number one stressful job, ahead of occupations such as air traffic controller, medical intern and firefighter (*Men's Health*, 1991). It has been claimed that many teachers are treated for symptoms similar to those which combat soldiers are likely to encounter (Bloch, 1978). There is also increasing concern among the teaching profession in the UK that its members are currently experiencing considerable stress. One of the major teaching unions, The Association of Assistant Masters and Mistresses (AMMA, 1990: 2), in *Managing Stress. Guidelines For Teachers*, points out that:

> Few would now dispute that teaching is a stressful profession, and it is widely acknowledged that the National Curriculum, LMS and other Education Reform Act developments are exacerbating an already tense situation.

Stuart Nattrass, Chair of the Health and Safety Executive's Education Service Committee in the UK, at the launch of their Guidebook on stress management (HSE, 1990), defined stress 'as the number one health problem amongst teachers'. A survey of British teachers in January 1991 revealed an increase of about 300% in the number of teachers leaving the profession through ill health since 1981 (Nattrass, 1991). A headteacher of an infant school, in a recent communication to the authors, identified a wide range of pressures:

> My post as head teacher of an infant school has changed dramatically since the passing of the 1988 Education Act. Political legislation has transformed the nature and scale of my work, minimizing my training experience whilst thrusting me rapidly forward – into budgeting, computing, site management, risk management, etc. – untrained and inexperienced.

What is stress?

Stress as a likely cause of illness, problems and personal misery is giving rise to growing public as well as medical and scientific concern. Hardly a day goes by without there being some reference to the phenomenon in the popular media, and magazines abound with 'questionnaires' for us to measure our stress levels. This media interest has both good and bad aspects. It is good in the sense that it brings the issues to a wider audience, but bad in that it can trivialise a serious subject. Most teachers now have an increased awareness of the effects of stress. They and their organisations would agree that the effects of stress, and long-term stress in particular, are severe.

There are many definitions of stress, some of which we will consider here. Ellison (1990) defines it as a biochemical response by the body to a threatening situation *(stressor)*. Although this response is meant to ensure self-survival, the frequent changes in blood pressure caused by regular exposure to stressors can lead to severe illness, including heart disease, in the future. Stress is specific to each individual. What one teacher might find stressful is not necessarily stressful for another. In addition, several teachers in the same stressful situation may respond quite differently. This non-specificity of the nature of stress makes it difficult to produce a simple cause and effect model (AMMA, 1987).

Stress, depending on how it is experienced, can be negative or positive. Teachers can find it stimulating and challenging, in which case stress is positive; or it can be the cause of varying states of anxiety and depression – here it can be harmful. Too much stress causes physiological and psychological problems for individuals. Although Selye (1956) described stress in a positive way, the term stress in common usage is usually found at the negative end of the spectrum.

> The word stress is used in the sense of 'distress' which people experience from too many or too few pressures and strains. Distress is something which occurs to all of us, as does happiness. It is only when there is too much distress, physical or mental, that problems start.
>
> (Bailey and Sprotson, 1987, Part 4: 4)

Hans Selye (1956) produced a model which had four dimensions:

1. *Overstress*: where there is too high a workload and the demands of the job are greater than the individual teacher is likely to manage.

2. *Understress*: where there is too little work to do and this leads to understimulation, boredom, depression and possibly lack of motivation.

3. *Good stress*: when there is something really challenging and motivating to do.

4. *Bad stress*: that which makes one feel exhausted, irritable and frustrated.

Cox and colleagues (1989: 1) described stress at work as:

> ... to do with coping, or failing to cope with the demands and constraints placed on the person. It is to do with the person's realisation that they have a problem which they cannot adequately or easily deal with.

Some studies have suggested a relationship between personality and stress. For example the work of Friedman and Rosenman (1974) suggested that certain personality factors were related to higher levels of stress. They identified *Type A* personalities (workaholics, restless and aggressive) as being more prone to coronary disease than their peers, whilst *Type B* (calm and relaxed) appear to be slower and steadier. However other findings suggest that it is not possible to detect particular traits which will definitely lead to stress; simply, it is more likely that there may be a vicious cycle of interaction between stress and certain personality traits, with one tending to reinforce the other (Rees, 1989). For the purpose of this chapter we will regard a stressful issue as being one which an individual feels he or she cannot cope with successfully and which causes him or her to experience unwanted physical, emotional or mental reactions. Stress will become a problem if there is a discrepancy between the demands on a teacher and his or her ability to manage. It therefore follows that the amount of stress which a person can withstand is differentiated according to the individual (Ellison, 1990).

Organisational stress

It is important also to consider the wider question of the stress that may be inherently present in an organisation. We must consider both the individual and the organisation in which he or she works. All forms of organisation are potential causes of stress. The AMMA (1987) Report was especially concerned that stress should be reduced and 'positively transformed', and suggested that organisational stress management and individual stress handling strategies should be employed in schools. If the organisation creates an imbalance by inappropriate demands on staff, in terms of the mismatch between the workloads of teachers and the abilities of individual teachers to meet them, stress reduction strategies must be implemented. On individual stress handling, the AMMA Report recommended that if teachers are given the skills necessary to manage their stress, both the individual and the organisation will benefit. An organisation that has a large number of highly stressed teachers will not be good for, or effective in, any organisational capacity.

Causes of stress in teachers

The causes of stress may be different for each individual teacher or group of teachers, but certain work related factors emerge as common:

- *Relationships with pupils*:

    - changes in pupil attitude and motivation;
    - anxiety over test and examination results;
    - perceived lack of discipline;
    - over-large class size;
    - mixed ability classes.

- *Relationships with colleagues*:

    - poor lines of communication at all levels;
    - lack of community spirit;
    - personality clashes;
    - lack of academic and social intercourse between departments;
    - workloads unevenly distributed.

- *Relationships with parents and the wider community*:

    - pressure from parents to achieve good results;
    - perceived impending threat of 'payment by results';
    - dealing with unrealistic expectations;
    - increased parental involvement and access, which can lead to possible conflicts;
    - general societal cynicism about the role of teachers;
    - poor pay and status;
    - media bashing.

- *Innovation and change*:

    - constant demands for change for no good reason;
    - feelings of powerlessness and failure;
    - rate of changes;
    - lack of information and resources to support and facilitate change.

- *School management and administration*:

    - poor overall school organisation;

- little real involvement in decision making;
- poor communication models;
- lack of staff development to meet new demands of job;
- lack of support from school administration in the face of increasing paperwork;
- inadequate staff facilities, storage areas and personal work spaces;
- poor technical back-up.

- *Time factors*:
  - increasing variety and number of tasks;
  - additional work demands outside the normal school hours, which can lead to conflict with family and friends;
  - frequency and ineffective organisation of meetings.

Not all of the above stressors may apply to all teachers. Some of them may be viewed as positive challenges. What is important, however, is that teachers identify, or are helped to identify, factors which are stressful to them. They should be encouraged to take the necessary steps to manage stress at a personal level and thus open up the debate whereby school staffs, governing bodies and local education authorities will be encouraged to take the matter seriously, and begin to identify ways in which teachers can be supported.

How individuals can manage stress

Individuals differ in how they respond to and manage stress. This is obvious during workshop sessions on our inservice training courses. Conflicting views about the nature and intensity of stress factors surrounding potentially stressful situations in schools are common. The essential issue to emerge is that individuals need to recognise and analyse for themselves the signs and causes of stress at work. A strategy which can be used successfully with teachers is to ask them as individuals to list the causes of stress within their schools. This approach generates a large amount of data which may prove difficult to analyse and manage at an individual level. A questionnaire designed especially for teachers (Brown and Ralph, 1994) may be more appropriate as this will enable the user to classify discrete areas, such as interpersonal relationships, school organisation, and role ambiguity, and produce a prioritised personal stress action plan. Management strategies might involve some or all of the following:

1 *Examining beliefs and expectations* – Are these realistic and achievable? Is there a need to set more attainable goals?

2 *Time Management* – Can time be used more effectively? Techniques such as prioritisation, delegation, objective setting can be considered.

3 *Assertion* – Learning how to communicate more confidently at all levels and to deal positively with conflict.

4 *Communication* – Looking at patterns of interpersonal communication and self presentation skills.

5 *Relaxation techniques* of all kinds, such as physical exercise, meditation, yoga, aromatherapy, and collection of bio-data.

6 Support networks – It is important to build and maintain support networks of family, friends and colleagues, both within and outside schools. One of the aims of our inservice work with teachers is to enable them to set up such self-supporting networks within their own schools. An extension of our work with teachers has been an investigation into the extent to which local education authorities have begun to consider how they might help teachers manage stress. This will be dealt with in more detail later.

How schools can manage stress

Much of the available literature on the management of stress has suggested 'coping' or palliative strategies at the individual level. How the school as an organisation creates and contributes to stress and manages stress problems has often been neglected. Many teachers on our courses identify school management as a major potential stressor. The HSE Education Service Advisory Committee Report (1990: 11) recommends that

> stress problems should be approached from both the organisational and individual levels, with each making an important contribution. Neither strategy on its own is likely to be totally effective.

There are a variety of ways in which middle and senior management in schools can help staffs to address problems of stress:

(a) Helping to *de-stigmatise* the idea of stress by putting it on the agenda for discussion.

(b) Encouraging the establishment of *self-help groups* to explore group problem solving of school stress factors and to develop appropriate solutions where possible.

(c) Developing an *empathetic ethos* and offering support for self-help management techniques.

(d) Identifying and liaising with *people who can help* within the local education authority and other relevant organisations.

(e) Drawing up a *school action plan* after schoolwide staff consultation. Factors to consider might include workloads, resources, discipline, relationships, environment, career progression, future staff development and training needs, parental and community pressures.

(f) Providing *appropriate staff development*, either within the school or at an outside venue.

(g) Making available information about *counselling services* and encouraging staff to use them where necessary.

Some plans may be easily and quickly implemented, whereas others may involve a radical rethink and restructuring of existing processes and procedures. It is crucial that managing stress is part of an ongoing debate in schools. It may be included in a school development plan and will need constant evaluation and reassessment.

How local education authorities can manage stress

We have collected evidence, as part of our research into stress, from 117 local education authorities in England and Wales. We were interested in the extent to which they were currently helping or intending to help school and school staffs manage increasing levels of stress. We were also interested in finding out the strategies the authority was using; for example, whether it was running stress management courses for headteachers, deputy headteachers, heads of departments and other staff, or any specialist counselling services which the authority might be making available to teaching staff. We discovered a rather patchy picture of provision nationwide. We were pleased to note that some authorities had adopted a pro-active approach and a number of innovative strategies were currently evolving. Three main strategies were identified.

First, many authorities were addressing the issue of stress management by running one-day courses for headteachers, deputy headteachers and other staff. These courses were of two kinds: (1) courses specifically dealing with identification and management of stress; and (2) general management development courses, using material developed within the authority or elsewhere, which included elements or modules on stress and time management. One or two authorities were also helping to organise whole school staff training days on stress.

A second strategy was the provision of specialist counselling services. This was available either through the authority's own personnel or other agencies. Referrals came either through self, line management, school, union, or school adviser.

Thirdly, stress formed part of the agenda of a number of joint union and local authority discussion groups, both formal and informal, and a few authorities had begun to develop means of surveying incidence of stress among their teaching staffs. Continued involvement of unions in this important area of teacher welfare is crucial and should form an integral part of local authority policy.

Among the more innovative local authority strategies we noted the following:

- a recognition that pupils also need to have the benefit of a stress management course (offered by several local authorities, notably Trafford);

- the development of a draft policy document for the whole county;

- the production and dissemination of a list of personnel whom teachers could consult on a confidential basis;

- an assessment of the amount of time teachers spent on standard assessment testing during the summer terms;

- research into stress incidence in a local authority through a locally based project;

- incorporation of work on stress in monitoring and evaluation reports on schools;

- the establishment of a stress review group, operating as part of a professional development consultancy, to monitor stress training provision;

- inservice development on a school cluster basis;

- provision of aromatherapy massage treatment at a local authority sports and leisure centre;

- training in self-help facial massage techniques for headteachers;

- dissemination of discussion papers and other relevant documentation, such as the Health and Safety Executive Guidebook (HSE, 1990);

- local health questionnaires and surveys.

One local authority reported also that its own officers were under a considerable degree of stress due to constant demands from government.

Conclusions

We need to note the importance of both organisational and personal factors in any examination of teacher stress (Brown and Ralph, 1992). It is their relationship which explains why many teachers find it difficult to address what they increasingly perceive to be the stigma of stress. Reflecting evidence from theorists on hierarchies of needs, most teachers say that organisational needs must be met before personal ones. However, teachers become more able to manage stress, even in the face of organisational constraints, if they have a substantial voice in deciding and initiating stress management strategies. School senior management also shares this concern.

Peggy, a primary school headteacher in a semi-urban area, reported the following:

> My attempts to alleviate stress are as follows ... firstly, I blocked up one of three doors into my very small office ... to reduce the three pronged attack! Secondly, I attended a stress management course at Manchester University, which helped me to plan my time more effectively and to regain control of my working life. I counsel myself to value myself and my life. Fortunately, we have a life-saving support group of headteachers within our area. We meet for 2 hours once a month – and laugh (the best therapy of all). We have decided on two residential courses a year, each based on a project to benefit all our schools; for example, all schools share a 'Good Behaviour Book' so that the same rules apply in all our schools, and we are working on a cross-phase policy at present. The greatest support is to know that you are not alone and can turn to a colleague who will understand your anxieties.

Change issues emerge as a significant factor in contributing to stress levels in schools. Teachers, for instance, say that a lack of time, professional development opportunities and funding can limit their interest in even thinking about change. Demands for change under these circumstances can result in excessive stress for teachers. Mary, a teacher of some 10 years' experience in a rural school, had this to say:

> The current political situation and the insistence on getting back to traditional (Victorian!) values in teaching have greatly contributed to levels of stress among my colleagues in school. Some of the changes which have been introduced since 1988 have looked positive at a superficial level, and yet the overall result has been the deskilling of many of my teacher colleagues, and has led to feelings of powerlessness and alienation in my school.

Contraction in school budgets has meant reduced opportunities for personal and professional growth for teachers. Appointment to a senior post in a school would usually be associated with expectations of change and growth, not with cut-backs and down-sizing. The following report from Eric, a senior teacher in an urban secondary school, echoes the comments of many other teachers:

> When I became a senior teacher I expected to be given the opportunity to be proactive and to introduce new ideas to the school. I expected to have some time for creative thinking, to engage in philosophical discussion with colleagues and to read educational journals and literature. Budget cuts, at both national and local levels interfered with my plans. I was unable to develop myself or my colleagues and I found this very frustrating. I lost all enjoyment in my job and am now looking forward to taking early retirement.

Since the introduction of the Education Reform Act in 1988, teachers' workloads have increased enormously. Some teachers, in order to survive, have had to learn time management and assertiveness skills. Pat, a male teacher in an urban school, is a typical survivor:

> As a teacher I find the major source of stress to be increased workload. Not

only is the volume of what one is expected to do increasing continuously, but also what one is expected to do and when. Many additional demands come in the form of administrative tasks to be completed at short notice as a matter of relative urgency. While such work is perceived as important by managers, it is not by me, as it is not teaching.

Coping with stress requires refusal, prioritization and subversive socialising. When I can say 'no' to extra work I do so – if it is not part of my job description, I will not do it. The work I must do, I attempt to prioritise, tackling important and urgent work first. Finally, I indulge in a good gripe with close colleagues as often as possible. This typically takes the form of contrasting the work required of us by managers in a limited time, with that required of them in more, and better-paid, time. Pointing up the hypocrisy and incompetence of those 'in charge' is very therapeutic.

David, a teacher of some 4 years' experience in an Inner City Secondary School, achieved an excellent first degree and is currently in his first job. Like many others, he is finding it difficult to cope, and even more difficult, to express these feelings and fears with his colleagues. He says:

I hate getting up in the morning. The thought of having to face Year 10 yet again fills one with despair. I cannot control them. They do not want to learn. I am terrified that my colleagues will hear the noise and call me a failure. I can't sleep at night and count the days to the end of term. I think it would help to talk to somebody about my stress, but I think then I would be labelled as incompetent. There is so much stigma attached to admitting that you are stressed. It's an admission that you can't cope. If I said this and lost my job, where would I get another one?

Having listened to teachers describe those factors which contribute to stress in schools at both personal and organisational levels, we find ourselves concurring with research findings which suggest that individuals differ in how they respond to and manage stress (Dunham, 1992). Conflicting views about the nature and intensity of stress factors are common. Teachers repeat the words 'stressed', 'tired', 'exhausted', 'frustrated' and 'alienated', over and over again when talking about teaching and stress. What we find most strongly expressed in the literature is that, in Britain at least, there appears to be a major stigma attached to the idea that individual teachers suffer from stress, and often teachers are afraid to discuss this for fear that it might indicate to colleagues and superiors that they are not up to the job. For example, we note from our own experience that teachers are concerned to conceal from others their attendance at stress management courses. It suggests that there is still a reluctance on the part of some teachers even to admit to themselves that they are experiencing stress. This appears to be a peculiarly British phenomenon, and may be linked to what is perceived as reticent British attitudes.

One of the central issues to emerge is that individuals need to recognise and analyse openly for themselves, signs and causes of stress at work, thus removing the real or imaginary stigma attached to it. They then need to decide upon appropriate strategies for its management. These themes lead to a focus on the importance of the teacher's voice as a bridge between organisational and personal stress reduction policies. These voices need to be heard at the whole school level, and senior management teams need to adopt a considered approach to the management of staff stress. Only an organisational approach can provide appropriate help for all teachers (NUT, 1990). This approach will have implications for those who lead schools, as they, too, need to recognise that to acknowledge stress in teachers is not a sign of laziness, weakness or incompetence. Ordinary teachers need to be reassured that they will not lose professional esteem or promotional opportunities by admitting to stress.

Those responsible for managing the Education Service at local level may have an added role to play, in the co-ordination of programmes to help teachers identify and manage their stress. We suggest that most of the work which has been done thus far has concentrated on dealing with the symptoms rather than removing the causes of stress. We would welcome more emphasis placed upon the encouragement of teachers to formulate action plans, which are followed up by school or local education authority, through stress reduction policies. Managing stress is, we argue, a whole school issue, and may well require a modification of cultural attitudes in many schools and local education authorities.

CHAPTER TEN

Supporting Staff Through Appraisal

John West-Burnham

The purpose of this chapter is to explore the relationship between the management process of appraisal and the importance attached to enhancing individual capability and performance. A tension can be identified at the outset between a formal, organisationally focused system and working to enhance the self-perception and motivation of individuals. The issue is the extent to which a bureaucratic system can meet individual needs. This chapter explores the following topics:

- values and staff management;

- the nature of appraisal systems;

- managing performance;

- barriers to supporting staff;

- developing a value driven model.

Values and staff management

One of the historic 'blind spots' of educational management has been an explicit understanding of the principles by which the adults in a school or college are to be managed. This is most frequently manifested in the lack of any reference to adults in the traditional aims or mission statement. This omission was further reinforced by uncertainty or ambiguity in the public definition of the components of management roles. Job descriptions of senior and middle managers are often vague to the point of obscurity, as to the precise nature of management responsibility for the work of other adults. This situation has been substantially modified by the introduction of statutory appraisal in schools, the requirements of government funded INSET activities and the movement towards Investors in People. However, there remains a significant level of confusion as to what constitutes an appropriate model for management relationships between staff.

This lack of clarity might be explained by a range of causes:

1. *The claim to professional autonomy* – Although this has been questioned by several factors, not least the introduction of appraisal, it is still a significant cultural icon. The fact remains that most teachers work in isolation, with very limited shared definitions as to the nature of effective classroom practice.

2. *The limited national and institutional debate on values* – The lack of explicit ethical standards about the nature of management relationships has led to management by exception; that is, there is a negative model based on legal and contractual requirements, but no positive synthesis as to what constitutes appropriate practice. The work on effective schools has developed a consensual model as to the components of perceived good practice, but these are generally described rather than explained or justified in moral terms.

3. *The deference to systems* – The impact of Local Management of Schools, the demands of the National Curriculum and the implications of the incorporation of colleges has led to a perceptible increase in reliance on systems-based approaches. A classic exemplification of this is the government's British Standard (BS EN ISO 9000), but the Employment Department's Investors In People scheme is also an externally accredited system which is imported into the institution. The increasing specificity of teachers' contracts (paralleled in further and higher education) is another manifestation of the introduction of a control culture, which is manifested in a hierarchical and bureaucratic dependency model. The School Teacher Appraisal Regulations are almost unique in introducing a model of staff management by statute.

4. *A limited understanding of management* – Although there has been an enormous amount of conceptual clarification as to what educational management might be, there is still a practical and semantic confusion between leadership, management and administration. The result is that educational organisations are often characterised by transactions rather than transformation – that is, based on reciprocity and conservation rather than change and growth. This is reflected in the complex hierarchical structures still found in secondary schools and colleges, the limited relationship between aims, development planning and the budget, and the emphasis on administration as the criterion for efficiency. The impact of OFSTED inspections has often been to reinforce the notion of transaction – that is, meeting specifications in order to obtain approval.

The combined effect of these factors has been to limit the formulation and implementation of a confident approach to the issue of values in educational management. Bottery (1994:150) argues that school management:

> Should be concerned less with efficiency, calculability, predictability and control, and the implementation of agendas set elsewhere, and more with empowerment, consciousness-raising and participation.

As will be demonstrated in my next section, appraisal, as a neutral system, has the potential to fulfil both of Bottery's approaches. It can be bureaucratic, yet it can also be empowering. The extent to which appraisal supports or controls staff is contingent upon the moral premises on which the system is designed. In the light of the four points outlined above, if there is not a systemic and explicit value system in place then a mechanistic model is almost inevitable by default.

The nature of appraisal systems

The publication of the Education (School Teacher) Appraisal Regulations (DES, 1991a) effectively ended a long debate as to the appropriateness of appraisal in educational organisations. However, the implementation and operation of the Regulations left LEAs and schools a range of options which would determine the nature of the systems. A fundamental assumption of the Regulations was that schools are rational systems. They implied a high degree of congruence about educational outcomes, roles and relationships and classroom practice. For example, they assumed an axiomatic relationship between the school development plan and individual targets.

Equally problematic was the very high significance attached to classroom observation. This assumed that (a) it is possible to infer valid conclusions from two brief periods of observation (b) common criteria exist which would allow meaningful dialogue and (c) that appraisers (and observers) are actually competent. The Regulations are full of such assumptions, which lead to a continuing tension as to the nature of appraisal. This tension between contrasting views can be represented as follows:

Formative	Summative
Diagnostic	Authoritarian
Developmental	Judgemental
Negotiated	Imposed
Anticipatory	Historic
Process	System

These tensions were exemplified in a number of organisational decisions made by schools. For example:

1. There was often an inherent tension in the stated purpose of appraisal – whether to improve the quality of children's learning, or to manage career development for teachers.

2. The decision as to who should appraise – the line manager, an expert appraiser or a friend?

3. The extent to which the agenda for each appraisal cycle was determined by the teacher, the school or a combination of both.

4. The nature and status of appraisal records, and the ways in which the information could be used.

5. The status of agreed appraisal targets, and the extent to which they were prioritised and resourced.

In the Report of the Leverhulme Teacher Appraisal Project (Wragg 1994:3) the following findings are noted:

> Sixty-nine percent (of teachers) felt appraisal had been of benefit to them, mainly boosting confidence and self-awareness, but only 49% felt it had affected their classroom practice.

By contrast with this significant mismatch between intention and outcome, most teachers (99%) were happy with their appraiser, although 44% of those who had an appraiser imposed expressed subsequent reservations. This split highlights an important issue in the management of appraisal – on the one hand, teacher satisfaction with the process in terms of outcome and relationship with the appraiser; on the other, the perceived impact of the process on the teacher's job in terms of classroom practice. This exemplifies the tension between enhancing self-esteem and relationships, and managing performance. This is not to argue that these elements are mutually exclusive, but rather to highlight the potential tension in terms of value, purpose and implementation. It is clear that appraisal in schools falls on the left-hand side of the model outlined above. Wragg (1994) states that there is little evidence of the data generated by appraisal being used in disciplinary or redundancy procedures, but equally it appears to have limited impact in terms of improvement.

Managing performance

According to Trethowan (1991:xiii),

> Unless teacher performance is managed successfully, no school will achieve its potential. Financial management, resource management, curriculum management and every other form of management all have their role, but they pale into insignificance beside the effective management of teacher performance.

For Trethowan, appraisal is an essential component of performance management. However, he argues that it is only one facet. It has to be matched by culture creation and goal setting, staff development and appropriate management (xi). It is this contextualisation of appraisal that can help to respond to the concerns and issues about appraisal, that have been identified in this chapter so far. However, there is still a fundamental conceptual issue to be addressed which is the extent to which it is possible to *manage* performance. This implies a superordinate function, which is usually characterised as personnel management or human resource management. Riches and Morgan (1989:2,3) define human resource management (HRM) as seeking:

> ....to start from a consideration of what the strategies of an organisation might be and then ask how the human resources can help formulate and accomplish those strategies, and what human development and motivation is required to meet those ends.

This notion of the organisation as both defining and facilitating performance is reinforced by Drucker (1988a:361):

> It is the test of an organisation to make ordinary people perform better than they seem capable of, to bring out whatever strength there is in its members, and to use each person's strength to help all the other members perform.

This view of HRM is strongly at odds with Guest's (1987) definition of personnel management, as being concerned with compliance and control through formal, bureaucratic and mechanistic systems. The concern about appraisal in educational organisations is the extent to which it avoids a systems approach and assumes organisational rationality. What is conspicuously absent from the Appraisal Regulations and from a largely anecdotal survey of LEA and school schemes is any notion that appraisal is a component of adult learning. Even the organic and developmental model of HRM assumes that the purpose of appraisal is to achieve compliance with organisational goals – a potentially naive aspiration in education, where such goals are at best problematic and at worst marginal or irrelevant. For Shipman (1990:143):

> The school is an organism, a body, living, growing, flourishing, decaying ... we are firmly in the land of culture, where values not structure, belonging, not organisation, are paramount.

Shipman raises the concern that without a high degree of consensus about values any organisational procedure, especially a complex activity such as appraisal, is likely to become marginal, superficial and irrelevant. An appraisal system which is derived from an Act of Parliament and is described in organisational terms is redolent of 'brute sanity', rather than support for development and improvement through learning. How such concerns might be understood and acted on will be the central theme of the final section of this chapter. Perversely, therefore, the antecedents and nature of the appraisal process might actually militate against its functioning effectively and achieving its stated purpose – something that the Leverhulme research quoted above would seem to confirm. Apart from this fundamental concern there are a number of other issues that can inhibit the effectiveness of appraisal as a means of supporting staff. These are discussed in the next section.

Barriers to supporting staff

Glover (1994:178) identifies some of the concerns raised by teachers about the operation of appraisal, which was

> … seen as 'being top down in a kindly way', 'imposed because a leopard cannot change its spots', and 'another example of collegiality in the things which don't matter and authoritarianism in the things that do'!

Two generic concerns emerge here: the issue of hierarchical management, and its effect on personal relationships. These concerns are extended and reinforced by Thompson (1989:109–110):

> If commitment to appraisal for professional development remains superficial and only thinly conceals the expectation that appraisal is about promotion for those with the right qualities – masculine ones – women's likely expectations for appraisal will be severely disappointed.

If an appraisal system is managed in an hierarchical way, with limited recognition of the importance of relationships and if it reinforces gender stereotypes, then its potential to support teachers must be seen as severely constrained. Trott (1994:87) synthesises the concerns:

> … if we are serious about '… assisting school teachers to realise their potential and to carry out their duties more effectively' (Appraisal Regulations) then this needs to include anti-sexist work and active addressing of equal opportunity, discrimination, gender bias, promotion and development systems, the gendered nature of organisational structures, as well as issues such as harassment and sexist attitudes.

In many ways the constraints on effective personal relationships implicit in hierarchy, poor personal relationships and gender issues are exemplified in Gray's (1993: 111) taxonomy, in which he contrasts the feminine or nurturing paradigm with the masculine or defensive/aggressive paradigm. He contrasts the two paradigms as:

Feminine	Masculine
caring	regulated
creative	conformist
intuitive	normative
awareness of individuality	competitive
non-competitive	evaluative

tolerant	disciplined
subjective	objective
informal	formal

According to Coleman (1994:190,191):

> Studies show that the effectiveness of schools is linked with qualities such as empathy, warmth, genuineness, concreteness ...

> Good management is seen to be the 'empowering' of others through transformational leadership. ...Women have far more interactions with both subordinates and superiors, and are more likely to be informal in style.... Women tend to give more importance to differences between individual students and to emphasize academic achievement and productivity of teachers.

Whilst it may be a partial caricature, it is possible to see large schools and colleges as conforming to an essentially masculine model of management. The potential for smaller schools to adopt a feminine model of management is often constrained by the limited opportunities for management to be practised. In the primary school, where the headteacher has a substantial teaching role, the opportunities for interactions between adults are severely constrained. In such circumstances 'management' may often have to focus on administrative and systems issues.

The issues discussed in this section – hierarchy, relationships and gender – are inextricably linked and can often be best exemplified in discussions about the culture of a school. Torrington and Weightman (1989:18) provide a definition of organisational culture as:

> the characteristic spirit and belief of an organisation, demonstrated, for example, in the norms and values generally held about how people should treat each other, the nature of working relationships that should be developed and attitudes to change. These norms are deep, taken for granted assumptions that are not always expressed and are often known without being understood.

By this definition the culture of many schools may make the effective management of appraisal highly problematic. The issues raised in this chapter so far can be summarised in terms of culture as:

1. Values which are often implicit and not shared.

2. A deference to systems approaches to management.

3. An emphasis on hierarchical models of management.

4. Uncertainty about the nature and purpose of management relationships.

If this analysis has validity, then the notion of appraisal supporting staff is compromised. The most that might be hoped for is that appraisal becomes a means of transmitting a particular definition of reality and securing compliance. The limited impact of appraisal on classroom practice reinforces this view, as common definitions of effective classroom practice are not always available or understood. The outcomes of the appraisal process will therefore inevitably concentrate on those matters in the public domain which are amenable to transactions between appraiser and appraisee, such as changing roles or attendance at training events.

For there to be a high degree of confidence that appraisal will support staff in the core purpose of improving children's learning, a number of paradigms need to be established. These are explored in the final section of this chapter.

Developing a value-driven model

If appraisal is to be effective then it must be consistent with organisational values. Although misgivings have already been expressed about the validity of many of the statements of aims provided by schools most of them will make some gesture towards learning. The purpose of this section is to explore how the Appraisal Regulations might be made consistent with what we know about effective learning. This immediately poses a problem, as very few educational organisations have a clear view of those ethical dimensions of learning which are translated into a meaningful definition, that can then be operationalised. If this is true about students, it is even more apposite when applied to adults.

The first problem is the extent to which the concept of appraisal as support is helpful in this context. Support has connotations of dependency and paternalism and the Appraisal Regulations reinforce this notion, notably in the powers vested in the headteacher. According to Pedler (1994:160):

> There is a recognition that the familiar hierarchical structures do not easily lend themselves to members taking responsibility for their own development ...

Appraisal systems could therefore act as a disincentive to individuals accepting responsibility for their own learning. The fact that there is a formalised system, operating on a regular cycle, could be interpreted as specifying that which is necessary and appropriate. Two or three targets per two year cycle could be interpreted as a somewhat minimalist model.

The concept of target-setting is highly problematic, as it divorces the learning from the task. A 'problem' is identified, extrapolated and defined and then remedial measures are identified. This contrasts directly with Schön's (1987:17) view of professional learning:

> learning *all* forms of professional artistry depends, at least in part, on conditions similar to those created in the studios and conservatories: freedom to learn by doing in a setting relatively low in risk, with access to coaches who initiate students into the 'traditions of the calling' and help them, by 'the right kind of telling', to see on their own behalf and in their own way what they most

need to see. We ought, then, to study the experience of learning by doing and the artistry of good coaching.

This is not to deny the significant advances achieved by action-research and mentoring approaches. However, it does call into question the potential impact of disjointed and incremental strategies likely to emerge from a bureaucratic appraisal process. Schön stresses the centrality to 'professional artistry' of reflection-in-action, the process by which the professional *understands* the implications of her actions. The skilled classroom practitioner undoubtedly exhibits this trait to a high degree; but it is potentially only marginal to the appraisal process, which leads to the conclusion that the learning arising from appraisal may be at best transient.

Schön also raises the issue of coaching, which calls into question the role and status of the appraiser. There is no guarantee that a line manager will possess coaching skills; it is equally uncertain whether skilled appraisers or peers will be able to operate in this way. Yet the ability to translate diagnosis into effective support for reflection-in-action seems axiomatic to a professional learning process. Wallace (1991:22) quotes Showers (1985) in identifying the potential of coaching, which

> ... implies that teachers observe each other in the classroom and give mutual feedback to see how far the skills are being practised; they examine the appropriate use of the teaching strategy; and they engage in collaborative problem solving and action planning sessions. A valuable spin-off from this way of working is the collaborative relationships and mutual encouragement it tends to generate among teachers in the same school.

This approach shows one of the ways in which appraisal might mature from a model of support based on dependence to a process based on interdependence. Wragg (1994) found that half of teachers in the sample had their appraisers chosen for them. This does not coincide with a model of effective learning for adults. Senge (1990a:10) challenges the notion of leadership as controlling or ordering:

> leader as teacher does not mean leader as authoritarian expert whose job it is to teach people the 'correct' view of reality. Rather, it is about helping everyone in the organisation, oneself included, to gain more insightful views of current reality. This is in line with a popular emerging view of leaders as coaches, guides or facilitators.

The emphasis on insight, and the assertion that reality may not be fixed, provides a powerful antidote to the dominance of knowledge as the basis for management, as exemplified in the framework devised by the Office for Standards in Education (OFSTED). Appraisal as support can be interpreted as senior staff helping others to implement that which is necessary to work effectively, or it can be seen as helping to define that which is necessary to work effectively. The problem with this approach is that it emphasizes the process of discovery and denies the possibility of 'right answers'. In describing their approach to research on quality schooling Aspin, Chapman and Wilkinson (1994:25) highlight the implications of this approach:

> we do not attempt to reduce everything to some absolute foundations of 'fact' and 'value', 'theory' and 'practice', or 'policy' and 'implementation', in the (vain) attempt to educe some 'analyses' of concepts and theories that can be completely 'correct' or 'true', ... Conceived of in this way educational policy and administration are like any science – an unending quest
>
> – to grasp the theories determining and predicting advance, and then
>
> – by critical theory appraisal and comparison, to show which of them is better and for what purpose.

For schools operating in an era of a prescribed curriculum, and with a model of accountability which is largely based on the demonstration of the acquisition of knowledge, this advocacy of contingency must be uncomfortable. However, the alternative is to perpetuate a hierarchical and bureaucratic model of professional development, which is at odds with a range of perceptions as to what might constitute effective professional learning. The decision is one that has to be based on the extent to which the values of the school or college are perceived to be significant components of management processes, or marginal to the reality of day-to-day management. The components of a value-driven model are summarised by Beave, Caldwell and Millikan (1989:106–115), who identify 10 'generalisations' about leadership which have clear implications for the concept of supporting staff:

1. Emphasis should be given to transforming, rather than transactional leadership.

2. Outstanding leaders have a vision for their organisations.

3. Vision must be communicated in a way which secures commitment.

4. Communication of vision requires communication of meaning.

5. Issues of value – 'what ought to be' – are central to leadership.

6. The leader has an important role in developing the culture of the organisation.

7. Studies of outstanding schools provide strong support for school-based management and collaborative decision-making, within a framework of state and local policies.

8. There are many kinds of leadership forces – technical, human, educational, symbolic and cultural – and these should be widely dispersed throughout the school.

9. Attention should be given to institutionalising vision, if leadership of the transforming kind is to be successful.

10. Both masculine and feminine stereotype qualities are important in leadership, regardless of the gender of the leader.

Seven of these factors refer directly or implicitly to the importance of vision and values to the effective school. It is also clear that these writers regard it as a preordinate concern of leadership. It is on this basis that it might be possible to develop a model of appraisal as support, which is not instrumental and mechanistic, while retaining a clear organisational focus and being primarily concerned with learning. In the next chapter of this book, John Isaac cites Schön's (1987:1) distinction between the *swamp* and the *high ground*. The swamp is characterised by vagueness, limited understanding and the inability to conceptualise alternatives. The high ground is the antithesis of the swamp. It may well be that one of the possible functions of appraisal is to help individuals move from the swamp. According to Campbell-Evans (1993:97) this can be done through a 'concerted effort of data collection, value articulation, recognition and consolidation'. Of these, value articulation is probably the most significant.

In the practical context of appraisal this would mean:

1. A high degree of involvement and collaborative working in the production of values and vision, which are then translated into Aims or Mission Statement.

2. Significant cross-referencing between the aims and the school development plan, job descriptions and policy statements.

3. The systematic translation of policy into specific criteria or illustrative material, to provide concrete examples of values-in-action. In essence this will involve the creation of a common language or shared stories.

4. The use of appraisal, as one of a range of management processes, to facilitate understanding and so allow reflection-in-action.

5. A movement away from appraisal targets as outcomes, to the specification of learning and improvement processes.

Underpinning these points is the need for vision and values to be as explicit about adults as they are about children, and for there to be a far higher correlation between intention and practice. Very often in schools the logical implications of a particular policy are not expressed in actual practice. For example, there is a problematic relationship between the secondary school timetable and most concepts of learning. Appraisal provides a significant opportunity to close the gap between intention and reality in terms of human relationships, the management of learning and the celebration of good practice. Parental love for a child is not meaningful if it is never more than stated – it has to be also expressed in action. Praise, recognition, advice and warnings have to be reinforced by practical help with dressing, homework, transport and all the things that children need to learn. But in the final analysis it is the display of affection that makes the greatest impact. For appraisal to support staff it has to encompass learning to enhance confident practice, but it also needs to address social and emotional needs. There is nothing in the Education (School Teacher) Appraisal Regulations that prevents this, if the system is seen as a formal expression of a culture centred on respect and improvement.

CHAPTER ELEVEN

Changing the Rules of the 'Men's Club': A Woman's Experience of Senior Management in Higher Education

Esmeralda Brodeth

> Never, 'for the sake of peace and quiet' deny your own experience or convictions.
>
> – Dag Hammarskjold (in Kane, 1976: 111)

A recurring theme in the chapters of this book concerns the need for fair opportunities for all, in educational management. However, as has been widely shown, the unfair conditions that exist for women in all jobs remain just as unfair in education. In the UK:

> Women are less likely to hold positions of responsibility in any area of paid employment. Davidson and Cooper (1992:11) quote that in 1988, women accounted for only 11% of general managerial staff. Despite the large number of female teachers, particularly in the primary phase, there are disproportionately few women in positions of authority in educational management.
>
> (Coleman, 1994:178)

As for further and higher education, Coleman cites a finding by Darking (1991) that females accounted for 4% of principals of colleges of further education, and 3% of professors in universities (*see also* Adler *et al.*, 1993; Davies, 1990; Shakeshaft, 1987, and also discussion of equal opportunities issues in Chapter 5 of this book).

What is the experience, however, of women who do get an entry ticket in what is the mainly 'Men's Club' of management? To investigate some critical issues that face women in educational management, this chapter draws on my experience as a woman manager and leader, in a higher education setting. Working outside my own cultural milieu, I served abroad as a University Library Director for 8 years, before returning to academic studies in educational policy and leadership.

Exchanging 'stories' for self-development

As will be argued by John Isaac in the next chapter of this book, it is now widely understood that a manager's professional development involves a crucial blend of opportunities for personal development, with the development of others in the organisation. A genuinely collegial approach to staff development requires us to have genuine opportunities for sharing experience with others. In this way our rich, reflexive experience can blend in a concerto of different voices, whose personal stories are circumscribed within a professional world that we share in common.

It is not, then, simply a self-indulgence, to listen to others' stories and to tell our own about what it means to 'manage'. Rather, this exchange provides an opportunity for transformation of our experience, into a better vision and better policies for our schools and colleges (Slack and Cornelius, 1995:337). Conversely, unless we draw truthfully from our own and others' actual experience, our leadership practice will be impoverished.

Personal experience, of course, cannot simply be applied directly to universal contexts. What we seek, rather, in an individual 'story' of someone's experience in management, are patterns of relationship in attitude or behaviour, that we can invoke elsewhere. *How* we do this is, of course, essential. We must use tact and intelligence, for 'voice' and 'touch' are as important as rationality, when we handle issues of power, politics and conflict, in order to devise empowering management strategies in the workplace. After all, it is in the spirit of equal opportunities, and evoking Blackmore (1989), that I wish to reconceptualise notions of leadership and power, to make our educational organisations more effective agents of change.

Bennis (1989: 4) equates personal growth and integration to the process of becoming a leader. Our character and experience are constantly in the process of becoming, and of being shaped for leadership practice. Through this interplay of 'one-is, one-becomes, while one-does', leaders grow in understanding their strengths and weaknesses. They can then learn to direct their lives, define specific goals, and work towards these. Within groups, the capacity to take personal charge of one's life (Bennis, 1989:5) can be directed to group goals, through effective translation into collaborative teamwork. We learn 'management' (sometimes painfully) early in life: at home and at school, where 'self-management' (in very simple terms) meant, for me, managing to combine classroom work with household chores. From these simple beginnings we learn a sense of responsibility, respect for others, and co-operative behaviour. Because management expertise is an essential survival requirement, it grows early;

family and friends, for example, help each other to 'self-manage' stress.

At the end of my university studies, when preparing myself to be a teacher, the world to be 'managed' widened enormously. Teaching was not just a matter of delivering a curriculum; it really meant caring for (and being supported by) others as well. Membership in an international Catholic association further opened this vision for me. It was from this group of predominantly women leaders that I also drew my role model of a caring, value-laden leadership. From this exposure to a variety of women's leadership practice, I encountered power in its life-giving, growth-generating aspects as well as in its subtle patterns of hostility, silence and passive aggression. Sometimes, subtle versions of power are more difficult to confront; yet they can be insidiously exploiting and manipulative, even in public arenas of the workplace.

Later, in my 8 years as library director in a university, I learned that the practice of leadership involves both giving and receiving. It means knowing when to talk and when to listen, as well as being open to learn from others (whether staff, colleagues or superordinates – *see* Duignan and MacPherson, 1993; Dunlap and Schmuck, 1995). Silence is the breeding ground for listening and learning. It generates reflection which, for one who has been fully engaged in action, is specially needed. Greenleaf (1977: 19) advises the servant–leader on the art of withdrawal, in order to re-orient oneself, to pace oneself and make optimal use of one's resources. Van de Pitte (1991: 149), in a similar vein, evokes Plato's advice, that wise leaders should spend a decent interval in administration, and then get back to their teaching and research, before they are unwittingly damaged by the power that they wield.

At the end of 8 years directing the library, I experienced mental exhaustion, and a deep need to 'withdraw', to make sense of my experience. Eight years had made me too involved in university politics, too self-important, and too comfortable with the 'taste of power'. I needed, more than I had realised, the discipline of self-critical and critical dialogue with others. Fortunately, my present academic studies now provide these needs.

Does leadership mean power?

Stodgill's *Handbook of Leadership* (1981) documented research findings on various studies of leadership covering more than three decades, but these provided no easy answer to the nature of leadership. In some studies the concept of leadership has also been linked with power. Greenfield (in Greenfield and Ribbins, 1993: 25) refers to leadership in administration as a matter of will and power: of bending others to one's will and being bent by others. This notion of leadership carries with it a view of power in relationships, which may imply either a mutuality in the social/organisational processes, or an asymmetrical power distribution.

My own management/leadership practice carried both mutuality and asymmetry, in social and organisational processes in the university. As a library director I formed part of the senior administrative team. This meant having to sit in two councils that tackled administrative and academic matters. The first was composed of senior officials (vice chancellor and vice presidents, deans and directors). The second council, chaired by the academic vice president, was composed of deans, directors and chairs of departments. I also had a team of four professionals in the library, together with four secretarial staff, an audio-visual technician, a binder and a cleaner. The first year, as I took over, the staff line-up and job descriptions seemed to be in place. Because I was new to the culture, the place and its people (others would call this an 'impression management strategy', of which I was oblivious then), I preferred to 'watch and observe', knowing that I too was being 'watched and observed'. The year after, we all saw the need to review library objectives and job stipulations. To do this I asked each member of the library staff to participate, by writing their job descriptions and work expectations, vis-à-vis the library objectives. Among other things, this meant the implementation of in-service training development programmes, as well as planning for periods of study leave to upgrade the professional preparation of the librarians. Gradually I saw the library staff's reservoir of talents, sense of responsibility and cooperative spirit begin to flourish. I made sure I mentioned this at the end-of-the-school-year commendation memos. Together we ventured into new enterprises: the start of the Library Liaison Team, with our faculty members; the establishment of the Faculty Study Area and the Special Collections Division; a Book Week Celebration held annually, which convoked school and university libraries. In short, our leadership vision, of quality service to the academic community, was being translated, on a day-to-day basis, through key management strategies such as cooperative endeavour and teamwork.

This did not mean, of course, that disputes were evaded; indeed, we tried to work out differences or misunderstandings when they surfaced. During my first year, I discovered that I made many rounds to orient myself to where my staff were deployed, in a four-storey building virtually unknown to me. I realised that while some staff felt happy at 'being visited', others were uncomfortable at what was thought of as 'snooping around'. Unaware of it myself, my 'management style' was being labelled, and was raising two quite opposite reactions among the staff. It was not long before I learned about this 'issue of intrusion', which I sought to clarify through a meeting. Hence, a once-a-month regular staff meeting and a more frequently-held interaction with the professional team were just two strategies I adopted, to improve communication among us.

Leadership, after all, is generally linked with power relations, since my post as library director (like that of deans) was in itself constituted in power and authority. The power to budget for human, material and physical resources was clearly stipulated in the Academic Staff Handbook of the university (for a small, young university of 1500 students and 200 staff, our organisation structure was firmly in place). If I carefully substantiated, with justified criteria, the proposed budget for different areas of expenditure, the amount I asked for was granted. Perhaps I was fortunate to have had a 'library oriented' administrator. Our library budget was gradually augmented (especially before the university's financial crisis), with a high priority placed on staff development. Two professional librarians (spaced within 3 years) went on study leave to the USA, and a rotation of staff for in-service training programmes was in progress. Naturally the staff and I worked even harder, in terms of stepping-up library services. Faculty Deans had higher book/periodical budget allocations, and students' reference/readers' services were upgraded. Our annual library reports carried our end-of-the-year accomplishments and projected activities – all geared toward boosting our own staff morale, and assuring senior administrators of our commitment to the university's overall goal of quality teaching and research. Here the power relationship – mediated by the Academic Staff Handbook – can be extended, as in a continuum from our senior administrator to myself as library director, and from me to the library staff. Through participation and power-sharing, we made such things happen, not as a magic formula, but through constant discussion, arguments and negotiations.

How, then, do 'voice and touch' operate in enlightened leadership practice?

Voice and touch in leadership practice

I use 'voice' in the qualitative sense (Schratz, 1993), given the chance to portray my leadership experience in an academic setting, with its attendant realities. On one level, I use my own voice as I make sense of the social world I live in as a woman, having assumed educational leadership/management duties in my own cultural setting (the Far East) as well as, more recently, in a predominantly patriarchal milieu (the Middle East).

And on yet another level, I also pay tribute to women and men who, in their own leadership practice, have shown me that our lives are intricately interwoven, not only in sharing vision and policies but also in listening to each others' personal aspirations. With them I discovered a common human ground of give-and-take, of an enriching synergistic relationship, with underpinnings of power and conflict.

Along with voice, I use 'touch' in its transforming sense. When things get rough and tough in the workplace, a soothing voice of reconciliation and a gentle, caring touch of affirmation can make a difference. Nelson (1983:22) says that without the humanising process of touch, speech and gesture from other persons, the infant would not learn personal meaning. This genuine personal presence, experienced early in life, is truly life-giving. It becomes a premise in the manager/leader's own relatedness, and paves the way for our relatedness with others, our communion with the world as we grow up and struggle for meaning in life. Harrison (1983:9) affirmed that to be in touch in this primary sense is to be reassured of our reality.

Words or actions that are consistent with what we say can touch other people, just as other people's lives touch us. In the home, at school, in the workplace touch can mean a word of praise, nod or a smile, a tap on the shoulder for an initiative sincerely given, or a selfless service rendered at a most opportune time. We do not touch to get back something, for that would be manipulating others for our own needs. The leader–manager (or the teacher) must allow freedom for others to be themselves. For instance, we just do not spell out objectives nor impose the curriculum, without considering the needs of our constituents. In this sense, we should be wary of certain manipulative utilitarian values: that our interest in the person is based on her or his usefulness to meet our own aims (as managers/leaders/teachers). Indeed, it is to lose sight of the essence of others as persons, when we look at them as objects, or perhaps pawns (as on a chessboard) that we can easily move here or there. To be in 'touch' in the right sense, we do not have to wait for great moments or seek elevating thoughts. In fact we may simply be ourselves, in that difficult quest for authenticity in our relationships with others (be they teachers or students). Perhaps, too, we have to begin to re-discover the quality of personal and working relationships, acknowledging the presence of another person before us (Nelson, 1983). As manager–leader, to be in touch is to be sensitive to the wear and tear, the stress our colleagues have to undergo, because of heavy teaching workloads or, perhaps, a family-related concern. Many studies of stress in organisations have, of course, reported views by staff, that stress is artificially caused by managerial actions and attitudes, and that it can be used as a management tool to put pressure on staff who are no longer needed in the workplace. Such action would be, surely, as wasteful as it is immoral, and would bring policies of 'flexibility' in staffing into dispute.

Against what Van de Pitte (1991) calls management ploys to manipulate others in the workplace (see Harrison, 1994: 182), those of us engaged in education may have to recover – in an era of conflicting views and confusing priorities – our belief in humanity, or the individual's presence as a woman or as a man. Whatever our educational ideology, the individual person is the subject of our respect, not an object to manipulate for our own goals or those of the school or state. In an increasingly competitive society, with free market and other ideologies competing, leaders, managers and teachers would have to gear educative efforts toward the active participation of students in their own learning process. Perhaps pragmatic considerations would not allow teachers to make this happen, in view of the constraints of the National Curriculum and the routine of the classroom syllabus. Yet the creative resourcefulness of educators is here put to the test, to develop their innate leadership talent, and to make classroom learning a meaningful experience for students. This requires us to listen to the students' voice, their needs, their expectations and the relevance of their learning in their lives. Students also need our touch: to be affirmed, to be guided in the difficult struggles of growing up and forging a future of their own, through their collaborative efforts, self-reliance and self-achievement.

As leaders and managers in education, our practice would embrace knowing when to lead and when to follow, inspiring others toward committed involvement in goals we have jointly made. This is easier said than done. Yet, when we attempt to adjust our vision, our need of others as persons in whom we invest our trust outweighs our need to compete. We set the primacy of the personhood of others over the slavish performance of tasks.

I recall here Anna Dengel's advice on the need for service in public life (quoted in Kane, 1976:73). Service in educational leadership would have to be the ideal norm. But service (which is sometimes dismissed as a 'soft' notion) sounds weak compared to 'leading', which implies being ahead, that is, being in control, creating a more powerful image, all of which are especially attractive in a patriarchal culture. Service, as Dengel proposed, entails a degree of selflessness. Supportive relationships at home and in any workplace enhance work and give meaning to life. A loving, serving leadership may sound utopian, yet organisations may need this for their very survival. We need to learn how to empower one another, to give each other's voice a chance to be heard, to harness the positive energies of power for growth and self-fulfilment. Our touch should have that redemptive force to restore the balance in our lives in a turbulent world. Without the vision of service, our education institutions may be effectively managed but poorly led (Bennis, 1989). Efficient management counts on cost and profit; a leadership of service counts on its human resources as its greatest investment.

Glazer (1991:337) states that the literature on management:

> continues to adhere to theories of leadership and organisation that discourage collaborative models of leadership and reinforce patterns of male dominance – female subordination.

While this is so it can be argued, that even in patriarchal cultures, women can best help themselves by doing their part to make their own distinctive voices heard.

To a certain extent, to join the hierarchical ranks might be a service to the feminist cause, through introducing 'reforms' – emphasising teamwork, collaboration, interdependence and collegiality, where individualism and competition prevail. To be outside the ranks, and uselessly swimming against the current of domination, is counter-productive. It reinforces patterns of male dominance and female subordination, if our voice and touch as women are absent in the higher echelons. Outright entry into the exclusive club of patriarchy, I believe, must be achieved through continuous intervention. The best political strategy is to work with the common purpose that proves to be stronger than differences of age, culture or gender.

Thus I should like to subscribe to the theory of androgyny (Langland and Gove, 1983; Meriwhether, 1984:38), which proposes that the androgynous individual exhibits both male and female characteristics, and integrates these qualities into single acts. The use and abuse of power is evident in the lives of women and men, as experiences of love and hatred, peace and violence in a person's life. History points to women leaders (Margaret Thatcher, Indira Ghandi and Corazon Aquino) whose inner strength and charismatic influence have earned them not only admiration and awe, but also fear and hostility, because they had learned to 'lead like men'. Yet we may overlook (or refuse to admit) that at times it can also be the woman in the more 'traditional' role who is the stronger, more dominating figure (at home, in the workplace or in public life). She can also work through an intuitive grasp of living particulars, especially of its personal elements. She has the special gift of making herself at home in the inner world of others (*see* Chervin, 1986:46). When such strength influences the external, objective environment of men, who are socialised in rational, detached patterns, then it may be felt, for good cause, to be threatening. This, at least, has been my experience.

Power and politics: A woman's insight and experience

I am deliberately using a woman's insight through experience, to underscore a personal, singular discourse. Singularity, however, does not mean a personal monopoly of, or alienating myself from the reconceptualisation of power and politics by other women writers. Singularity connotes uniqueness, for every personal experience is unique and contextualised. Before it can be identified with worldwide perspective, it springs first from personal, localised experience.

In my experience as an administrator, I 'fought' not only for women's rights but for those of all my staff. Our sociopolitical situation (characterised by military occupation) meant that we were all subject to harassment and oppression. No one in the workplace was spared of discriminatory practice. However, this did not mean that there were no specific issues of gender to tackle. In a predominantly patriarchal society, it would be illusory to say that women are treated as equals by their male counterparts. What has happened is that women's struggle for equal status has become subsumed in the common national struggle for freedom and sovereignty. As the peace process progresses, women's 'second class status' and oppression (Peterson and Ingalls, 1993; Peteet, 1991) would have to be high on the agenda in both academic and political circles. Democratic mechanisms would certainly have to tackle equal opportunities and rights.

Flowing from experience, power and politics have eventually become constitutive elements of leadership practice, in my own conceptual framework. With power games and political ploys I found the need of a leverage, where values and moral issues can be confronted; where situations of oppression can be dealt with, and justice can restore equality and empowerment. Other authors (such as Bottery, 1992; Hodgkinson, 1991; Greenfield and Ribbins, 1993; Harrison, 1994) have dwelled, of course, on the need for an ethical/moral framework in educational management.

Women have been led to accept (usually silently) that power and politics belong to the men's club, which will always 'call the shots', while women have their own subordinate, less powerful 'sub-club' (*see* Cantor and Bernay, 1992). Against this, women and the more outspoken feminist movement have, over many years, taken up the cause of liberation. One of their aims is to reconceptualise leadership and power. Blackmore (1989: 3) proposes the reconstruction of:

> Leadership (that) can take other forms than having power over others and leadership skills that can be used in a different way.... Leadership and the power that accompanies it would be redefined as the ability to act with others to do the things that cannot be done by an individual alone.

In the library, we found that working together, in ways that counted on what each other person can offer as talent or expertise in joint projects, empowered us to accomplish things more effectively. Not only did we pool our resources together, but we also learned how to convince the rest of the university, and mobilise teachers to support our projects and activities. Because we were predominantly women (by a ratio of nine to three), it was easier to think as 'one mind', although it is also fair to say that of the three men in our group only one was openly 'power-oriented', in 'male-club' ways. Nevertheless, my male colleagues did not put up obstacles to our co-operative endeavours, nor were they unhealthily competitive.

My experience of the 'male club' power and politics was clearly more frequent in the administrative circle, where the struggle for economic resources was stiffly competitive. Deans and directors represented their respective faculties and departments in terms of budget allocations. But I was keen, here, to use my own forms of communication: by directly dealing first with my senior administrator, and presenting needs and projected activities in the annual report. Such processes required a range of refined management and political skills, such as the ability to negotiate, to give and take, and to empower others as well, in working towards decisions that were good for the library (and, therefore, for its staff).

Conclusion

I began this chapter with Dag Hammarskjold's advice to give voice to experience, and to declare our beliefs. Recounting my management/leadership experience has been a healthy exercise, of taking stock of my vision and values, amongst the people and institution where I worked.

I have suggested that power can be viewed in relational terms, as enabling others to discover in themselves centres of self-leadership (Cabot; in Pigors, 1935). Hence, in practice, leadership/management and its accompanying power can take on a more favourable connotation, of enabling or empowerment. Leadership practice in education also involves a triad of power-relations (managers ◄—► staff ◄—► students) that can be characterised by a give-and-take process. In this give-and-take, circumscribed within social/organisational processes, conflict occurs. Personal and organisational goals may not always synchronise, even when 'agreement' may seem to have been reached, between interested groups.

In a conventional pattern of leadership–followership, there are those who lay down the rules of the game and those who follow. Yet if this is done as a more democratic process where consultation, communication and participation operate both ways, power tends to be more diffused and shared, while conflict can be reduced to a minimum. Against the blatant view of power, as oppression, injustice, domination is an obverse view: when we work together, we pool talents and resources to contribute more effectively to our schools and colleges. This should further move us toward interdependence, acknowledging our need for one another, rather than a hard-nosed individualism and competition. Women, together with men, who are willing to work in new ways, can redefine those hard-line versions of leadership/management and power that was the legacy of that exclusive, now discredited patriarchal club.

CHAPTER TWELVE

Self-Management and Development

John Isaac

The case for managers to work on their own development was made in a study by Constable and McCormack (1987) of the needs of UK industry and commerce. This Report suggested that managers should:

- Own their own career, and positively seek out continuous training and development.

- Acquire the learning habit early in their career.

- Recognise when new knowledge and skills are required and seek them out.

The School Management Task Force also supported the idea that, as a matter of principle, there is a need for a high degree of individual initiative in career development and improving personal management performance. They made it clear too, that all teachers are managers and need management development (DES, 1990).

This chapter will review the issues about the place of the 'self' in self-development; how self-development links to knowing about the self, and how the whole issue of taking control of your own development as a manager means learning both about yourself and about how you work.

The 'self' in self-development

Most work on the self-development of managers makes little reference to the 'self', although Pedler *et al.* (1986: 4) proposed that:

> We define self-development as personal development with the manager taking primary responsibility for her or his own learning and for choosing the means to achieve this. Other commonly held views on the meaning and purposes of self-development are:
>
> – career development and advancement;

- improving the performance in an existing job;
- developing certain specific qualities or skills;
- achieving total potential self-actualisation.

Experience of working with my own development, and that of others, suggests that it is important to develop the concept of 'self' as part of self-development. The self-actualisation idea of Maslow (1954) coincides with the feeling that most of us have, that we could in some ways move towards a better life with a better 'me'. He describes such people as having a more efficient perception of reality and more comfortable relationship with it. They also have more acceptance of the nature of themselves and others. It is interesting to see Maslow's ideas being incorporated in the recent work of Senge (1990b:141), in his section on 'personal mastery':

> It means approaching one's life as a creative work, living life from a creative as opposed to reactive viewpoint.

So the examination of the 'self' as part of planning self-development is an important step. Hamachek (1992: 4), in a study of development of the 'self', sets out a definition:

> Broadly defined the self is that component of our consciousness that gives us a sense of personal existence. Defined more specifically the self is the sum total of all we refer to as 'mine'. As a central aspect of our existence the self houses our total subjective and intrapersonal world; it is the distinctive center of our experience and significance.

Hamachek goes on to list the four primary attributes which make up the 'self' physical, social, emotional, and intellectual. It becomes clear that the 'self' is not stable. It changes over time and is influenced by circumstances. Thus individuals may change some aspects of themselves as the environment changes.

Time influences self, mostly through the experiences that time spent gives us. Furthermore, through time certain goals either are attained or may recede as impossible.

The aspects of self that may be partially or fully hidden may be revealed through either the influence of the environment or the passage of time. The Johari window has long been used to illustrate the way in which parts of ourselves may be hidden from others or hidden from ourselves. The way in which the window may be used in giving feedback is detailed in Whitaker (1993: 126–27) (Figure 12.1)

A preliminary approach to a more detailed picture of the self can be gained by getting feedback directly from others – for example, through 'Positive Post Box', where all in the group write positive statements about all the others, which are then posted to them. Pedler and colleagues (1986: 31–46) have a full self-analysis questionnaire for managers. However,

	What is known to self?	**What is unknown to self?**
Known to others	**PUBLIC AREA** You know and others know	**BLIND AREA** You don't know but others do
Unknown to others	**HIDDEN AREA** You know but others don't	**UNKNOWN AREA** You don't know and others don't know

Figure 12.1 (after Whitaker, 1993.)

they suggest that the exercise should be carried out with a partner, since unsupported introspection about your own attributes is extremely difficult to achieve.

Argyris and Schon (1974:7) developed the useful idea, that managers have 'espoused theory' (which is what we say we believe in) and also 'theory-in-use' (which is what we actually do):

> We cannot learn what someone's theory-in-use is simply by asking him. We must construct his theory-in-use from observations of his behaviour.

For the self-developing manager this raises the paradox that Argyris and Schon go on to explore. How do you change behaviour that you are not aware of? Except for accidental and random effects, management development without awareness is clearly not possible. This may partly explain why, after so much has been stated about self-development through reflection, little seems to have happened.

Reflection in action

The action research movement has gained many followers, and most teachers are familiar with the terms, 'reflection on practice' and 'action research'. The approach of action research links with the action learning ideas of Revons and others (as discussed in McGill and Beaty, 1992). Much has been gained by the application of these ideas and they are rightly well supported. However, there is a danger that these terms may be used without a full understanding and commitment to their concepts and processes.

Gaining control of our development is linked to the way in which we visualise the relationship with the world of events around us. To what do you attribute the causes and events that make up your working world? Taking responsibility for the control of your own development is crucial. Tajfel and Fraser (1978: 247) identified this in their section on attribution theory:

> At one extreme, 'internals' attribute the cause of reinforcements to their own personal attributes or endeavours; at the other extreme 'externals' see such reinforcements as due largely to chance or forces beyond their own control.

It would seem likely that those in management posts would be 'internals'. They will probably attribute their management position to qualities that they themselves possess, rather than to luck or other external factors.

Managers may well find it particularly difficult to reflect effectively because of the sense of role and position that they hold. They may depend for their confidence on the belief that they are functioning well. There is some possibility that managers have the greatest difficulty in learning and in developing through learning, for this reason. Any recognition that their competence is less than adequate leads to the dilemma of a mismatch between 'ideal' and 'real'. The 'self' has means of guarding our theories-in-use from such threats, and Argyris and Schon (1974:32-33) list what managers do to protect theories-in-use:

1. Compartmentalise various aspects of performance.

2. Give selective attention – where areas of weakness are simply not attended to.

3. Use micro-politics within the organisation to suppress data – so that evidence of anything less than perfect performance as a manager is covered up.

4. Act violently to remove offending elements – items that threaten performance are attacked.

5. Act in subtle ways to produce self-sealing, self-fulfilling prophecy.

6. If forced to make a change, they make marginal changes and leave the core features whole.

Some teachers believe that they manage in a particular way, and defend their mental picture of the 'self' against any evidence that they are really acting in a different way.

Reflecting – what has happened?

Two papers, which explored the issues involved in reflection related to the action of teaching, are helpful in considering the processes of reflection in management development (Day, 1993; Griffiths and Tann, 1992). Day (p. 84) lists the four assumptions which support an operational definition of reflection in teaching:

1. Engaging in reflective practice involves a process of solving problems and reconstructing meaning.
2. Reflective practice is manifested as a stance towards inquiry.
3. Reflective practice is seen to exist along a reflective spectrum.
4. Reflective practice occurs within a social context.

He goes on to describe the processes that he thinks are involved in reflection: *describing, informing, confronting,* and *reconstructing*. It is the stage of confrontation that is the important feature identified by Argyris and Schon, and on which Day (1993: 88) comments. Here action and reflection are exposed to examination:

> However, as we have noted, reflection is a necessary but not sufficient condition for learning. Confrontation by self or others must occur.

It is that confrontation, or reflection under examination, that is essential if higher levels of development are to be reached, and the defences of 'self' broken through. This stage really needs the help of some skilled helper or helpers as Day describes (p. 88):

> Those involved as 'skilled helpers' must be special people, critical friends, trusted colleagues and who have not only technical abilities but also human relating/interpersonal qualities and skills as time energy and the practice of reflecting upon their own practice.

Griffiths and Tann (1992: 78) suggest that a weakness has been to see reflecting as a process that takes place at only one level. They define five levels – some for reflecting as the action takes place, and others for reflecting after the action:

(A) Reflection-in-action

1. *Rapid reaction* – almost automatic.
2. *Repair* – on-the-spot rapid reaction to a situation.

(B) Reflection-on-action

3. *Review* – thought and reflection after the actions are completed, possibly resulting in change of existing plans.
4. *Research* – systematic and sharply focused observations. You reflect on the information itself and its validity and reliability.

5. *Re-theorising and reformulating* – the person's own theories may be changed, and accepted theories are challenged.

This framework is a developmental one, which provides a real structure for the developing manager. Griffiths and Tann make the point that espoused theory and theory-in-use have to be related, if change and development are to occur.

The practicalities of reflection are that individuals must be able to deliberate on some kind of evidence, to see whether it supports the case that the theory-in-use links with the espoused theory. To do that, the various defences that become set to safeguard us against any form of attack on our view of 'self' have to be overcome.

The way forward has to be in becoming more sensitive as individuals, with the help of critical friends in the same school or elsewhere, who can review the evidence and test out the theory-in-use that appears.

Learning as a manager

Self-development involves learning which links to knowledge of different kinds. The main approach we are considering here is to reflect on knowledge-in-action, or process knowledge, with an awareness of how this subjective understanding may be made more valid by raising awareness. This is partly dependent on sharing of experience with others. However, the process of building on tacit process knowledge is difficult, as is shown by Eraut (1994: 7):

> This requires considerable self-awareness and a strong disposition to monitor one's action, and cross check by collecting additional evidence in a more systematic manner with greater precautions against bias.

Developing yourself as a manager depends on the extent to which you recognise issues from your reflection, and learn to change your behaviour. Managers in professionally based organisations, such as schools, could be expected to be proficient learners but Argyris (1991:100) found difficulties with managers in general:

> Put simply, because many professionals are almost always successful at what they do, they rarely experience failure. And because they have rarely failed, they have never learned how to learn from failure. So whenever their single-loop strategies go wrong they become defensive, screen out criticism and put the 'blame' on anyone and everyone but themselves. In short their ability to learn shuts down precisely at the moment they need it most.

Senge (1990b:142), writing on personal mastery, makes it clear that today's managers have to be learners:

> People with a high level of personal mastery live in a continual learning mode. They never 'arrive'. People with a high level of personal mastery are acutely

aware of their ignorance, their incompetence, their growth areas. And they are deeply self-confident. Paradoxical? Only for those who do not see that 'the journey is the reward'.

The process of learning as a manager within education can seem a risky process. There are a series of areas of risk-taking that face such people:

- The risk that the system will break down in an organisation where for each learner each year, term or week is a once and for all experience. If making a change means that things go wrong, that group of learners lose an opportunity that cannot be retrieved.

- The first risk arises because trying out new activities can lead to a de-skilling process. You leave something at which you have a skill, in order to attempt a new approach.

- This in turn leads to a risk of conflict with others – both with learners and with colleagues who wish to leave things as they are.

- Increased risk of stress arises from the other features.

Thus learning and developing means making changes, and this involves risk. Senge's idea, that those with personal mastery face ignorance with confidence, rests on the basis that such people are learners. They have learned before and can learn again.

The mind-set of some managers also seems to result in what Argyris calls 'single loop learning', in contrast to 'double loop learning'. Single loop takes place when you learn to solve a problem directly. Double loop is when you start to learn about the causes of the problem, and the strategic questions of what the organisation should be trying to do. Hawkins (1994) elaborates on the learning of managers, and raises the issues of a treble loop, which he terms 'transformational learning'. The question at this level is, 'Who or what are we serving in this endeavour?'. It is about facing the operational, strategic and service levels of learning.

A major issue in dealing with management learning is the basis of what kind of knowledge is needed. Eraut comments (1994:103) that even if you ask education managers how they work it is likely that you will get a confused answer:

> Many areas of professional knowledge and judgement have not been codified; and it is increasingly recognised that experts often cannot explain the nature of their own expertise.

Eraut's work is particularly helpful in discussing the various forms of knowledge that professionals use. Here teacher–managers are taken as being professional, although in many cases the professional knowledge is in teaching rather than in managing.

Propositional knowledge

Propositional knowledge is that which is commonly understood in education. Eraut (1994) lists three sub-categories:

- discipline-based theories and concepts;

- generalisations and practical principles in an applied field;

- specific propositions about particular cases.

This propositional knowledge may be in action in one of four ways: *replication, application, interpretation* and *association*.

Process knowledge

Process knowledge is that which is about knowing how to do things. Examples given by Eraut include: *acquiring information, skilled behaviour, giving information, and meta-processes* for directing and controlling one's own behaviour.

Professionals learning are a particular group operating in complex situations. Effectively, all managers only learn that process knowledge is valid, by trying the process and accepting it for themselves. Professionals in action seem to have a type of knowledge which they apply without conscious thought – a level that relates to the Griffiths and Tann (1992) 'reaction' level of reflection. Schon (1987: 28) and others have recognised this as 'knowing-in-action':

> The knowing-in-action is tacit, spontaneously delivered without conscious deliberation; and it works, yielding intended outcomes so long as the situation falls within the boundaries of what we have learned to treat as normal.

These experiences lead to learning and development if they can be brought out of the level of tacit understanding and made public, as Eraut (1994:7) shows:

> The problem for professionals however, is not to exclude such experiential learning, they would be lost without it. But to bring it under more critical control.

Through a clearer understanding of self, reflection and learning we can develop the ability to reach the Senge stage of personal mastery. How do we make progress towards this, in the practical world of the education organisation?

Self-development

Many teacher–managers have been involved in the *Investors in People* programme, to support management development. Giving time for a programme of self-development is a practical issue that has to be faced.

Much of the development that can be carried out within a self-development programme of this kind fits within the time already involved in work. In some ways it is not the work that expands, but the thought and reflection involved. Through the establishment of critical friends, much of the data on the work that is being carried out can be collected with no additional time taken. Where skills are improved, the result is that better decisions are made, which are more effective, thus saving time.

To begin a programme it is helpful to carry out a personal management audit, based on one of the schemes that list the full range of management abilities that are needed for the fully functioning education manager. Pedler *et al.* (1986:31–35) provides a useful analysis list for managers. Management Charter Initiative (MCI) competency standards have been designed for managers in commerce and industry. School Management South (SMS: Earley, 1992) is a consortium of schools across a number of Authorities in the UK which revised and evaluated the MCI standards for use in schools and colleges. However, SMS standards have been researched in school contexts, and are clustered into four areas:

- *Manage policy*: – Review, develop and present school aims, policies and objectives.

  – Develop supportive relationships with pupils, staff, parents, governors and the community.

- *Manage learning*: – Review, develop and implement means for supporting pupils' learning.

- *Manage people* : – Recruit and select teaching and non-teaching staff.

  – Develop teams, individuals and self to enhance performance.

  – Plan, allocate and evaluate work carried out by teams, individuals and self.

  – Create, maintain and enhance effective working relationships.

- *Manage resources*: – Secure effective resource allocation.

  – Monitor and control use of resources.

For each of the listed units there are a range of standards given in the documentation (Earley, 1992). The personal management audit should include an audit of the skills, knowledge and understanding that an individual already has, for comparison with the SMS list of standards. If those involved wish to gain an award, or be credited with the MCI standards, they should approach a local institution of Higher Education.

At this point it is impossible to get an NVQ award on the SMS standards, since the only body recognised as able to fix standards is MCI. However, there is relatively little difference between the two sets in the features covered, except for the terms used by them.

A personal audit needs the help of a critical friend, if possible. This would best be someone in the same school or college, who is also working on their own development scheme. If such a colleague cannot be found, then it is important to seek as much feedback as possible from others.

Evidence can be built up as diary entries and daily thought records, but there are advantages in using video or audio-tape records of the action; a tape-recorder left running in the classroom may be easiest to operate. All such records become difficult to analyse afterwards, but the teacher–manager often knows the section of any interchange that illustrates some theory-in-action. The time required to review the tapes and to consider them with a colleague may not make this option possible. One approach to developing competences has been to use behaviourial event records, or critical event records. This is where the teacher–manager selects an item of action in the week that seemed to be important, and reviews the action, following a pattern of analysis. This can be developed in various ways; one that has been used successfully by teachers is: '*The critical incident*'.

It might help to reflect on a critical case through some of the following dimensions:

- Who?   Draw a diagram of the role connections between the people involved.

- You
  - What were your feelings?
  - What caused those feelings?
  - Did you express your feelings?
  - If not, why not?

- What?
  - Define what the incident seemed be about.
  - What was it really about?

- How?
  - How did you manage it?
  - What kind of authority did you use?
  - How did the organisation of the school influence the issue?
  - Did gender/class/ethnic or cultural difference matter?

- With what?
  - Did you use skill (such as understanding the timetable of the Key Stages of the National Curriculum)?
  - Did you use skill in dealing with people and establishing

relationships?
– Were global skills used of being able to see the issue from a wider context, such as the need to relate to parents and governors?

- So what? How did it all matter?

- Now what? What do you now need to learn?

With the critical incident it is helpful to get a variety of views of the event, and to discuss it with others.

There is obviously a danger that defences will come in, at the point of deciding what event to record, but this can to some extent be met by the comments of the critical friend. If there is no critical friend who can share and exchange the review function, then the teacher–manager is left with self-review. For this, evidence is even more critical, and data might be best left after recording, for a period of several days before trying to review the events. From analysis and confrontation stems the learning, which is the essential feature of all development.

Argyris and Schon (1974) used an interesting approach, of recording a meeting or other event on the right-hand page and an analysis of it on the left. Where records of meetings or other events are available, this is a useful (but possibly time-consuming) way of getting more information from an experience.

It is at this stage of making meaning from the account that teacher–managers need to think of single, double or triple loops of learning. Feedback from others is especially valuable. However, feedback sources need some careful selection. In exposing the more concealed parts of the 'self' we make ourselves vulnerable. Feedback needs to be open, and positive, as well as pointing to areas in need of development. Serey and Verderber (in Bigelow, 1991: 14) explain the skill needed in coaching for managerial improvement:

> It takes time, skill and courage to confront poor performance. Providing this coaching directly but gently is an absolute necessity if students are to become competent managers. When we provide course feedback and coaching to students in our skills course, we try to balance the need to provide honest feedback with the need to protect the self-image of the student.

When managers find areas in which they lack experience or expertise there comes the stage of building up a portfolio for development. This might be physical, in the form of a loose-leaf folder, or simply a process of reflection. The process is one of gaining experience, or strengthening areas where required. Sometimes it is possible to do this through job rotation. Senior Management Teams can see the advantage of building up the strength of the team, and moving certain experience around is a way of doing it. In some areas it is still possible to attach staff to another school or non-educational organisation for short periods of experience. In the field of human relationship skills, it is nearly always possible to gain experience that is needed, by structuring things to provide the required learning conditions. In areas of technical skill, such as computer management systems or accounting, it may be necessary to attend workshops or courses.

The main point about progress towards what Senge (1990b) calls *personal mastery* is that through systematic self-development, we never stop learning and developing. True self-development is not aimed at self-advancement but at personal growth. Both may arise, but it is personal growth that feeds the 'self' and leads to a better quality of work life.

Membership of the British Educational Management and Administration Society provides some wider contacts with whom to discuss issues of self-development. The society publishes two quarterly journals, and its national conferences provide an opportunity to meet with others who are working as managers in education.

Part Three: The Successful School/College

CHAPTER THIRTEEN

Improvement Through Inspection

Brian Chaplin

Introduction

Contrary to popular belief, a remarkable feature of national education policy in the UK, during and since the 1980s has been the degree of consensus about the principles on which it should be based and the objectives it should attain.

In the context of an increasingly competitive and complex economic and technological world, the principles included:

- a common curricular entitlement for all pupils of compulsory school age;

- a common examination for all (or nearly all) at 16+;

- a framework to cater effectively for pupils with special educational needs, including the most able as well as those with special difficulties;

- a system in which decisions about spending are placed as close as possible to the teacher in the classroom;

- schools which are more responsive to parents and the communities they serve.

Each has largely been achieved, although the ways and means of their attainment have been and still are the subject of bitter political dispute and public controversy; some of these are examined in later chapters of this book. For example, David Jesson (Chapter 19) argues for fairer standards of assessing school achievement, and Jon Nixon (Chapter 18) scrutinises critical issues in the curriculum. When the 1988 Education Reform Act set up the National Curriculum and its assessment to secure a common curriculum for all, it lacked a philosophy for the whole curriculum, and became so overloaded that it has had to be drastically pruned. None the less, the first section of the 1988 Act still requires schools to provide a broad and balanced curriculum for all pupils.

GCSE is a common, single subject, public examination system which encompasses over 90% of 15–16 year olds. Its hurried introduction, uncoordinated with the National Curriculum, also caused controversy but now nearly all pupils nationally gain at least one graded result in the examination. Indeed, over 40% of entrants gain five or more subject results at the three highest grades. Prospectively, GNVQ and other vocational courses may complement the GCSE system at 16 to meet the full range of pupils' needs.

Following the Warnock Report (DES, 1978) on Special Needs in Education, the 1981 Act transformed its structure and brought more pupils with special needs into main-stream education. Again, adequacy of resources and quality of provision for these pupils in the main-stream has been controversial. Subsequent legislation set out to improve the assessment of their needs and the appropriateness of the education provided, by creating statements of special educational needs and a Code of Practice.

Arrangements for the local management of schools (LMS) in the 1988 Act took detailed financial control away from LEAs, amid considerable debate. Financial resources and decisions about their use are now delegated to institutions, with the intention that spending should reflect the particular needs and priorities of each institution.

The role and responsibilities of governors as an educational 'board of directors' for each school have increased substantially with each new piece of legislation over the last decade. The parents and the community now have a much stronger voice on governing bodies. Parents (or, more precisely, some privileged groups of parents) also feature strongly in other, more controversial initiatives: for example, in the extension of 'parental choice' through more open enrolment, and the creation of grant maintained schools and city technology colleges. None of these have become any the less controversial with the passage of time.

If these are the broadly agreed principles on which the national education policy has been built, then its more precise objectives have been equally clear and acceptable. They have been to:

• raise standards;

• make schools more accountable, particularly to parents;

• promote values and attitudes appropriate to a responsible society.

Again, controversy has centred on the strategies used to attain these objectives. Legislation can create a highly centralised curriculum, determine the means of assessment, give powers to parents and governors, delegate finances and specify the values it thinks are important. But a set of statutory instruments cannot tell the government or the electorate how well any of those delegated responsibilities are being implemented, or whether they are leading to improvements in the system. Other strategies, again controversial, have been necessary to try to ensure that policy objectives are being achieved. These have focused specifically on the learner, the teacher and the school.

The performance of the learner as an individual is measured largely by his or her performance in public examinations and National Curriculum tests, where the results have to be communicated to parents. These tests proved controversial with the teaching profession, and publication of the aggregated performances of all pupils in a school, as well as those of other local schools for comparison, is equally contentious. The league tables, whose provenance is bitterly disputed, are designed to stimulate parental demand for high standards. If the school fails to achieve them, the thinking is that parents will transfer their children to other, more successful schools. Because money follows the pupil, income will be lost by failing schools and will be gained by schools that deliver high standards. In theory, therefore, market forces apply strong incentives for schools to establish good standards, at least when an alternative school is near at hand.

Improving the quality of teachers was centred on two independent, yet interdependent approaches. The first was a radical remodelling of the initial teacher training system, which placed more emphasis on work in the classroom with experienced teachers than on the training in institutions of higher education. The second was the introduction of a national system of systematic teacher appraisal, which evaluates each teacher's performance but is linked to identifying and meeting teachers' needs for professional development.

Institutional performance was to be raised not only by the publication of league tables but, more importantly, by independent inspection of all schools – primary, secondary and special – once every 4 years. The report of each inspection must be published and a summary of the report must go to all parents and staff. So, too, must the action plan, which has to be prepared by the school and the governors to remedy any deficiencies which the inspection identifies. The implementation and outcomes of the action plan are monitored by parents, to whom the governing body must report progress at least once a year. Again, parents and market forces are intended to apply pressure on schools to improve. The publication of the action plan recognises, at least, that inspection of itself does not raise performance, any more than you can fatten calves by weighing them.

It is therefore worth looking in more detail at the rationale, structure and operation of external inspection, to see whether it brings about the intended internal improvements in schools, and whether the process can be used for self-evaluation and institutional development, independently of the 4-yearly inspection cycle.

Inspection rationale

The establishment of the inspection system and the Education (Schools) Act of 1992 focused precisely on national policy objectives. Each school is assessed on:

- the standards it attains and the quality of learning and education it achieves;

- its efficiency and the value for money it provides;

- the spiritual, moral, social and cultural values it achieves.

These outputs are the central feature of the inspection schedule in the Framework for the Inspection of Schools (OFSTED, 1994a), the instrument by which schools are inspected and which has the force of law.

Inspection is a form of educational audit, a snapshot of the school at a particular time. If it is no more than that, intended to weigh rather than fatten, then it would be perfectly possible to read a school's performance indicators – its assessment and examination figures, truancy rates, exclusions and pupil destinations – rather as a gas meter reader might do, and tick the appropriate box. However, inspection under the Act is intended to lead to improvement. The Framework recognises that schools are complex organisms, constantly changing and developing partly to respond to the demands of society, partly to accommodate the year-on-year changes in staff and pupils. The Framework therefore sets out the means to look at the schools in the round, and not merely read the meters. It is based on the former full inspection schedules of HM Inspectors of Schools (HMI) and draws on their years of accumulated experience. The publication of the Framework forced HMI to systematise and rationalise their schedules and, more importantly, reveal the criteria by which they judge schools. The publication of the criteria and the guidance to inspectors may do more to achieve conformity to government standards than the inspections themselves: at last, schools know what is expected of them, and they can use these carefully defined expectations to monitor and improve their provision quite independently of inspection itself. None the less, the prospect of an external audit every 4 years tends to focus a school's mind wonderfully – although, as Wilcox and Gray show in the next chapter, questions need also to be asked about the aims and quality of OFSTED inspections.

The inspection process not only assesses the products – the school's standards and quality, its efficiency and the values it conveys – but also the processes by which these outputs are obtained. The result is a comprehensive survey of all the major contributory factors which explain why a school's performance is as it is. Used by schools, the factors provide senior and middle managers with a structure for quality assurance similar to Investors in People standards but specifically geared to education. The areas covered by the current schedule of inspection are:

Outputs (products):

Standards achieved and quality of education provided overall (3.1, 3.2)

Efficiency (4)

Pupils' personal development and behaviour including their spiritual, moral, social and cultural development (5.1, 5.2, 5.3)

Contributory factors (process):

Standards achieved and quality of pupils' learning in each subject of the curriculum (6)

Quality of teaching (7.1)

Assessment, recording and reporting (7.2)

Quality and range of the curriculum (7.3i)

Equality of opportunity (ii)

Special educational needs (7.4)

Management and administration (7.5)

Staff, resources for learning accommodation (7.6 i, ii, iii)

Pupils' welfare and guidance (7.7)

Links with parents, agencies and other institutions (7.8)

(figures refer to sections in OFSTED, 1994a)

A consistent rationale is applied to the inspection of each of the contributory factors, as well as the main outputs:

- evaluation criteria are stated;

- evidence which must be considered is specified;

- areas on which judgements must be reached and reported are identified.

In this way, consistency can be established between different inspectors – which is necessary when the number of inspections runs close to 1000 each year in the secondary sector. Inspection teams must apply all the Framework criteria and use all the evidence in order to provide secure, first-hand and valid judgements, collectively agreed by the whole team.

Self-evaluation, using inspection

Schools have not been slow to use the criteria and the evidence for themselves, either for review/development or for quality control. The inspection schedule's use for review/development is not only valuable in preparing for inspection, but also contributes to the cycle of school development planning. Major re-casting of school development plans usually occurs every 3–4 years, and increasingly such reviews are geared to the inspection and action plan cycle. Annual revisions, up-dating and refinement of the short- medium- and long-term objectives can also draw profitably on the Framework.

The constituent parts of a secondary school – subject departments, mechanisms for pupil support and management – can each exploit parts of the schedule for their own purposes. They can also use the inspection methodology to reach their objectives, to:

- examine the documentation;

- observe the work and activities of the pupils directly;

- discuss the outcomes with those involved.

Subject review

Subject review:

In undertaking review/development, a subject department might well use the criteria from the following sections of the schedule shown in Tables 13.1–13.3 and ask itself the accompanying relevant questions.

Table 13.1

3.1 STANDARDS OF ACHIEVEMENT	
Criteria	*Relevant Questions*
What pupils know, understand and can do in the subject at least meets national expectations of average pupils nationally.	How effectively are pupils covering the relevant National Curriculum or other programmes of study? What evidence shows their knowledge, skills and understanding?
Standards delivered at least meet national norms in the subject.	How does the school's profile of attainment compare with the national profile in NC assessments, GCSE, A-level or other nationally assessed data?
Standards achieved at least match pupils' abilities.	Given the pupils' abilities, are performances in line with or below or above expectations?
Pupils are competent in reading, writing, speaking, listening, number & IT.	How are these skills evaluated in the subject? Are pupils performing below, above or at expected levels?

Table 13.2

3.2 QUALITY OF LEARNING	
Criteria	*Relevant Questions*
Pupils make appropriate progress in knowledge, understanding and skills in the subject and in reading, writing, speaking, listening, number and IT	What gains have been made and sustained over a period of time?
Pupils acquire appropriate learning skill in relation to their ages and abilities: – observation and information seeking – looking for patterns and underlying reasons – pose relevant questions – solve problems by applying what has been learned – communicate in various ways – evaluate their own work	To what extent does the subject provide opportunities to develop the skills at levels appropriate to pupils' abilities and with what results?
Positive attitudes to learning: – motivation and interest – concentrate and work productively – cooperate	How well do the various approaches to learning promote and maintain positive attitudes to learning?

Table 13.3

7.1 QUALITY OF TEACHING	
Clear objectives for groups, understood by pupils	Does the planning and the teaching make clear intended outcomes? Do pupils know whether they have achieved them?
Secure command of the subject	Are programmes of study covered in sufficient breadth and depth?
Lessons have: – suitable content – activities which promote learning of content	Are the teaching approaches suitably varied to provide different routes to learning? Is the work differentiated for different abilities to maintain momentum? Does the feedback to the pupil from marking, tests, reports and informal assessments lead to improvement?
Teaching methods: – engage, motivate and challenge – enable progress to be made at a suitable pace – make pupils aware of progress and achievement	Overall, what are the priorities for INSET?

In addition a subject department wishing to undertake a comprehensive annual review of its performance might also use the sections in Tables 13.4 and 13.5.

Table 13.4

7.2 ASSESSMENT, RECORDING AND REPORTING	
Pupils are assessed regularly and the arrangements are manageable	Are assessment and marking procedures consistent across the subject? Do they consume too much time and energy for the results achieved?
Accurate records are kept of individual pupils' achievements	How consistent, reliable and secure are pupils' records?
Outcomes are constructive and inform subsequent work	Are assessments solely summative or are they used to modify approaches to meet learners' needs?

Table 13.5

7.6ii RESOURCES FOR LEARNING	
Criteria	*Relevant Questions*
Sufficient	Which aspects of the subject are inadequately supported by books materials and equipment (including IT and the library)?
Accessible	At what points in the scheme of work are learning resources less readily available to teachers and pupils to support the work in the classroom and at home?
Of appropriate quality	In what respects do the resources available fail to support the teaching and learning of pupils of different ages and abilities?
Used efficiently	Are the funds available sufficient to refresh and develop resources for the subject? Is expenditure targeted to defined priorities and are simple cost : benefit analyses undertaken? Which resources are under/over used and bring least/most learning advantage? (e.g. cost : benefit and opportunity : cost)

Management Review

The provision for special needs or equal opportunities, staffing and accommodation needs, and the school's curricular provision, are aspects on which the management will need to make strategic decisions. The sections shown in Tables 13.6–13.9 may be useful in helping the management team and ultimately the governors to make informed decisions.

Table 13.6

7.3i QUALITY AND RANGE OF THE CURRICULUM	
Criteria	*Relevant Criteria*
The content, structure and organisation of the curriculum in the school: – helps the achievement of high standards	Are time allocations appropriate? Is the curriculum accessible to all pupils?
– reflects the school's aims	Do the schemes of work and the work in the classroom make explicit the links with school objectives?
– has content which meet pupils' needs, interests and abilities	Do particular components in the courses need revision or replacement? What are pupils' views of the courses?
– is effectively organised	Are teachers' programmes well supported by appropriate grouping of pupils, documentation and resources?
– prepares pupils for adult life	Does the work in the subject offer effective springboards into the next stage of education/training/employment?
– is enhanced by extra-curricular activities	How well do visits, fieldwork and club activities support work in the classroom?

Table 13.7

7.3ii EQUALITY OF OPPORTUNITY AND 7.4 PUPILS WITH SPECIAL EDUCATIONAL NEEDS	
Criteria	*Relevant Questions*
All pupils, regardless of gender, ethnicity, ability or social circumstances have access to the whole curriculum	Are any barriers built into option systems or setting arrangements which disadvantage particular pupils?
They make progress commensurate with their developing abilities	Is the work adequately differentiated? Is continuity and progression built-in? Are targets and individual learning programmes appropriate?
Statutory requirements are met	Are the necessary sex discrimination and equal opportunities policies in place? Are the governors meeting their obligations for SEN, statementing and the Code of Practice?

Table 13.8

7.6i STAFF	
Criteria	*Relevant Questions*
Staffing to achieve required standards and quality of learning	
Availability – sufficient staff – appropriately qualified staff – appropriately rewarded staff	Are there enough qualified and experienced staff? Are they paid at levels which reflect their contributions and responsibilities?
Deployment – staff used to best effect	Is the staff's experience, expertise and interests matched to the pupils and programmes they teach.
– appropriate allocation of responsibilities	Are duties effectively and equitably distributed (including workloads and non-contact time)?
Development – appraisal linked to professional development	Does appraisal identify individual training and development needs? Are these blended with the needs of the subject departments and the school as a whole?
– knowledge and skills continuously up-dated	

Table 13.9

7.6iii ACCOMMODATION	
Criteria	*Relevant Questions*
Sufficient general and specialist spaces in good condition	Which aspects of the subjects' work are constrained by inadequate, unsuitable or poor condition accommodation?
Spaces suitable for numbers and ages of pupils	In what ways do the spaces available promote/limit the range of approaches to teaching and learning?
Accessible and efficiently used	Are there ways in which the location and timetabling of spaces could more effectively promote the teaching and learning in the subjects (including clustering rooms, storage and administrative space)?

As long as procedures do not become unduly bureaucratic, considerable advantages, may, arguably, accrue to the senior management of the school if systematic annual reviews are undertaken by each subject of the curriculum. Many schools are already using the inspection schedule's criteria, as the basis for each subject's development plan by which they bid for funds and outline priorities for the following year. In these cases, senior managers and governors then have an overview, from which they can distil priorities for the school as a whole to incorporate into the school development plan. Inspections have placed considerable emphasis on the school development plan. It is increasingly seen as the business plan for the school. An effective school development plan is likely to contain:

- Short (1 year) medium (2 years) and long term (3–4 years) priorities in relation of the school's mission and objectives.

- Each short-term priority will need to be analysed to show:
  planned expenditure, means of implementation, personnel involved, necessary training, target dates for completion and success criteria for evaluation.

- Budget forecasts and implications for staffing, resources, accommodation.

Two sections of the inspection schedule are specific to the management function, and are being increasingly used by senior management as part of their own review and quality control processes: Management and Administration, and Efficiency (Tables 13.10 and 13.11).

Table 13.10

7.5 MANAGEMENT & ADMINISTRATION	
Criteria	*Relevant Questions*
Aims and objectives promote good standards and quality of learning and pupils' spiritual, moral, social and cultural development	Are aims and objectives explicit in prospectus and staff handbook? Do schemes of work and pastoral programmes relate to school objectives?
Leadership by governors, head, senior and other staff promotes the school's aims and objectives	Are group and individual goals set and met? Are areas identified for improvement? Do governors, head, senior and other staff act as partners in formulating and implementing policy? Is there common ownership of policies and pride in the institution? Are there clear lines of reference and responsibility? Is there a clear view of future development?
Plans are relevant, achievable and effectively implemented	Are plans the result of accurate assessments of strengths and weaknesses? Do they prioritise effectively areas for development? Do they allocate appropriate finance, staff and training to implement them? Are there appropriate means of evaluating progress and outcomes? Do they make any difference in the classroom?
The routine administration and organisation of the school is effective and efficient.	In what ways do administrative and organisational arrangements meet/not meet needs? How well planned and executed are daily routines? How effective are the management information systems?
Governors, staff, pupils and parents work together to achieve common goals; internal and external communications promote effective operations and public relations.	What mechanisms are there to inform, involve and motivate the various constituencies in the school's development? Are they effective? Are lines of responsibility and channels of communication in the school appropriate and effective? How effectively are the school's image and achievements projected?
The school evaluates its work effectively.	What quality assurance mechanisms have the governors put in place? What quality control mechanisms has the school put in place?

Table 13.11

EFFICIENCY	
Criteria	*Relevant questions*
Financial planning and management are geared to appropriate objectives.	Are procedures for determining spending priorities and allocating finance effective? Are governors and staff involved in decision-making? Is budget setting geared to school objectives?
Staffing, learning resources and accommodation are deployed to match school objectives and spending priorities.	Do staff, resources and accommodation match the curriculum? Is time used effectively? Are there sufficient non-teaching staff in the right jobs? How effective are review and planning procedures? How is what happens in the classroom assessed?
Financial control is effective.	Do the governors exercise appropriate oversight? Are budget decisions separated from budget administration? Is expenditure monitored and are information systems in place? Are the accounts regularly audited?
Cost effectiveness is evaluated.	Does the school undertake cost benefit and opportunity cost analysis before spending? Does it monitor and evaluate development items? How do the school's performance and cost indicators compare with local and national figures? How does the school measure inputs/outputs to decide value for money? How does the school canvas and use parents' views?

The Welfare and Support of Pupils

Senior management has to coordinate the work of subject departments with mechanisms which oversee the welfare and support of the pupils – the pastoral system. The main purpose of the pastoral system should be to maintain and monitor pupils' progress within the curriculum. Indeed, the pastoral system often has a direct stake in the curriculum, for example personal and social education courses, tutorial programmes or careers and guidance provision. However, the remaining areas of the inspection schedule are focused on broader aspects of the school's activity, which set out to create happy and committed pupils who can benefit from the curriculum provided. The technique of applying the inspection schedule's criteria to the various areas of the pastoral provision is also being used by schools to assess performance and strengthen accountability. These sections centre on the pupils' personal development and behaviour; their welfare and guidance; and the ways in which the school supports the community and seeks support from it (Tables 13.12–13.16).

Table 13.12

5.1 PUPILS' SPIRITUAL, MORAL, SOCIAL AND CULTURAL DEVELOPMENT	
Criteria	*Relevant Questions*
Spiritual: Pupils respond effectively to opportunities to reflect on their lives and the human condition.	How effectively does the school reflect the human spirit and explore fundamental questions across the curriculum and within assemblies? Are the agreed syllabus and acts of collective worship in place?
Moral: Pupils understand right from wrong; they respect people, truth, justice and property.	How are pupils helped to come to an understanding of moral questions? To what extent have shared values been established among staff and pupils? Is PSHE effective? How are pupils' possessions and the school building treated?
Social: Pupils understand how societies function through the family, school, local and wider communities.	How effectively does the school explore contemporary and other societies with the curriculum?
Pupils relate well to others, they take responsibility, exercise initiative, work successfully in groups and participate productively in the school community?	What contributions do pupils make to the functioning of the school? Are a wide range of groupings and social experiences offered inside and outside the classroom? How is responsibility for others promoted?
Cultural: Pupils understand aspects of their own and other cultural environments: religious, social, ethnic or aesthetic.	In what ways does the curriculum provide experience of their own and others' heritages within and outside the curriculum?

Table 13.13

5.2 BEHAVIOUR AND DISCIPLINE	
Criteria	*Relevant Questions*
Discipline (inputs) The school's policies, procedures and practices promote; – good behaviour – development of self-discipline – good quality of life in school – an orderly community.	Are relevant and effective policies in place? Do rewards and sanctions promote good behaviour? Is exclusion used responsibly? Are the means to prevent and deal with bullying effective? Are 'safety nets' in place and operational? What means exist and how effective are they to promote independence and self-discipline inside and outside the classroom?
Behaviour (outputs) Pupils' attitudes and actions promote – appropriate standards – effective learning – good quality of life in school – an orderly community.	How good is pupil behaviour inside and outside the classroom? How extensive is bullying and tormenting? How effective is the extra-curricular programme? Do pupils take responsibility for self and others?

Table 13.14

5.3 ATTENDANCE	
Attendance exceeds 90% in all classes and year groups.	Are attendance/absences analysed and compared with local and national averages? Is the action which follows with pupils, parents and other agencies effective? Is internal truancy checked?
Recording of attendance complies with DES Circular 11/91.	Check Circular and registers.
Pupils are punctual at the start of the day and for individual lessons.	Are means of monitoring punctuality effective? Are rewards as well as sanctions in place?

Table 13.15

7.7 PUPILS' WELFARE AND GUIDANCE	
Criteria	*Relevant Questions*
Pupils' needs are identified and progress monitored.	How effective are the school's arrangements to monitor pupils' well being and link pastoral support with curricular performance? How effective are arrangements to identify and monitor pupils' personal and social needs?
Pupils are involved in defining their needs.	How well are pupils involved in setting expectations and recording their achievements? How effective are tutorial support and PSHE in involving pupils actively in planning their future?
The support and guidance provided meet pupils' needs, promote progress and enhance standards.	How effective are pastoral and subject mechanisms in meeting pupils' needs and supporting progress and standards? Are the guidance arrangements, including careers and work experience, effective in preparing pupils for the next stage of their development within school and beyond?
The health and safety of all those in school are protected.	Is the school's health and safety policy effectively implemented? Have issues been assessed and are safety and emergency procedures well practised?

Table 13.16

7.8 LINKS WITH PARENTS, AGENCIES AND OTHER INSTITUTIONS	
Criteria	*Relevant questions*
Parents are well informed	How effectively does the school communicate its intentions and achievements to its parents? Are parents satisfied with the nature and cycle of reporting pupils' progress?
Parents contribute actively to the life and work of the school.	Are the mechanisms to involve parents in school appropriate? Does their contribution enhance standards and quality?

Conclusion

With only one cycle of secondary school inspections completed by 1995, it is too early to claim that inspection is raising standards and improving the quality of education. Many issues identified by inspection and included in governors' action plans are, in any case, fairly long term and will take some time to be completed and evaluated.

None the less, it is possible to identify some outcomes from the OFSTED inspections already undertaken. They have claimed to reveal the following.

Standards

- In most schools pupils achieve standards which are at least appropriate to their abilities in 70–90% of the lessons seen.

- When judged in relation to national expectations of average ability pupils for each age group, schools' performances are strongly dependent on the profile of ability of their intake, although the majority add at least some value to pupils' performances over 5 years.

- Standards of listening are high and those in reading are at least sound, extended discussion to clarify thinking and extended writing to consolidate and communicate ideas are less frequently used and attainments in these skills are therefore more modest.

- Competent standards of numeracy are reached across the curriculum but those in information technology vary widely from subject to subject.

- Social and economic deprivation is a factor but not always the dominant factor in the attainment of high standards: they depend more on effective leadership of the school and high expectations in the teaching.

Quality and Education

- In most schools the quality of learning is at least sound and often better in 70–90% of lessons seen; pupils generally make good progress in the knowledge and understanding required by the National Curriculum; attitudes and motivation are generally good; the weakest learning skills are pupils' inability to transfer learning from one subject or aspect to another and their inability to evaluate their own work as a basis for improvement.

- In most schools, the quality of teaching is at least sound in 66–85% of lessons seen and is often better.

- The least able pupils are generally well supported; much of the teaching is directed at the middle of the ability range; the work is least well matched to the most able pupils.

- Although schools assess pupils regularly, the outcomes are rarely used to adjust the next stage of the work to accommodate weaknesses or increase the challenge for individuals or groups of pupils.

- Virtually all schools incorporate the National Curriculum at Key Stage 3 and a considerable majority meet its current requirements at Key Stage 4. Although religious education is usually incorporated in the curriculum for all pupils at Key Stage 3, it is much less consistently included at Key Stage 4.

- Time allocated to subjects, other than the core foundation subjects, varies widely.

- All pupils, regardless of gender, ethnicity or ability, generally have good access to a broad and balanced curriculum at Key Stage 3 but breadth and balance are less secure, particularly for less able pupils at Key Stage 4.

Efficiency

- Financial control is effective; a typical budget profile is: staffing 80%, premises 10%, educational resources 7%, other 3%; reserves are generally 4–6% of income but large balances up to 10% are held by some schools.

- Financial planning and management are generally focused on appropriate short-term objectives; longer term planning is weaker; the link between educational priorities in the school development plan and the financial and resource implications is often made late in the planning cycle.

- Governors are closely involved and helpful in setting policies and budgets; their understanding of the curriculum and their mechanisms for quality assurance are less well developed.

- Expenditure on learning resources is generally only just adequate and tends to support existing curricula; that on libraries is inadequate.

- Deployment of staff and match of qualifications/experience to programme taught is generally good; women are numerically less prominent in senior posts.

- School and subject development planning infrequently defines success criteria or the means of evaluating the effects of expenditure on standards; evaluation of cost effectiveness is therefore weak.

- Successful schools tend to have strong but collective leadership, clarity of purpose, shared values and ownership of policies, and consistency in their application.

Pupils' Personal Development and Behaviour

- Intermittent attendance affects the standards attained particularly at Key Stage 4; in many schools it is not unauthorised absence but absence authorised by parents which damages continuity and progression in pupils' work.

- The great majority of schools are orderly, happy institutions which work hard to create a climate conducive to learning.

- Pupils' moral and social development are effectively promoted in most schools.

- Pupils' spiritual development is more patchy: consistent provision of an act of collective worship remains a difficult objective to obtain; religious education for all is not adequately provided in Key Stage 4 in many schools; other aspects of spiritual development through art, music, literature, drama are more consistently provided.

- Schools find some difficulty in including adequate recognition of other cultures in the curriculum and outside it.

- Extra-curricular activities complement the curriculum and help establish responsive relationships in many schools.

- Pastoral systems are increasingly aligned to monitoring and supporting pupils' experience and attainments in the curriculum.

Most Frequently Identified Points of Action

- Extend the range of approaches to teaching and learning to meet the needs of pupils of differing abilities, particularly those of the most and the least able.

- Use assessment and marking more effectively to inform planning and match the work more closely to pupils of differing abilities.

- Improve planning at department and school level to ensure that appropriate priorities are defined, costed and implemented, and that the criteria by which their success will be judged are specified.

- Improve the means of review and evaluation at departmental and school level to provide a clearer view of cost effectiveness and value for money.

As has been suggested, important questions remain about the aims, scope and methods of OFSTED inspections, some of which will be raised in the next chapter. Readers are also referred to Peter Ribbins' final chapter (20) which interrogates some key aspects of the Chief Inspector's first annual Inspection Report (OFSTED, 1995).

As Brian Wilcox and John Gray point out in the next chapter, there are some doubts about the appreciation of inspection methods and more work may need to be done to refine procedures. However, at this early stage, one encouraging outcome of these inspections is that very few schools are failing or are at risk of failing – and that has to be good news.

CHAPTER FOURTEEN

Inspections Under Scrutiny: Implications for Future Programmes

Brian Wilcox and John Gray

Introduction

Until comparatively recently most teachers in Britain had little or no experience of being inspected. In the mid-1980s the extent of 'full' or 'whole school' inspections carried out each year by local education authorities (LEAs) was probably less than 1% of all schools (Stillman, 1989). Even when the efforts of Her Majesty's Inspectorate (HMI) are taken into account the inspection rate was only boosted by a further $1/2\%$ or so (DES, 1989). The chances therefore of a school being comprehensively inspected were about 1 in 100. It was thus possible for many teachers to go through a whole career without encountering this kind of inspection. Inspection, although part of an enduring educational folklore, was for most teachers essentially something that happened to other people.

This situation was to change when the British Government announced, in the summer of 1991, that the existing arrangements for inspecting schools would be replaced by new inspection teams under the direction of *independent* registered inspectors (RgIs). RgIs were to tender for inspection contracts on a competitive basis – an idea popularly referred to as 'privatising the inspectorate'. The new proposals were rapidly enshrined in the Education (Schools) Act 1992 which came into force in September 1993 and 1994 for secondary and primary schools respectively. Henceforth all schools would have a full inspection once every 4 years. Inspections would now be coordinated by the Office for Standards in Education (OFSTED). From being a rare experience in teachers' lives full inspection would become a relatively common one.

The inspection model which has been introduced is very much a development of the approach used in recent years by HMI. It is, however, more comprehensive in its coverage, concerned not only with curriculum and teaching but also with all aspects of the organisation and management (including financial aspects) of schools. It incorporates some novel additional features – for example, the inclusion of a 'lay' inspector in the team, and the organisation of a meeting to hear parents' views. Unlike the former practice of HMI, however, the details of the inspection procedures are set out in a publicly available handbook (OFSTED, 1992, 1993, 1994b), discussed by Brian Chaplin in Chapter 13. Inspection is now ostensibly out in the open.

How will teachers react to this intensive approach to inspection? What effect will it have on them and on their schools? How effective will the inspection methods be? We have had the opportunity of exploring questions of this nature in the course of our study of LEA approaches to assessing the quality of schooling. As part of this study we were able to follow-up six OFSTED-style inspections in five different LEAs. The schools and inspections are simply designated anonymously as A, B, C, D, E and F in the account which follows.

The inspections studied

The inspections were carried out to give the LEAs experience of using the OFSTED *Handbook for the Inspection of Schools* (OFSTED, 1992) before the introduction of OFSTED 'for real' in September 1993. The inspections took place between October 1992 and February 1993. Some of the inspectors at that time had already participated in the national OFSTED training programme. Although not all of the OFSTED features were included in the inspections (for example, the inclusion of lay inspectors, the use of parent meetings) all followed the essential elements of the 'inspection schedule' (set out in the Handbook (OFSTED, 1992)) specifying the evaluation criteria to be used and the evidence to be considered. The inspection reports produced generally conformed to the prescribed format, although there were vestiges (more marked in one inspection than the others) of the style of report previously adopted by the LEAs.

The schools varied in the nature of their catchment areas, ranging from the disadvantaged to the relatively advantaged. In terms of their effectiveness they generally reflected that broad average swathe of schools which are neither outstandingly 'good' or 'bad'.

Our approach was to interview representative samples of school staff and inspectors for each inspection on three separate occasions:

1. Shortly after the inspection when the report had been circulated and/or the staff had been informed of the general findings of the inspection.

2. About 9-12 months after the inspection.

3. About 6 months after that (15–18 months after the inspection).

The later interviews (at stages (2) and (3) above) were concerned with the implementation of inspection report findings. The results from these interviews are described in detail elsewhere (Gray and Wilcox, 1995) and will not be considered here. The emphasis of this chapter is on the process of inspection rather than the outcomes of implementation.

Results of the study

We focus here on three important aspects: general reactions to inspection; reactions to inspection findings; and reactions to the methods of inspection.

Reactions to inspection

The prospect

The prospect of being inspected caused anxiety amongst at least some of the teachers in all six schools. This was sometimes influenced by previous experiences of inspection. In three of the schools (B,C,F) there was some recollection of the previous occasion of being inspected – memories which in the case of one inspection were certainly the cause of initial anxiety. Teachers felt generally more at ease if they had had positive relationships with the inspectors previously.

The timing of the inspection was considered awkward in two schools, coming just after 'open week' in school B and immediately after Christmas in school C. However, all headteachers welcomed the opportunity of an inspection, not least perhaps because this was thought to ensure being spared a 'real' OFSTED inspection in the immediate future.

Pre-inspection meetings between members of the inspection team and school staff were considered to have been useful in clearing up problems and reducing staff anxieties. In school D, the headteacher had attended a local course on OFSTED inspections and had fed back the insights gained at a meeting with heads of department. This had been important in preparing staff for the coming inspection.

A major task for the schools was the production and collation of a range of school information. Much of this information was not easily and readily available. The information gathering activity and the involvement in meetings with inspectors to plan the inspection arrangements took a considerable amount of additional time. The brunt of this was borne by the headteacher and deputies and in total amounted to between 3 and 5 day equivalents in four of the schools. In the other two schools (A and D) the total headteacher/deputy time was 18 and 12 day equivalents respectively, although the former included time out of school for the headteacher to attend OFSTED familiarisation courses. Other staff reported spending up to an additional 2 day equivalents on preparation of one kind or another.

Inspection team leaders were particularly heavily involved in preparing for the inspection, and estimated times ranged from 4 to 10 day equivalents. Most other inspectors were involved for up to 2 day equivalents on preparation, although for some the range was from 4 to 9 days. In two cases (D and E) the times were considered exceptional since inspectors were having to adapt to the new OFSTED arrangements and this had necessitated *inter alia* the organisation of additional team meetings.

The reality

All schools experienced some additional stress and strain during the inspection. The headteacher of school E discerned a variation in staff's reactions throughout the week:

> The first couple of days there was an artificial euphoria – a 'Dunkirk spirit'. By midweek niggles rose to the surface, for example, teachers were saying 'I wasn't seen enough' – a sort of midweek blues. At the end of the week people were saying they quite enjoyed their inspection.

Teachers in school A were generally happy with the way the inspection was conducted, although the comment of the head of special needs was 'as bad as I had feared'. In this case, however, the teacher taught across many departments and was observed in each, and was thus probably 'over-inspected'. Teachers differed in their approach to being inspected; this was reflected in views ranging from 'we did nothing we would not have done normally' to 'you were aware you were performing and made sure you were well prepared'.

A common comment of headteachers and their staff was that the inspection week was physically exhausting. Inspectors also found the week – consisting not only of full days but also late nights spent reflecting on and analysing the data collected – fatiguing and pressured. Inspectors too could have their own sources of anxiety:

> I always feel that we won't get the evidence and have time to sort it out. At the start I was optimistic and then became despondent, feeling that we won't get the task done. Then I became a lot more optimistic. (Inspector, D)

Inspectors commented incidentally on aspects of the OFSTED procedures. Generally these were commended – 'much better than anything we have done before' (A). Inspectors in school F considered the procedures to be more professional and to lead to a 'more balanced and objective picture' than their former approach had done. The team leader for E, however, thought that the OFSTED approach was more frenetic, and emphasised the need for a meeting at the halfway stage in order to refocus.

Inspectors experienced some stress as a result of applying the new OFSTED procedures for the first time and, in the case of team leaders, organising larger inspection teams than accustomed to previously. All inspectors, however, were generally satisfied with the experience and the outcomes of the inspection.

Teachers' reactions to inspectors were generally favourable. Valued personal qualities included being unobtrusive, helpful, supportive, empathetic, sensitive, positive, flexible, and willing to listen to teachers' concerns – although there was some variation between staff. In only one school was there any indication of an inspector being considered less than tactful and lacking in sensitivity in dealing with a teacher.

Where negative assessments were made of inspectors these were associated with professional skills rather than personal attributes (although a sharp line cannot easily be drawn between the two). Professional credibility can be a key issue. In one inspection (C) the headteacher noted the absence of specialist inspectors in certain subject areas. As a result it was considered that sections of the inspection report dealing with these subjects lacked credibility. The same headteacher contrasted local inspectors somewhat unfavourably with HMI:

> If it had been an HMI team there would have been more to criticise. If the inspectors had the 'terrier-like' approach of HMI and their sophisticated methods and sharp minds then the report would have been less good ... the inspectors didn't find out some things we knew were wrong.

The team leader in school A commented that some information gained in the inspection had been inaccurate and that the credibility of the (primary) inspector involved had been challenged by the school.

Reactions to the report and its findings

A common response in all schools was that the inspection – although it highlighted, reinforced or confirmed issues that had already been identified – had not resulted in any real surprises: 'That is our school, we are like that' (deputy head, A). This lack of surprises led one head of department in school B to raise the question whether the inspectors 'have reflected the image we ourselves have put forward and, in the time available, can they do anything more than this?' The headteacher thought that although the report was a confirmation it was important nevertheless:

> As headteacher for 7 years there is a danger of becoming institutionalised – it

is important to know you have got it right – so it was worth the time.

In three of the schools (D, E and F) however there was an admission of some personal surprises and a realisation that some things had not moved as had been hoped, or that some areas had come off worse or better than had been expected. The headteacher of school A admitted to learning two things about the school: that the libraries were closed during the lunch break and that negative attitudes were being expressed by pupils towards pupils with special educational needs.

The extent to which inspectors were surprised by the findings was related to their prior knowledge of the school or of its specific departments. Those who had such knowledge were in some cases pleasantly surprised by the outcome. For example, the team leader of inspection C found that preconceptions of the headteacher's style had not been borne out by staff comments and that the school was performing better than had been expected.

Occasionally, rather than being accepted, findings were contested and opportunities of learning from them were rejected, for example the suggestion in school A that the withdrawal scheme for corrective reading was denying children their National Curriculum entitlement.

In two schools (E and F) the headteachers vigorously contested the emphasis given by inspectors to detailed job descriptions, as a requirement for effective line management of staff.

Despite disagreeing with some of the findings, school staff generally considered that their inspections had been of real value in clarifying and reinforcing priorities for future development. A common belief was that the inspections had given a 'seal of approval' to recent initiatives and a general 'morale boost' for teachers. Headteachers and senior staff tended to feel that reports strengthened their positions and lent weight to existing and proposed developments. For example, in school E the headteacher commented that the inspection had provided some hard evidence on departments – 'some bullets to fire' – which would be useful in the curriculum review currently being conducted. There was, however, the occasional dissenting voice – 'the inspection had limited value since there had been no expectation of [subsequent] support and advice' (head of department, E).

Reactions to the methods of inspection

Classroom observation

Being observed is always potentially stressful. Some teachers put on a 'special show' for the benefit of the inspectors; others claimed that they treated the lesson being observed as a 'normal' one. Inspectors' views on this issue could be regarded as inconsistent by teachers:

> [Inspectors] said they didn't want to see showpiece lessons but during the inspection one said 'to score a [grade] one you have to put on a mega-galactic happening'! (teacher, school F)

Teachers could be concerned if they were observed in a lesson which was considered atypical in any way; for example, being observed when 'covering' a lesson for another colleague or at the end of the afternoon with potentially 'lively' classes.

A common complaint was the difficulty experienced in getting feedback at the end of a lesson on how it had been perceived by the inspector. Although this could vary from inspector to inspector, the major problem was the lack of time available to the inspector before moving onto the next lesson. The problem was particularly acute where only parts of lessons were observed.

Another potential issue was whether or not classroom visits were timetabled in advance. Teachers generally preferred to know when they would be observed and were disappointed if, for any reason, inspectors could not be present as expected. In contrast, inspectors generally preferred the additional flexibility of not being constrained by a timetable.

Ensuring an adequate coverage of teachers, without over- or under-observing particular individuals, was sometimes difficult:

> Some teachers were visited two or three times – for example, in order to see work across the years in departments with only two teachers. Also on 'pupil pursuit' it is pot luck which teachers you observe – one newly appointed teacher had four visits. In contrast, in the science department of 13 staff the inspector was fully stretched to see everyone. (team leader, C)

In inspection E one head of department remarked that the sample of Year 11 teachers and classes had been insufficient because mock examinations were held on one of the days. A similar problem was encountered in inspection A, where cover for absent staff and mock examinations had not been checked. In school E the inspectors were conscious of having moved to observing part lessons (as allowed under OFSTED) in order to ensure coverage. There was however a difference of view about the desirability of doing this.

The grading of lessons and the aggregation of the gradings in order to give overall measures of quality was an innovation for all of the inspectors. They referred to some disquiet in the schools about the five-point grading scale used and the meaning to be ascribed to the mid-point of '3' or 'satisfactory':

> I was amused but disappointed by the making of subjective judgements and then converting them into statistics. For example, 70% of lessons were satisfactory – it is not clear what 'satisfactory' means. It gives an undeserved legitimacy to the whole exercise. (head of department, E)

Interviews

Formal interviews were held with teaching staff in all inspections as well as more spontaneous talks in the classroom and elsewhere. This more informal approach was the general rule in talking with support staff, pupils, parents and governors. Only one inspection (E) used formal interviewing with a specifically drawn sample of teachers and representatives of these other groups. Inspectors' comments indicated a need to develop further the techniques of interviewing by the clearer formulation of interview questions or by otherwise improving existing interview instruments. Some individual teacher comments suggested that they would have welcomed more time for being interviewed, and/or the opportunity of talking more generally, or more interviews with all members of staff.

Some concern was evident in schools D and E at what was seen as an apparent over-reliance by inspectors, on comments made by individual teachers which were not thought to be entirely justified:

> Interviewing – I am more worried by this and I am not convinced of the objectivity. Things come through from teachers 'flying kites' which are not necessarily checked out or set in a wider context. Some things were said in the report which indicate that the inspectors had been nobbled – the claim that middle management was over-burdened. Not sure of the body of evidence for this and it raises doubts about the impartiality of the process. (deputy headteacher, D)

Other inspection methods

There were few comments made on other inspection methods. Inspection team C were aware that they were currently better at some things than others. For a long time they had followed the HMI practice of inspecting pupils' work. Nevertheless they were aware of the difficulties of looking at pupils' total output and making refined judgements on it. They recognised the need for developing more rigorous procedures for assessing the level and appropriateness of the work. The team leader of inspection A commented that there was no time to gather data satisfactorily.

An inspector in team B drew attention to the importance of being able to look critically through the school documentation submitted before the inspection and knowing what was relevant to select from it. The chief inspector in team C thought that their approach to dealing with the pre-inspection information needed 'beefing up' – time spent on this was very valuable as it enabled inspectors to know what to look for when they visited the school.

Other issues related to methods

The potential problem of reporting on cross-curricular themes was identified in inspection D:

> PSE [Personal and Social Education] took a hard knock – it relied on all the inspectors collating their views, which is not a successful method of inspection.(deputy headteacher)

Inspection teams consist of a small core of inspectors present for the duration of the inspection, and a larger number of specialist inspectors who generally attend for only part of the week. This can lead to difficulties:

> The [Information Technology] inspector wrote his piece on Wednesday before seeing what other people had said on this. It may be better to involve such inspectors in the inspection later in the week. A similar problem arose for the assessment section. (team leader, D)

These last two examples point up the general issue of how an inspection team establishes collective judgements about cross-curricular and whole school aspects. This task can only realistically take place in team meetings held during and immediately following the inspection. An inspector in F thought that a lot of time had been spent in these meetings discussing and reporting back on individual subject areas. As a result the agenda concerned with whole-school matters had not moved on as much as it might have done.

The issue of atypicality or unrepresentativeness was raised in most of the inspections. In school D the inspectors commented that they had not seen the rich multi-cultural provision which the context of the school had led them to expect. The headteacher explained that this was because the week of the inspection was not a typical one. One teacher felt that inspectors assume that every aspect of a school's range of activities is fully running during the inspection week. Clearly that would be an unreasonable expectation and so it is important that other evidence is sought on those features which, although not apparent during the inspection, nevertheless normally take place. Similar concerns were evident in school A – one teacher thought the account of the department was not representative of the actual teaching time; in another department group work and lower ability classes were not seen.

A related issue is that of comprehensiveness – the aim of covering all aspects of a school as set out in the *Inspection Handbook* (OFSTED, 1994b: 2,7). Although there were no major areas omitted in the six inspections, teachers and/or inspectors recognised that there had been some minor omissions or aspects which had been inadequately reported. Some of these not surprisingly coincided with those findings which the schools tended to contest. Fully comprehensive cover at a level considered satisfactory by all teachers and inspectors is likely to be difficult to achieve. The inspectors in team D particularly referred to the difficulty of fitting everything into the time available, despite having given more time to the process than would be possible in future under the OFSTED arrangements.

Conclusions and implications

Some of the issues discussed here may be viewed as 'teething' problems, with which schools and their inspectors, as they gather more experience, may learn to deal more effectively or, alternatively, come to terms. The value of these 'early accounts' of experiences of inspection stems from the extent to which they reveal the general kinds of concern that are likely to attend any inspection-type activities.

Psychological and physical effects

External inspection is always likely to be stressful for teachers. This is perhaps to be expected, since teachers are likely to associate inspection with their experience of its most characteristic feature – the observation of classroom teaching. To be observed teaching is to offer up a window on that most jealously prized of all teacher attributes – the 'professional self'. Some teachers may be sufficiently robust to take this in their stride and claim to act no differently from normal; others, however, may experience varying degrees of anxiety.

From an inspector's perspective the importance of any one lesson is the contribution it makes to a putative sample, from which judgements are subsequently derived about teaching generally. From the teacher's viewpoint, however, the situation is intensely individual and personally significant – it is *their* teaching which is being observed. As a result, as our study indicates, teachers are likely to be concerned that inspectors see them in 'typical' lessons, understand the context in which these lessons take place and, most importantly, provide feedback on how the lessons have been regarded. Given the highly programmed nature of the inspection week it is difficult for inspectors to find the time to meet the latter requirement.

The situation may be different for headteachers and their deputies. They are generally involved only to a minimal extent in teaching, their primary task being increasingly that of management. Usually acts of management are not directly observable and inspectors have to rely on inferring their quality from their presumed effects. This may be difficult to do, as at least one inspector acknowledged. Managers then do not risk in quite the same way the direct exposure of 'professional self' as teachers in the classroom. However, in none of the inspections was management generally regarded as a major weakness. When this is not the case (that is, when management is reported to be poor) then headteachers are likely to experience extreme discomfiture, particularly when the findings of an inspection are made public (*see* Wilcox and Gray, 1994).

The substantial additional work that fell particularly on inspectors and senior school staff, both within and beyond the inspection week, led to feelings of fatigue and pressure. Already there is an indication from RgIs engaged in the OFSTED programme that some at least find the pace of inspection very intensive, and are anxious about their ability to sustain such concentrated work on successive inspections (OFSTED, 1994d:24).

Inspection – no surprises

Given the considerable input of people's time and efforts and the consequent real costs involved, substantial gains in knowledge about the schools might have been expected. This was certainly so for the majority of inspectors. School staff, however, generally indicated that they had learned little that was new to them about the school and that there had been no real surprises. Headteachers tended to feel that if they had been surprised then this would have meant they had not been doing their job properly. Can we really take this notion seriously? Can a headteacher really claim to know a school in its totality? However, staff also emphasised that inspections had a confirmatory role. It may be argued that public confirmation has the effect of strengthening and making existing beliefs more secure.

Some staff *were*, in fact, prepared to admit that there had been some surprises. These were of two kinds. There were surprises that were accepted, and others about which staff remained unconvinced or even specifically rejected. Of course, the biggest surprise and potential gain in understanding is when an inspection pronounces a school to be very much 'better' or very much 'worse' than the staff had supposed. None of the inspections studied, however, fell into either of these two extremes.

The trustworthiness of inspections

The 'trustworthiness' of inspections and their findings rests ultimately on the credibility of the methods employed to collect and analyse different kinds of evidence. Although none of our interviewees offered a sustained critique of the inspection methods employed, all expressed their concerns about at least some aspects. The majority of these related to classroom observation. This is not surprising, given its centrality to the inspection process – at least 60% of the prescribed minimum inspection time is to be spent in lessons (OFSTED, 1994b: 3,12) – and its greater familiarity to inspectors. Some inspectors' comments indicated their need to know more about other methods of inspection such as the analysis of school documentation and the scrutiny of pupils' work. A later survey has also indicated that RgIs generally would welcome guidance on how to scrutinise pupils' work (OFSTED, 1994d:64).

Other comments identified perceived inadequacies in some of the applications of inspection methods and raised doubts about individual inspection findings. In brief, these reflect concerns that:

1. Adequate *coverage* is ensured in order to avoid undue emphasis being given to the atypical lesson or programme, and the tendency to assume that things not seen during the inspection do not occur at all.

2. Judgements are adequately *corroborated* by more than one piece of evidence.

3. Where several inspectors are involved in examining the same aspect of a school their separate items of evidence should be brought together effectively to yield a *consensus* judgement.

Although these concerns are recognised in the *Inspection Handbook,* surprisingly little guidance is given on *how* they might be overcome in practice. For example, on the issue of collective or consensus judgements the *Handbook* states:

> Reaching consensus about the quality of a school is most easily accomplished through discussion involving all team members towards the end of the inspection. If some members are unable to attend such a discussion, alternative ways of obtaining their views about the main findings will need to be established.(OFSTED, 1994b:3,20)

and again:

> ensure that where more than one member has evidence on the same matter, the evidence is carefully collated, synthesised and evaluated. (OFSTED, 1994b: 3,27)

These injunctions are eminently sensible, but they beg questions about how they are to be carried out. Reaching a 'true' consensus in meetings of a dozen or more individuals is not easy, nor are the strategies of doing so transparently obvious. Operations of collation, synthesis and evaluation are deceptively straightforward terms which, in practice, refer to complex tasks of reducing and transforming what are essentially qualitative forms of data.

There are clear indications therefore that a further level of training for inspectors is necessary which concentrates on methods of inspecting and analysing qualitative data.

Concluding note

This study essentially frames a fundamental question. Do OFSTED inspections, given their not inconsiderable costs and the potential physical and psychological effects on those involved, result in trustworthy and truly informative accounts of schools?

Although this study has not provided a definitive answer to the question it has identified some of the issues which will need to be considered. Further research is required, based on case studies of a wider range of school inspections in the primary and special school sectors. Such a study would need to explore in particular the relationship between individual and collective judgement and the nature of inspection evidence. In the past inspections have been a much neglected area of educational research. Now that they have become a more pervasive instrument of government policy a more intensive research scrutiny is demanded.

Acknowledgements

The research reported here was part of a larger study supported by a grant from the Economic and Social Research Council (R000233227). We should particularly like to thank the necessarily anonymous teachers and inspectors for their willingness in being interviewed about their experiences of the inspections described here.

CHAPTER FIFTEEN

Planning for Success in the Senior Management Team

Bernard T. Harrison and Stephen Knutton

Consultative Management: 'High gain, high strain'?

Chapter 5 of this book examined critical issues in management through teams in education; in its concluding note, it recommended the need for whole staff development in the Japanese art of *'Ringi-Ko'*, or consultative decision-making. This present chapter returns to issues raised there, through a more particular focus on the performance of senior management teams (SMTs) in secondary schools. Some general discussion will be followed by initial studies of SMTs in action in two secondary schools.

SMTs are an established part of college and secondary school culture, and are increasingly familiar in primary schools. They are based, now, on quite well-established theory and practice. Marsh (1994: 28–34), for example, traces the influential work of Caldwell and Spinks (1986), on the development of *Collaborative School Management* (CSM) programmes in the planning for school effectiveness. Caldwell and Spinks proposed six phases in the cycle of CSM, to be operated by school managers:

1. goal-setting;
2. policy-making;
3. planning programmes;
4. preparing budgets;
5. implementing plans;
6. evaluating programmes.

CSM, as seen by Caldwell and Spinks, involved thorough day-to-day school programmes for each of these phases, with regular targeting of new areas for development and review.

Marsh acknowledges that the SMT approach is 'eminently practical', and that 'it does seem to work' (p.33). Yet he notes several criticisms of CSM programmes that have emerged. These concern, especially, dangers of inflexibility in operation, 'top-down' direction, over-concern with financial detail, and too heavy demands on school staff. In its emphasis on 'rational/logical/ordered process' (p.34), it tends to evade 'the spontaneities, wide-ranging discussions, outburst and arguments that so often occur in schools'. These might be illustrated, for example, by the challenging views of those middle and senior managers, who were recorded in Chapter 5 of this book. Criticisms of these earlier programmes have also, in a number of ways, been acknowledged by Caldwell and Spinks themselves, whose later work (1992) emphasised the importance of 'human', 'educational', 'symbolic' and 'cultural', as well as 'technical' leadership in the management of education. An over-preoccupation with 'technical' aspects, imposed on the school or college by the Department for Education or other outside bodies, denies essential contributions that an individual organisation can make to its own future. This can produce, in Hargreaves's (1992) well known phrase, a 'contrived collegiality', where managers are reduced to acting as technicians, working on instructions from above.

A vision for a 'whole' education service, however, depends on the free initiatives of teacher–managers. As the National Commission on Education (1993: 340) predicts, a well-designed educational system would 'encourage professional teachers and trainers, also educationists, to contribute to the running of the system'. In an illuminating comparative study of management across various kinds of organisations Bottery (1994: 135) suggests that, in the non-profit sector, 'No-one will stay within a hierarchical structure for the sake of it: it is simply an evil that is tolerated'. Seeking an even less hierarchical version of educational management than the CSM programmes envisaged, Marsh describes a *'People-Centred Action Model'* (PCA), which has 'no normal hierarchy of policy-makers'. PCA would depend essentially on *interaction* of middle and senior managers with all staff, in order to identify essential planning needs and achieve required changes. With PCA, organisational improvements can be proposed and implemented by any staff member, regardless of status. Encouragement of initiatives would be an essential component of normal staff development, and good initiatives would need human and material support, to ensure success. Since PCA gives little attention 'to the formal structures of a school such as the school boards and senior staff positions' (p.41), Marsh acknowledges, 'it might be argued that this emphasis upon personal relationships is over-stressed', at the expense of 'harnessing the power of formal groups within the school'.

Are schools and colleges really ready for consultative management?

A PCA approach might, perhaps, commend itself to some of the interviewees who were consulted in Chapter 5. However, as Peter Ribbins shows in Chapter 20, only a small minority of schools have moved away from traditional headteachers' leadership. Secondary schools may still regard the SMT itself as a sufficiently radical and experimental departure from the traditional autocracy of a headteacher. Writing, for example, in a Scottish context, Warren (1994: 186) depicts a rigid hierarchy of management, from headteacher/rector down to senior teachers, that she regards as the general pattern of promoted posts in Scottish schools. Although the school in her case-study has an active SMT, one of her findings was that 'staff at the "chalk face" of the school have apparently little knowledge of the nature and functioning of the management' (p.197).

A more optimistic picture of 'whole staff' involvement in management processes is provided in *Effective Management in Schools* (DFE, 1993b:25). This Report, which investigated 57 schools and visited 12 for more detailed study, found that, in those 12 schools:

> all 12 headteachers espoused an essentially democratic approach to leadership and management. All of them insisted that they sought to lead in conjunction with colleagues, more especially senior colleagues, this being variously referred to as 'collegial', 'democratic', 'team-oriented', 'open' and 'consultative'. None was autocratic in the traditional sense of management by 'dictat'.

On the other hand, there was 'considerable variation' in the ways that individual heads approached their role: 'This was most apparent in relation to their prominence in the school and whether they were seen as strong, distinctive leaders'. The self-views of headteachers revealed a blend of concern to show leadership, and to operate consultative and team aspects of management (p. 26). The views of their staff, however, dwelled more on the authority of the heads: 'She's in command of everything, she's definitely at the helm' ... 'one doesn't mistake who's the head of this school' ... 'I truly think he's quite authoritarian' ... 'the headteacher is forceful but not dictatorial' ... 'she is the main catalyst in school development' (p. 27). Overall, this DFE Report reveals the values that teachers themselves still place on strong leadership from the head and the senior team, as essential components in effective school management. Consultative management was of secondary importance:

> Most respondents appeared to want a combination of firm leadership and consultation over policy matters that directly affected their working lives. Most did not want to be consulted over detail ... (p.125)

This concluding finding suggests that 'whole staff' management is not as strongly rooted as might appear from the rhetoric of some school heads and SMTs. Teaching, it seems, remains a fairly conservative profession, which prefers to move only slowly, and with some caution, to more open systems of decision-making. A more enterprising view of opportunities, for deputy heads, at least, to take management initiatives is provided by Weeks (1994: 251), who claims: 'There has always been an opportunity for creative management in secondary schools'. Yet, after describing his own successful completion of a project as a deputy head, he also acknowledges that the 'formal hierarchical structure of some schools perpetuates bureaucratic processes' (p.262). As a result, staff may feel tied down to a system that does not encourage them to be innovative. However, schools, and particularly SMTs, must be committed to the idea of encouraging initiative and embracing failure.

Weeks attributed the success of his project to the 'full and active support of the headteacher' (p. 263), and of the SMT. He was working in a school that had developed a 'change' culture through a collegial approach, 'with as much staff and pupil involvement as possible' in the teams that had the task to achieve change (p. 262). Yet this pattern of collegiality cannot be taken for granted, as is shown in a study by Cowham (1994: 285-286) of senior management attitudes in a newly incorporated college. The 'first phase' interviews in Cowham's enquiry revealed extremes of outlook. These included a principal who described himself as 'power–coercive' in approach; a deputy principal who claimed: 'I believe in strong central direction and have been called a Stalinist, which I guess is fairly accurate'; and a vice principal who spoke of the 'primarily educational' mission of the college, and of the need to be 'more collegial'. In the 'second phase' interviews, however, Cowham noted 'a perceptible change' in management culture and management style, and a 'higher degree of collegiality' (p. 288). Senior management was beginning to move away from 'power–coercive' towards 'empirical–rational' modes of managing change (p. 289).

Given, then, that many educational organisations are likely to be still working to implement versions of 'Collaborative School Management' as outlined by Caldwell and Spinks (1986), and that 'People-Centred Action' models of school/college management, as envisaged by Marsh (1994) are virtually non-existent, this suggests that educational leaders are likely to require solid evidence that consultative management actually *works* in schools and colleges, before they are likely to consider further management reform.

In the first complete book on the operation of SMTs, Wallace and Hall (1994b) reported on their full year's study of six SMTs in secondary schools. They identified significant successes, and also a number of drawbacks and risks involved, in operating consultative management through the SMT. They concluded that SMTs involved a 'high gain, high strain' strategy, and that schools need to take account of both of these. In their 'balance sheet for SMTs', Wallace and Hall (1994b: 197) find that one of the most important 'gains' is that a successful SMT can empower the head, through the support of all SMT members. It can create a strong sense of job satisfaction, and may release powerful synergies, which achieve far more than might be expected of individuals acting on their own. On the other hand, SMTs curtail a head's power to act unilaterally. This may be no bad thing in itself, yet just one destructive member of the SMT can destroy the work of the team, by producing unresolvable internal conflict. Other 'potential strains' include the time-consuming nature of genuinely consultative teamwork; the danger of SMTs operating in isolation from the rest of the staff; and the ultimate accountability that a head must accept, when teamwork falls.

All the gains, and some (but not all) of the strains identified in the Wallace and Hall study were evident in the two studies provided below, of SMTs in secondary schools. In each school, individual members of the SMT and other staff were interviewed, and SMT meetings were observed on a number of occasions.

Northside School

The setting

Northside School is located in what has been described as 'possibly the largest council estate in Europe', where unemployment figures are even higher than average for the ageing industrial city to which it belongs. Northside is a secondary comprehensive school of 1,300 pupils, aged 11–16. Its headteacher has earned considerable respect in the city, for initiating innovations that have had a city-wide impact (for example, in planning records of achievement). Having worked previously at the school as a senior mistress ('Can you imagine being called a "senior mistress" these days?'). Claire had returned to Northside with a mission to 'start afresh', which she explained in her first address to the staff: 'So now, the first day back, the staff expect me to give them a sort of "state of the nation" address about where the school is at'.

In the first interview with her, Claire emphasised that she was 'ultimately responsible for everything that goes on in the school'. She expressed initial reservations about the term 'open' management: 'I have seen a school that I will not name destroyed because of so-called open management, where decisions were being made by people who had absolutely no accountability'. Her reaction against 'open management' was understandable, given this disclosure. As Stewart and Barsoux acknowledge (1994), different management terms can have quite different connotations for individual managers, according to their different kinds of professional experience. However, Claire soon disclosed that she wished the school to run, in fact, on genuinely consultative lines. Nobody, including herself, could claim to have 'total autonomy' in decision-making. She said that a key task for herself was to ensure that any recommendations from planning teams

> matched school policies, and school philosophy. If you like, I'm the spider at the centre of the web who can try and bring coherence to all the various policies.

Organisation of the SMT

Writing on 'Managing in a constructive environment', Lawrence (1994: 65–83) recommends six key areas of responsibility that must be shared in all organisations:

1. *Production management* (that is, for schools and colleges, the curriculum);
2. *Personnel management* (all staff);
3. *Customer services management* (care for students/pupils);
4. *Research and development;*
5. *Strategic planning;*
6. *Financial management.*

In schools of more than 30 staff (such as Northside), Lawrence suggests, headteachers would need, ideally, a non-teaching finance manager and five other staff (apart from the head and senior deputy) to be responsible for other portfolios.

Claire's arrangements for her SMT at Northside were within a similar framework, but more streamlined. She had reduced the team from eight to five, including herself, each of whom had one of the portfolios identified by Lawrence, above. Claire herself took direct responsibility for two of these. Each member of the SMT carried a 'code card', which was produced after long discussion, and with the full agreement of them all:

NORTHSIDE SCHOOL SMT
  Together We Can:
    Be Fair
    Be Consistent
    Show High Standards
    Collaborate
    Share Our Vision
    Follow School Aims

Communicate
Participate
Enable Others
Celebrate Success
Reflect

How, and how far, did the SMT succeed in these aims? Evidence from interviews with individuals on the SMT, and from observation of the SMT in action revealed a strong commitment to the 'code card', and of a shared team responsibility for each of the areas identified by Lawrence (above).

1. Curriculum management

Claire disclosed that this large area of responsibility was, inevitably, shared by many teachers outside the SMT. Subject department leaders had asked if they could run their own group independently of the SMT, so that they could work out their programmes without direct intervention from 'above'. Both Claire and John, the deputy head who carried the curriculum portfolio, shared some unease that this was a 'self-led group, which contains some of our strongest middle managers'. In practice, the arrangement was working well, but there was a risk that the 'whole curriculum' responsibility which John carried on behalf of the SMT might clash with the particular interests of the main subject blocks. The SMT did not feel that this was 'out of control, but such a group with different people in it, might become a problem'.

Interviews with John, Claire and senior curriculum leaders, and observations of SMT discussions showed that the SMT was vigorously committed to a 'whole curriculum' view, and that they expected full consultation with the subject leaders' group. They required this overview to ensure successful development of curriculum policy. Furthermore, of course, 'whole curriculum' discussions were inextricably tied to the school's overall financial policy, which was clearly a task for the SMT.

Discussions with senior curriculum leaders revealed that they appreciated the autonomy granted to their group, but that they also valued the guiding relationship provided by the SMT. Contrary to fears that autonomy for the curriculum 'barons' might lead to trouble there was, in fact, a strong common purpose shared between the SMT and the curriculum leaders, in policies for curriculum development. The SMT looked to its curriculum group for effective regular management of agreed 'whole school' curriculum policy; the curriculum group looked to the SMT for good forward planning. For example, the SMT was observed making plans, up to 2 years ahead, for reform of the large Craft, Design and Technology Department. These plans involved change in personnel and resource investment and would require consultation with the curriculum leaders group, at a later stage.

John emphasised that the quality of the SMT depended, above all, on the quality of its whole school planning, in all areas. He thought, too, that the 'inevitable gap', between the heads of even the largest sections, and the 'whole school' view of the SMT itself, had implications for staff management.

2. Staff management

SMT members realised, through Claire's own example, the importance of both vision and balance in their forward planning. Their ideals should not allow a particular enthusiasm to distort the whole picture. The art of good staff management is, in part, to form a 'disinterested' whole view among all the 'interested' voices of the staff. An aspect of the 'inevitable gap', though, revealed the need for staff *development*, to give staff opportunities for wider experience. Linda, a deputy head who had been recently appointed to Northside, disclosed her interest in this area. Although she had some criticisms of the management in her previous school (mainly, concerning the 'almost total absence of forward planning', and the consequent dependence on 'crisis management') she had been glad, as the head of a large subject area, to gain a place on the school's SMT. The only real way of learning how to bridge the gap was, she thought, to *do* it. She thought that this opportunity for direct experience must have helped her in getting the deputy headship at Northside, and she wished to contribute to effective staff development policies in her new post.

As the study in Chapter 5 showed, senior people in education are as keenly aware, as in other organisations, of their needs for staff development. Claire herself, for example, revealed her plans to be seconded to a commercial/industrial context for some months, in order to gain comparative insights into managerial expertise. Staff development needs were reflected, too, by another member of the SMT (Stephen), who disclosed that he had been initially reluctant to take the 'whole school' view that membership of the SMT required. He had, however, been 'dragged screaming' by Claire into accepting the new role, and now found much satisfaction in it.

A further example of concern for staff development was observed, when the SMT conducted a progress interview with a project team. After the team left at the end of the interview, the SMT discussed not only the points made about progress on the project, but also how each individual on the team had handled the interview. In particular they noted, with approval, that one of them had been more assertive in her presentation, and more effective in representing her team.

3. Management of students/pupils

Observations and interviews revealed the lead provided by the Head and the SMT in this area. At breaktimes, Claire was to be seen mingling with pupils and staff in the public areas of the school's main building, just as John was a regular and easily visible presence in the second site. Despite his claim that he was 'less directly involved, these days, with pastoral duties', the interview arranged with him had to be delayed by a 'critical incident' concerning a certain pupil and a fire alarm.

Operational pastoral responsibility for the pupils was shared between the two heads of sites, Stephen and Len, both of whom were full members of the SMT. They felt however that, just as they undertook to contribute to all the policies of the school through their work on the SMT, their responsibility for pupils was fully shared amongst the team. On the obverse of the code card (cited earlier), that each member of the SMT carried, was:

NORTHSIDE SCHOOL: FOR THE STUDENT
Together we can:
Be caring
Realise full Potential
Foster Partnerships
Enable Students
Foster Happy Relationships and Co-operation
Foster Moral Values
Ensure Entitlement
Provide a Stimulating and Secure Environment

This summarised an ambitious programme, easier to state than to achieve; yet, at least the policy was firmly in place, and the school was in no doubt about the personal contribution that all SMT members were determined to make, to the 'whole school' care of all pupils. In this way, the rhetoric of the code card might become reality.

4. Managing research and development

A good example of team commitment to research and development was observed at a SMT meeting which discussed school policy on handling bids for 'Raising Achievements and Participation Projects' (RAPP). The school had won a previous bid, and the team was now planning a more ambitious bid. Members explored the complexity of the bidding process, including the need to co-ordinate with other schools; and to develop expertise in making bids, to avoid the frustrations of failed bids. This discussion revealed detailed understanding of the 'enterprise' rules that governed such bids, and a critical insight into opportunities and constraints that needed their attention.

The SMT were then joined by staff who were responsible for operating the successful RAPP bid (which concerned differentiation and targeting the needs of more able pupils). After listening to their progress report, the SMT raised questions. There was discussion about the variability of teachers' response, in handling insights gained from research and development such as this. Clearly, both the SMT and the RAPP teams were determined to implement the research that they felt the school now *owned*. This stress on ownership was reiterated by Claire, who urged that teachers must be encouraged to feel that they were leading the reforms that were needed. John pressed the RAPP team for an early interim report, so that they could plan action in the next school year; Claire suggested that pupils should be invited to monitor the project – will they themselves perceive that they are being stretched by the new scheme? These were good probes; when the RAPP team left, the SMT exchanged some acute – and sensitively expressed – remarks on how their 'middle' management colleagues had handled the enterprise to date. This discussion showed that they recognised the importance of the staff development aspect to the project.

5. Strategic planning

As indicated earlier, all members of the SMT were agreed, in seeing strategic forward planning as their essential reason for existence. Each member was generous in praise of the skills of others on the team, and thought that the present team was both strong and harmonious. However, they all commented on the severe pressures of time on their work, and on the continual temptation to choose 'quick fixes', instead of the (time-consuming) patience that genuine planning requires. Len, who describes himself as 'a practitioner by instinct', felt, 'after all, that *vision* is even more important in critical times'. John agreed that, despite the 'intense pressures' of their work, SMT members had so far avoided serious illness, because they shared strong values and a strong sense of common purpose. All members of the team singled out Claire's leadership in promoting good strategic planning for special praise: 'she just insists that we should ask the best of ourselves – and gets it'.

However, the SMT was observed, at several points, to voice its frustration about the 'short-termism' that was imposed on them from outside, at local and national levels. As Linda remarked, 'The trouble with trying to achieve good forward planning is that you keep coming up against reality'. This was, of course, most evident in areas of financial management.

6. Financial management

Although the financial administration was handled by a 'superb finance clerk', Stephen was the SMT member who had recently taken on specific responsibility for examining budgeting processes, and for initiating discussions on financial policy and planning in SMT meetings. In this, he received the support and detailed advice that he needed for his new work, from Claire and others in the SMT.

Northside School is generally under-resourced and, in some critical areas, its needs are urgent. This reflects the weak finances of the Local Authority, as well as the particular location of the school. Buildings and equipment were in a poor state, and staff:students ratios were too high.

Although several members of the SMT confided their personal criticisms of both Government and Local Authority, about the urgent financial needs of the school, SMT discussions were wholly concerned with the practical issues – with 'what can and must be done', to ensure that scarce resources were well used. Inevitably, uncertainties about future financial provision frustrated the SMT's long-term planning. These involved uncertainty about school numbers, as well as national and local political factors. Clearly, however, the team had accumulated many years of experience, in devising coping strategies to counter the vagaries of these external forces. This produced, at least, a high quality of analysis in their financial discussions, even if solutions were not always available.

As will be seen in the study below, some important similarities and differences emerged, in the SMT policies and practice of a secondary school in a quite different location.

Hillcrest School

The setting

Hillcrest is a comprehensive school, located on a single site, 3 miles from the centre of a large industrial northern town. The school serves predominantly residential areas as well as rural villages. Three months before our visit the 12–16 school was reorganised into an 11–16 establishment, and student numbers increased from 815 to 1135. This involved the admission of 482 new children into Years 7 and 8, the appointment of 18 new teachers (of whom 12 were newly qualified) and the commissioning of four new buildings, as well as alterations to two others. This was all accomplished in less than 6 months – an achievement that was commended by the Director of Education. The school has a strong reputation among parents who, by and large, expect the school to deliver good academic results at the end of compulsory schooling.

Prior to this study the school Senior Management Team described themselves as atypical, in that they were a small, balanced (two female/two male) team of head and three deputies, who had worked together for 10 years. Although rotation of responsibilities had occurred in the past it no longer featured in their current operations. The origin of the team's sense of common purpose was graphically described by the head, Carole, when she recalled having to suspend a member of staff within 2 weeks of taking up appointment. The disciplinary matter resulted in so much work that, effectively, she had to leave the running of the school to the deputies. As Carole says, the experience was

> traumatic, but, in reality for bonding a Senior Management Team, you couldn't beat it, because instead of myself and the original two deputies eyeing each other and wondering how we were all going to get on with it, we got on with it.

The stability of the SMT is also mirrored by the stability of the school's staff. Although, 2 years previously there were no teachers under 30 years of age, they now made up almost one-third of the staff. Whilst the SMT did not perceive its own stability as problematic, it viewed an ageing teaching staff, and high associated salary costs, as a cause for concern. It was glad to have an opportunity to appoint a cohort of younger teachers.

Interviews showed that all members of the SMT shared similar views on management, even though their backgrounds were diverse. Three members had held senior pastoral roles, which had influenced their stance in handling pastoral issues. All three commented that their senior pastoral role had been extremely demanding. Consequently pastoral responsibilities were shared by the SMT, to ensure that the heads of year were not over-burdened. Despite their agreement on most issues, members of the SMT identified, as one of the key strengths, their differences in terms of their variety of subject backgrounds, personalities, experience in different schools and varied interests. Brian identified the death of ambition (in the raw sense of climbing the promotional ladder) in each member as a virtue, in that they could all devote themselves to the school. Therefore, the need to rotate responsibilities was no longer an issue. They all knew enough to cover for each other's absence and could specialise in one particular area of interest to them. Carole pointed to a parallel from industry, where 'they don't expect the finance director to swap with the personnel director and the marketing director at regular intervals'.

The SMT was agreed on their understanding of consultative management, and the ways in which they perceived their own approaches to be genuinely open. They believed that managers had a responsibility to manage, but this did not mean being autocratic. What mattered was not pseudo-democratic decision making, but genuine consultation through appropriate avenues. Each member of the SMT was strongly opposed to collective decision-making at staff meetings, on the basis of bad experiences elsewhere. Carole and her deputies emphasised open-door policies, and developing mechanisms to enable all those with knowledge and appropriate experience to get involved when particular issues need to be tackled. Yet the SMT could not abdicate its responsibility to manage – it had to demonstrate leadership whilst involving others in its decisions.

In the first interview Carole described various formative experiences in her own career progression, and her approach to management. In particular she stressed the importance of capitalising on *opportunities* whenever they occurred. During early stages of her career Carole had been given important responsibilities, which played a significant part in preparing her for a future leadership role. An important task of management is to recognise these opportunities when they arise and to act on them. This involves taking risks, but benefits can be enormous. It also provides opportunities for creativity in management. This was echoed by Diane, another member of the SMT, who pointed out, 'It behoves the management team to try and produce opportunities for staff who wish to take them and ... ultimately it may lead on to cash incentives'. Further discussion of this in the context of cross-curricular themes is explored in the section on staff management below.

1. Curriculum management

Carole takes a keen personal interest in curriculum management at Hillcrest. She likes to anticipate national curricular requirements, and makes full use of her contacts to steer the curriculum at Hillcrest in appropriate directions. Most notably this occurred in the case of Technology where the SMT anticipated curriculum changes, and decided in 1993 to make it a core subject for all pupils. This has not been without its problems, since the national debate had not progressed as fast as expected, and parents of able children do not always appreciate its educational value. Yet the school has developed excellent facilities for teaching the subject, and has recruited high quality teachers. The move towards technology as a core subject required some creative time-tabling, in order to protect Food Studies – which is a successful and popular subject in Years 10 and 11.

Planning at Hillcrest is driven by the curriculum and the needs of pupils. This was most evident at a SMT meeting, where the impact of reducing from nine form to eight form entry was debated (see also strategic planning, below).

Whilst the SMT regard the direction of policy on curricular matters to be their responsibility they leave subject area decision-making, such as which GCSE syllabus to adopt, to individual departments. Consultations take place between individual departments and the SMT. However, the advent of the National Curriculum resulted in such rapid changes that a

National Steering Committee was formed. This committee, involving members of the SMT and Heads of Departments, oversees the integration of statutory requirements, provision of facilities and sharing the effects of change across the curriculum.

A striking success at Hillcrest was the creation of a cross-curricular week, in which the timetable of all Year 9 pupils is suspended and time devoted to cross-curricular themes such as environmental education, health education, economic and industrial understanding and citizenship. This is taught by staff volunteers, and proved to be a powerful way of developing staff, promoting whole school approaches, and avoiding some of the dangers of subject compartmentalisation for younger teachers. The development is given status by Carole's presence in chairing the staff planning group.

2. Staff management

Carole's own formative experiences, of seeking challenging opportunities and significant responsibility early in her career, are reflected in her approach to personnel matters, where she is keen on delegation:

> I don't think that you can ask people to take accountability without giving them responsibility. I expect everybody in this school who has responsibility, and that is down to the last standard scale teacher, to take responsibility. Each of our teachers has their own classroom and I expect them to make that a pleasant place to be, I expect them to inform the deputy with responsibility for sites and premises if there is anything unsafe, or whether it needs any work doing on it. I expect the head of department to have an overview and support them, but all teachers have their own base, with their own classroom.

This was most evident in the cross-curricular development, which sought to give pupils a different curricular experience. It also provided opportunities for staff from different subjects to work as a team and, for younger staff, the chance to negotiate with fairly senior colleagues, including the head. In the years since its inception the cross-curricular week had flourished, and many of the co-ordinators had moved on to greater responsibilities. At the time of the study the SMT was seeking volunteers from staff without responsibilities to act as assistant co-ordinators, with a view to offering them opportunities for career advancement.

Colin has responsibility for staff development and deployment of INSET funding. This is closely linked to the School Development Plan, and great care is taken to ensure that, where staff take up new responsibilities, INSET resources are identified and appropriate courses sought out. The SMT is particularly concerned to ensure that ancillary staff are also included in entitlement to staff development.

An important feature of staff management at Hillcrest is that all staff should feel able to raise any issue or problem with any member of the SMT, whom they choose. Diane remarked, for example, that she would be 'hurt if I thought staff didn't feel my door was permanently open'.

3. Management of students/pupils

To Carole, caring means 'educating every individual child to their full potential', and to that end pupils must come first. Yet, as Diane observed, 'A school can only be successful in student care if it is successful in people care – pupils, teachers, ancillary staff'. Every working person in the school (from Year 7 pupil to the head) has personal needs that require management attention. Brian commented that all staff and pupils are well supported. He thought that the absence of a binary pastoral/academic structure was a considerable strength in highlighting the responsibilities of all staff; this was even more important now that the school had grown. Historically Hillcrest had a strong pastoral care bias – so much so, that Carole could talk of losing the balance between support and challenge. Because heads of year have less time for their pastoral roles than in many schools, the SMT handled most serious disciplinary cases; a member of the SMT would involve the welfare sub-committee of the governors, where required.

4. Research and development

Research and development issues feature as a regular agenda item for the SMT, though Carole admits that the National Curriculum has reduced scope for flexibility, compared with her days as a deputy in a neighbouring city. The cross-curricular week was itself a manifestation of the SMT's aims to develop the curriculum. The main curriculum development at Hillcrest has been in the area of Technology, where the school anticipated national directions and mounted a successful bid for a £250,000 Technology Schools Initiative (TSI) to equip the school. Further technology developments occur through involvement with 'Neighbourhood Engineers'.

Another example of curricular development is the SMT's approach to vocational development, where Carole keeps a watchful eye, and plans to build bridges with the local college rather than act unilaterally. Brian, as systems and finance manager, undertakes developmental work which results in software, for solving problems identified in strategic planning. He also undertakes analysis of value-added aspects of performance by the school in conjunction with Year 11 information systems. This provides more reliable information, with which the SMT can identify issues for special attention.

5. *Strategic planning*

Strategic planning is the main feature of SMT meetings. Reflecting on the school's development, the SMT was convinced that the school reorganisation had gone so smoothly because of its attention to planning detail. One example relates to staffing, where the curricular and timetable needs for the school had been worked out in such detail that it was possible for advertisements for 18 new posts to be prepared, in anticipation of approval being given, and to appear within a few days. In this way the SMT was in good time to choose new staff with care. Detailed advance planning enabled them to avoid awkward timetable splits. In their plan for growth, for example, they decided to appoint a full-time, rather than part-time scientist. To fund this they decided not to budget for supply teachers, but to cover supply needs from within their increased staffing.

In anticipation of forthcoming cuts in the school budget the SMT had asked the deputies with responsibility for the timetable and finance to prepare alternative plans, not only for the next financial year, but for future years. The effects on staffing needs of restricting Year 7 to 240 pupils and reducing from nine forms to eight was considered. The effect on Years 8 and 9, and on staffing in subsequent financial years was investigated. The analysis was then taken a stage further by examining the subject teaching expertise required by these plans, and comparing these with known staff expertise and flexibility. This provided early information for prioritising staff replacements. This analysis was conducted within a clearly defined set of principles, related to the main purpose of the school – the education of children. Brian pointed to the strategic nature of planning when he observed that 'nothing is allowed to happen naturally'. Where a potential problem is seen, the SMT seeks to clarify the problem through talking about it, tries to agree on a strategy, and selects one of the team to take what action is needed.

6. *Financial management*

Our study took place at a time when schools were determining their financial and staffing planning for the new academic year. At Hillcrest the SMT had made a policy decision not to employ a bursar. By maintaining academic control they sought to emphasise the educational basis of decisions, such as ensuring priority for teaching children and providing necessary resources. Of course, clerical assistance was required for the settling of accounts, but it was the responsibility of a designated SMT member to provide a full financial picture for the team. Some responsibility for finance is delegated to Heads of Department, who receive capitation for their subject areas. Departments can bid for additional funds, in line with agreed school priorities. This enables the

SMT to monitor spending against the aims of the School Development Plan. The deputy with oversight of finance commented that departments were able to make honest and reasonably accurate forecasts of their financial needs. Interestingly, finance was identified by three of the SMT as one thing they would like to change about the school. The impact of just a small amount of extra money to be spent on the school environment could, they thought, make an enormous difference to the quality of educational experience in the school.

Northside and Hillcrest: a summative note

We noted some important differences, in this exploratory study, between the styles and outlook of the SMTs in these two schools. For example, Northside regularly changed round the portfolios of responsibility, so that each member of the SMT could develop a full view of school plans and policies. By contrast, Hillcrest opted for stability, as no one in the SMT claimed to be interested in promotion. A critical issue arises here, perhaps, in distinguishing between 'self-development' and 'self-advancement', which deserves further investigation.

However, the similarities that we found between these two SMTs were far more notable than the differences. Our interviews and observations revealed that these highly committed SMTs did not evolve by accident. Rather, they had grown through the careful design of headteachers, who had directed their leadership to developing genuine consultative management amongst SMT members. When investigation is extended to the experience and attitudes of less senior staff we may find, of course, that the impressive sense of collegiality, which was in evidence amongst the members of the SMT, might not be so widely shared amongst the whole school. However, informal discussions with some teachers outside the SMT suggested that the consultative patterns established at the top were also influencing other working areas of these schools.

Claire and Carole undoubtedly earned their reputations as headteachers of rare quality. Yet, when asked about their own effectiveness as a leader they both preferred to talk about their school rather than themselves. In this, they – and all members of their SMTs – illustrate a point made by Kim and Mauborgne, who wrote on 'Parables of Leadership' in the *Harvard Business Review* (1992:123):

> What is leadership? The essence of leadership cannot be reduced to a set of particular roles and activities. It is like the challenge of describing a bowl: we can describe a bowl in terms of the clay from which it is made. But a true picture must include the hollow that is carved into the clay – the unseen space that defines the bowl's shape and activity.

This might, at first sight, seem to be a 'mystical' view of leadership. Yet it offers an exact analogy, in the cases of Northside and Hillcrest, since the achievement of their headteachers was to create the 'unseen space' that defined the actions of the SMT. The 'leadership' of the schools was enacted in that space, where all members of each SMT showed

> the ability to hear what is left unspoken, humility, commitment, the value of looking at reality from many vantage points, the ability to create an organisation that draws out the unique strengths of each member.
>
> (Kim and Mauborgne, 1992: 23)

CHAPTER SIXTEEN

The Management of Quality

Judith Bell

It is rarely possible to read educational journals, or even daily newspapers without coming across articles about quality. What is it? How do we know it is there? Why isn't there enough of it in our schools, colleges and universities? Statements from ministers have left little doubt that in their view, we are short-changing our pupils and students and that academic standards are falling.

Some of the statements about falling standards give the clear impression that there has never been any systematic attempt to enhance quality in this country. That is certainly not so. All the committed teachers and education managers I have known have as a matter of course looked back at their work and come to conclusions about the effectiveness of their teaching, their budgeting, their assessment procedures and their students' overall learning experience. They may not have used the words now in common usage, and they may not have kept systematic records, but they did the job. Good teachers always wanted to do better and to provide the very best for their students. The difference was that their quality assurance was a private matter, limited to the conscience of individuals or small groups. They did not make their methods public, *because no one ever asked them to do so.*

That approach worked perfectly well for the committed teachers and managers. The problem was of course that there was no check on those individuals who did not have the same commitment, skill and enthusiasm for the job.

Everything is not perfect in education. We all know that, though we may be reluctant to admit it in public. Every organisation has its dead wood (industry and government included), but the dead wood in education can have a devastating effect on the students who are unfortunate enough to be in their care. There are very few bad teachers, but the effect they have on the rest can be serious. They are the ones who do the minimum amount of work, who never take their share of the disagreeable or difficult jobs, who have no sense of commitment to the students. They are the ones whose classes start late and finish early, who mark work late, hastily and unhelpfully, who are never available to see students and who do not feel that time needs to be spent on preparation. They are there, and we know they are there, so why haven't education managers done anything about it? Just try proving it, if there has never been any attempt at formal quality assurance or quality control. We may 'know' they are doing a poor job but in the past there has rarely been any hard evidence to prove it.

My years as one of Her Majesty's Inspectors of Schools left me in no doubt that the vast majority of teachers and education managers are committed, skilled and overworked. The point of my argument is that there is a tendency for the sins of the few to overshadow the virtues of the many. Ministers have been quick to point to the deficiencies of the education system and individual examples of such deficiencies are not hard to find. 'One of my constituents told me', or 'the other day I was talking to a parent who …'. It is all too easy to cast doubts on the quality of the entire teaching profession by reference to individual cases.

Until the mid-1990s, in only a few cases were serious efforts made systematically to judge the quality of the education we provide and to record the evidence. Now, all educational institutions are being compelled to address the problem of quality. Central government directives, many linked to finance, have forced us all to do what we should have done ourselves years ago. We have always balked at making judgements about colleagues or even about ourselves and we have comforted ourselves by saying 'it's not my business', 'it would be a gross infringement of personal liberties', 'teachers must at all costs retain their autonomy', 'it can't be done in my subject' and 'there's nobody here capable of making judgements about my teaching'. I have heard them all, and they have often been accepted as reasons for doing nothing and leaving newly-qualified and inexperienced teachers to their own devices in their early years of teaching.

Unbelievably, I have been through seven probationary periods in my time; two in English universities, two in colleges of further education, two in the Department of Education and Science and one in an American university. In six cases, I had a congratulatory letter at the end of the first year notifying me that I had successfully completed the probationary period and was now permanent/established/tenured. I can honestly say that no one really knew whether my work had been of a good or even satisfactory standard – apart from the Americans.

At the University of Wisconsin my teaching was observed on eight occasions during my first year. After each visit, I was interviewed and points of teaching style were discussed. I did not like those unannounced visits, any more than I imagine teachers in this country welcome visits from inspectors, assessors or evaluators. Student feedback at the end of each course was automatic and an accepted part of the process. Our abilities, strengths and weaknesses were known and documented. If weaknesses were identified, efforts were made to help us to improve. If we did not improve, we were not re-appointed.

Looking back I think there were several reasons why that rigorous regime was accepted by staff. Procedures for quality control were automatic. No one was exempt and everyone knew that. The unannounced visits provoked anxiety but they too were normal practice. Moreover, there was no doubt that the observers were themselves good teachers. They knew what it was all about and were able to talk openly about their own practice. Student feedback was just one strand in a much wider scheme of appraisal and evaluation.

In my early years as an HMI, I came across a few institutions or departments where similar, thorough systems of quality assurance and control were in place but I also came across a great deal of resistance to the idea that such practices should even be considered. All the signs were that Ministers would not permit such a state of affairs to continue and this was made clear through a sequence of Education Acts, the most far-reaching of which was the Education Reform Act of 1988 – though concern about the quality of education was the subject of public debate long before the Reform Act reached the statute book.

In the late 1960s and 1970s, the 'progressive' approach to the teaching of young children proposed in the Plowden Report (1967) was challenged by Peters (1968) and others. The Black Papers (Cox and Dyson, 1969 and 1970) led the attack on 'liberal' approaches to teaching which, they alleged, paid insufficient attention to the skills children needed.

Disturbing evidence from HM Inspectors and from public enquiries confirmed that all was not well. The much-publicised case of the William Tyndale School, which resulted in a public enquiry (Auld, 1976) highlighted ways in which weak management can, albeit exceptionally, result in something approaching chaos.

The report of this enquiry provided rich pickings for a government determined to take action to improve the quality of education in our schools: in fact, knowledge of the ways in which the school had been allowed to operate were of equal concern to many teachers. All branches of the media joined in the condemnation of an LEA which could allow such a breakdown to occur, and of the teachers, several of whom had done their utmost to support the pupils in what must have been extraordinarily difficult circumstances.

At the time, reports of biased curricula and left-wing orthodoxies being pedalled in the classroom were common and demands for more control and better value for money in education accelerated. We were repeatedly reminded that 'Education, like any other public service, is answerable to the society which it serves and which pays for it' (DES, 1977).

Looking back, central government's move towards greater control was probably inevitable. The argument was that if teachers and LEAs could not put their own house in order, then the government would.

The new order

No sector of education has been exempt. Schools, colleges and universities have all been included in the drive for greater efficiency and effectiveness. The message to all has been clear. You must get into line. You must account for yourselves and your finance. You must demonstrate how you are providing value for money. You must do better.

Central government directives have now forced institutions to implement systems of appraisal, to introduce formal monitoring and evaluation procedures, to identify ways in which judgements can be made about quality – and to manage finances efficiently. In order to make sure we conform, we are *all* now subjected to inspections, quality audits or assessments.

Schools, further education institutions, the former polytechnics, Colleges of Education and all adult education providers funded wholly or partly from the public purse were accustomed to visits and inspections carried out by LEA advisers/inspectors and by members of Her Majesty's Inspectorate, but it became clear that the new-style inspections carried out by 'registered inspectors', trained and assessed by the Office for Standards in Education (OFSTED) and by the Further Education Funding Council (FEFC) were to be more frequent and to have the power to enforce change which HM Inspectorate never had.

Institutions of Higher Education which had a major role in the education and training of teachers were to continue to receive visits and to be inspected by HMI, pending decisions from central government about the future of teacher training. In 1992, all polytechnics became universities and so were then subject to the same conditions as universities, but universities discovered, possibly to their surprise that they too were to be included in the quality awareness and assessment exercise.

Schools

From the beginning, it was clear that registered inspectors would be required to carry out inspections according to specific guidelines laid down in the *Framework for the Inspection of Schools* (OFSTED 1993a), discussed by Brian Chaplin in Chapter 13. OFSTED was able to draw on many years of HMI experience, but placed greater controls over the conduct of inspections than had ever been the case with HMI. Some schools expressed concern that inspectors would spend too short a time in schools to enable valid judgements to be made about the quality of work and that they would have predetermined ideas about the 'right' ways of doing things. Possibly to allay such fears, the OFSTED discussion document *Improving Schools* makes the point that:

> There is no single route to the improvement of schools, nor any single point on a school's route to improvement at which it can stop and call the process complete. Schools have much in common with the provision they make and the framework within which they operate. However, in the ways they deliver that provision they are infinitely varied. They are also infinitely improvable. The evidence of HMI inspections shows that planning for improvement has not been a strength in the majority of primary and secondary schools.

and goes on to state that

> there is no magic formula for bringing about school improvement; nor is it easily achieved, particularly by schools in socially deprived areas. Nevertheless ... even schools suffering from high levels of deprivation can achieve genuine improvements through careful, rational planning and the commitment of teachers, heads, pupils and governors.
>
> (OFSTED, 1994c: 5/7)

Improving Schools was reporting on HMI follow-up visits made to three schools in 1992 and 1993. Each had had an earlier inspection and HMI had made firm recommendations about the need for improvement in specified areas. The follow-up visits provided evidence of ways in which the schools had addressed the recommendations and in so doing, had raised standards, enhanced quality and improved efficiency. The inspectors reported that if improvement is to be achieved, there has to be a climate for improvement.

They write:

> The improvement of schools cannot be achieved overnight. If planning is to be effective, certain conditions have to be present. The schools referred to in this discussion document share some or all of the following characteristics:
>
> - they have clear educational aims and objectives and high expectations about achieving them;
>
> - both staff and pupils demonstrate faith in the school's ability to improve itself;
>
> - priorities are set out clearly and the reasons for them are widely understood;
>
> - they understand the importance of value for money and that financial management achieves efficiency as well as effectiveness;
>
> - they have faith in the pupils and high expectations of them;
>
> - leadership is strong (improvement is often brought about the insistence of a

new head teacher, however subtly it may be expressed, on a change in the school's culture and by the head's standing firm in the fact of resistance to that demand);

- they take openness and consultation seriously; the purposes of initial audit and its outcomes, as well as the subsequent planning, implementation and review, are shared with staff who are invited to be partners in a corporate enterprise;

- their plans are practical and simple enough to be clear to all; the roles of all participants in the work are clearly defined as are the expectations of what is to be achieved within suggested timescales;

- they specify criteria at an early stage in their planning and refer to them regularly;

- they maintain rigorous monitoring and evaluation;

- the implementation of plans is not left to look after itself; professional criticism, praise and support are given in the right proportions in order to motivate all staff and pupils;

- there is consistency between the values the school claims to espouse and the working realities it demonstrates; in other words, the leaders live what they believe.

(OFSTED, 1994c: 41)

It is interesting to note that in the period between the first inspection and the subsequent follow-up visit, the staff of these improving schools had themselves identified the mistakes they had made in the past. These were reported as:

- failure to move from review and analysis of the process to planned action

- lack of success criteria

- financial factors not taken into account early enough

- unrealistic timescales

- failure to spot the need to update or revise the plan

- 'losing' targets which are not met by the date planned

- the wrong use of questionnaires

- failure to involve governors appropriately

- insufficient attention to the impact of what has been achieved on the quality of learning.

(OFSTED, 1994c: 42–43)

I imagine most education managers and teachers will recognise the ease with which each of these 'mistakes' can be made when each day seems to bring with it another set of priorities and deadlines. And this raises what to me is a key question, which is: *would these schools have found the time or have given priority to rectifying these mistakes if a follow-up visit were not on the horizon?*

I suspect not, because schools have been under such pressure to survive in turbulent times that they just might have put off certain tasks until … Well, until later, and that would have been a great pity, because they just might not have been able to achieve the impressive quality enhancement reported in *Improving Schools*. So, might it be claimed that in these cases improvement had been achieved through inspection? It seems so, and if OFSTED can provide more evidence of this kind, then the cost of inspections may well be justified.

The specific criteria which determine the ways in which school inspections are now carried out aid the speedy production of inspection reports. HMI and staff of the institutions they inspected were frequently dismayed at the time it took before a report was issued. There were many reasons for this, amongst which were the difficulty of summarising what amounted to a forbidding amount of documentation, the problems of extracting reports on time from team members and the numbers of hands through which draft reports passed before clearance could be given.

The new-style reports are produced quickly and so recommendations can be implemented speedily. There is some plain speaking in some reports and schools which are regarded as being substandard are left in no doubt about their failings nor about what has to be done before the next team visit.

At a recent conference of inspectors and advisers in London, Her Majesty's Chief Inspector of Schools is reported as saying that:

> children in one in 20 primary schools are getting a "raw deal"… OFSTED evidence showed that in 5% of schools, teaching was unsatisfactory or poor. The standards of achievement in 10% of secondaries inspected during 1993-94 were also at the low end of the scale. (*Times Educational Supplement*, 16 September 1994)

Put another way, the evidence showed that in 95% of primary schools and 90% of secondaries teaching was satisfactory or better. Even so, no child should be expected to get a 'raw deal' during school days and though some reservations about the role of registered inspectors remain, particularly amongst the education professionals themselves, if the evidence demonstrates that the poor have been forced to improve and the good to become excellent, then so much the better.

OFSTED is satisfied with the way the new-style inspections have gone, and the review of the inspection system based on the first 100 inspections of secondary schools reports that:

The new inspection system has made a remarkably good start. OFSTED has succeeded in establishing through the *Framework* a basis for inspection which commands wide support. Sufficient inspectors have been selected and trained to ensure that the inspection programme can continue in all schools well into 1995 and beyond.

The monitoring of inspections and procedures to survey the views of those involved in or affected by inspection have contributed very significantly to assuring quality. These aspects of our work will continue. OFSTED's attention is turning to the standard of the written reports and summaries, where early evidence shows that some improvements may be needed. We are beginning to monitor the action planning process in a sample of schools in order to inform further guidance on action plans. We shall also undertake longer-term studies to evaluate the quality and implementation of action plans and the effects of inspection on school management.

It has been too early to judge the value for money of the new system although OFSTED will be investigating this to ensure that public money is well spent. The total cost of the inspection of a large secondary school, including preparation costs for the school, is equivalent to a small proportion of 1% of the school's income over 4 years, though the school, of course, does not pay for the inspection.

The proof of inspection will be in its effects on school improvement. As the Secondary Heads' Association says to its members: 'The new system of inspection is a great opportunity for schools' (Dunford, 1993). To fulfil this expectation, independent inspectors and OFSTED must continue to ensure that inspection is of the highest possible standard.

(OFSTED, 1994d: 39)

It is probably too early not only to judge the value for money of the new system, though it is not yet clear how that calculation will be made, but also to prove whether inspection does in fact have a positive influence on quality enhancement in the long term. I hope it does and as long as high standards of inspection are maintained, and central government continues to provide a significant proportion of the costs, there appears to be no reason why the new inspection system should not fulfil a continuing valuable role in assisting schools to identify and eradicate weaknesses and to build on known strengths.

Further education

Until the incorporation of colleges and the establishment of Further Education Funding Councils for England and Wales, all institutions of further education, like schools, were subject to visits and inspections by HMI and LEAs, but in addition, they experienced regular visits from awarding bodies, assessors and verifiers, and examining and validating bodies. They were also well accustomed to being questioned about their quality procedures. Such experiences should have placed them in a good position to account for themselves. However, most FE institutions are large and therefore costly. In the mid 1980s, the non-advanced further education (NAFE) service in England and Wales cost well over £1 billion and government was looking to ways of reducing that ever-increasing sum.

Anxiety about costs was heightened following a report of the Audit Commission (1985), *Obtaining Better Value from Further Education*, which indicated there was significant scope for improved management and increased efficiency in colleges. Following that report, the DES and local authority association officers embarked on a joint study in order to consider how greater efficiency could be achieved. The report of that important study, entitled *Managing Colleges Efficiently*, recommended a number of ways in which colleges might manage their resources better and emphasised that:

> the ability to measure efficiency and effectiveness is a mark of good management. Any indicator of efficiency, the ratio of input to output, must be based on sound proxies for input and output. The efficiency of a college is therefore tied inextricably to the results of the educational process .....

(DES/Welsh Office, 1987: V)

The era of unit costs and performance indicators had arrived. In order to drive home the messages of Managing Colleges Efficiently, the DES asked the Further Education Staff College to produce a manual of guidance on ways in which college management might be improved (Birch, 1988). The government wanted value for money, not unnaturally, but continually stressed that improvements in efficiency should not be at the expense of educational quality. The manual, *Managing Resources in Further Education,* has long been out of print, but it remains an invaluable reference source and has formed the basis of many quality assurance systems.

In spite of the guidance included in these two publications and the invaluable support provided by the Further Education Unit and the Further Education Staff College, reports of HMI inspections indicated that still more needed to be done to improve the quality of management and of educational provision.

The Further Education Funding Council was established and assumed responsibility for the control and distribution of funds, but also for a new-style system of inspection, different from but on similar lines to that planned for schools.

Independent inspectors were trained, assessed and recruited. Precise guidelines were laid down and a format for reports produced. The message, as always, was that improvement was being sought through inspection.

FEFC inspectors look not only for statements of intent, but for evidence that policies and procedures are being implemented. The FEFC circular *Assessing Achievement* (Circular 93/28) informs colleges that inspectors' main sources of evidence will be:

- direct observation of the delivery of the curriculum: that is, the observation of training, teaching and other activities designed to promote learning

- inspection of students' work

- discussions with individuals or groups with a interest in, or view on, the quality of the college's provision, e.g. students or former students, college staff, governors, parents, employers, representatives of local training and enterprise councils, and community representatives

- examination of documentary evidence provided by the college ...

Four types of documentary evidence will be particularly useful in setting the context of any inspection activity:

- the college's mission statement or statement of purpose, its strategic plan and annual operating plan, the college charter

- the college's standard set of performance indicators as agreed following consultation between the Council and the sector, together with any internal performance indicators used by the college staff to help assess the extent to which they are achieving the targets which they set for themselves

- reports from examining, validating and accrediting bodies, and the college's responses to those reports

- the findings of the college's own quality assurance procedures as expressed in an internal quality assessment report.

(FEFC, 1993a: 9)

Inspection guidelines are quite explicit and there is little excuse for college management who misunderstand what is required by the inspection team. For example, under the heading of *Teaching and the Promotion of Learning*, the guidelines indicate that course and programme teams would be expected to demonstrate that they:

- devise coherent programmes which meet the needs of students and have clearly identified aims and objectives which are shared with students

- keep records of students' achievements, regularly inform them of their progress and identify targets for further progress

- assess and meet the needs of students with disabilities and/or learning difficulties

- devise teaching and learning schemes which
  — ensure adequate coverage of the topics on the syllabus and specified competencies

— ensure that all the aims and objectives of the programmes are achieved

— challenge and extend students' skills, knowledge and understanding and encourage their personal development

— take account of the different abilities of students on the programme

— include a regular schedule of setting, marking and returning work to students within agreed deadlines

- devise assessments which are at an appropriate standard and test the achievement of all the agreed aims and objectives of the programme

- ensure that assessments are consistent and fair, that appropriate appeals procedures are in place, and that achievement is certificated where appropriate.

In addition, in their dealings with students, staff:

- establish good relationships which promote the achievement of learning

- set the learning in the context of what has gone before and make it clear what it is intended to achieve

- ensure that the interest of students is engaged and sustained

- choose a variety of teaching and learning approaches which are appropriate for the subject being studied and encourage students to work on their own or in groups

- reinforce learning through the use of teaching and learning aids

- display sound knowledge and understanding of their subject area

- provide information or instructions clearly, at a pace and level which meet the needs and abilities of students

- check regularly that learning has been achieved.

(FEFC, 1993a: 13)

I imagine most colleges would claim that they conformed to these and similar guidelines, but providing the evidence may well be another matter. Demonstrating these qualities and skills to an inspector who visits one class is likely to be difficult, but as any inspector knows, the value to a college is the preparation done before the inspection.

The inspection guidelines are not (or should not be) unchangeable and unchanging. There is invariably more than one way of enhancing quality and each college has its own particular characteristics. The guidelines recognise this and make it clear that

Responsive colleges adapt to changing circumstances, as do views on what constitutes a strength or weakness. The inspection process itself can be expected to identify strengths other than those listed in the guidelines. In other words, quality assessment is a dynamic process involving a constant dialogue between the assessors and the assessed.

(FEFC, 1993a: 12)

As long as these principles are maintained, there seems little doubt that though further education inspections are likely to provoke anxiety – and, it has to be said, are costly and time consuming – the outcomes should be positive.

Adult education

Adult education (AE) managers feel, perhaps justifiably, that they have to face more problems than institutions which have a predominantly full-time student body.

The FEU Bulletin of June 1990, *Performance Indicators in Education and Training of Adults* draws attention to the problems of transferability of models designed with full-time students in mind. AE institutions are faced with the problems of managing courses and programmes of varying lengths. Students generally attend on a discontinuous basis and AE and continuing education services do their best to provide for what the Russell Report described as the 'life-long but discontinuous modes' to 'correspond with the unpredictable development of people's abilities and aspirations at all ages' (Russell Report, 1973: 16, para 50).

Crude measures of efficiency are not likely to be sufficient to take account of the variation in mode, content and timing of continuing education activities, and more will need to be done to ensure in particular that non-accredited AE is not swept along the performance indicator route without due consideration being given to the particular circumstances in which programmes for adults are provided.

In addition to the problem of the transferability of models, AE providers point to the very large number of courses (and therefore tutors) involved, the geographical spread, the wide range of subjects and levels, and the relatively small number of full-time staff to deal with the whole diverse issue of the management of quality.

They refer to the difficulties of producing evidence of the quality of teaching when there are several hundred part-time tutors for courses held in numerous venues miles apart from each other. The Universities Association for Continuing Education (UACE) survey of quality assurance procedures in Departments of Adult and Continuing Education (UACE, 1995) discovered that a range of approaches was adopted, including class visits, tutor self-assessment, tutor feedback and evaluation, staff appraisal and peer review. Each had its own set of problems and a number of departments reported they had run into difficulties by not clarifying policies at the outset and in particular by failing to identify who was responsible for what. Resolution of problems proved to be time-consuming and raised issues of management responsibility which departments had found difficult to resolve. Even the apparently uncontentious issues presented problems. For example, most agreed it was important to obtain feedback from students, but differences of view about how precisely it was to be done quickly emerged. Questions were raised about:

1. The purpose of student feedback/evaluation. What did the department actually want to find out, and why? Were questionnaires the best way?

2. The time of year when questionnaires should be distributed. It was common practice to distribute them at or towards the end of the year, but this practice was questioned on the grounds that it would be better to obtain student views earlier, while there was time to deal with any problems.

3. How should completed forms be returned to the department? Via the tutor (in which case the department might not receive all of them)? Direct to the department by post (which would be costly)? Collected by staff tutors, administrators or clerical staff (which would be time consuming and expensive in the case of widely dispersed courses)?

4. What was to be done with completed forms? Whose job would it be to analyse them? Whose job to take action if problems emerged? Whose job to check that action had been taken?

5. Should the same questionnaire be used throughout the department regardless of subject or level, or should separate areas operate systems of their own? Differences emerged amongst specialists who tended to claim that their subject 'was different' and therefore needed special treatment.

6. Should only a sample of courses and tutors be selected for the exercise and if so, how should the sample be drawn?

The shared experience of Departments of Continuing Education which participated in the UACE project has been invaluable in highlighting areas of difficulty and in providing examples of successful practice. Most providers now accept the fact, though not always willingly, that they must provide evidence of the quality of their programmes. Funding is dependent on such evidence but in any case there would be no justification for excluding adult education from the mainstream quality enhancement programme. To do so would be to assume that AE is of so little consequence that it can easily be dispensed with. Questions have always been asked about justification for spending public money on 'leisure time' activities and adult educators have not always found it easy to demonstrate the difference between 'leisure' courses and educational courses which are carefully designed to enable students to progress, to increase their 'knowledge, skills, judgement and creativity' (The Russell Report, DES, 1973: 3). Nor have they found it easy to provide evidence of the quality of teaching and of student learning.

Adult educators may need to adopt different procedures to suit their context, their resources and their student population, but the quality issue cannot be swept under the carpet, nor should it be allowed to do so. If sensible quality assurance mechanisms can be devised, then the likelihood is that students will receive a good educational experience and the evidence of quality should greatly improve the chances of programmes of study for adults continuing to be funded in the longer term.

Universities

Schools and FE institutions had, albeit infrequently, received visits from HMI and, even more infrequently, experienced full inspections, but with the exception of Departments of Extra Mural Studies, which until 1992 were funded direct by the DES and were therefore liable for inspection by HMI, universities had maintained their autonomy. However, warning noises emerging from government sources made it apparent that even the universities would be required to demonstrate that they provided value for money and to produce evidence that their products were of high quality.

The Committee of Vice Chancellors and Principals (CVCP) recognised the signs and took the initiative. They established the Academic Audit Unit (now the Division of Quality Audit of the Higher Education Quality Council) with the remit to enquire into the extent to which quality assurance procedures were in place in universities.

In an interview with Rosalind Yarde for the *Times Higher Educational Supplement* of 6 July 1990, Peter Williams, the then head of the AAU made the wry comment that 'universities maintain that they produce quality products. But it always struck me that they opened themselves to criticism if anyone said "prove it".' He stressed that the Unit was not being established because of concern that standards were falling but because of 'a need for universities to show and explain to the world at large what they are doing'. He was concerned to ensure 'that universities don't disadvantage themselves by ignoring the question'.

The AAU, and later the HEQC, trained auditors and embarked on a series of audit visits. I imagine it must have been quite a shock to the system for universities to discover that a team of auditors intended to enquire into their procedures for quality assurance but, with one or two exceptions, they appear to have found the visits useful. It was made clear from the outset that the auditors (drawn from the universities themselves) would make no attempt to impose set procedures. The approach was, and still is, to enquire, to ask questions and to attempt to understand how universities' quality assurance systems actually work. The questions they ask are valid across the whole education system:

- What are you trying to do?

- How are you trying to do it?

- How are you doing it?

– Why are you doing it in that way?

– Why do you think that is the best way of doing it?

– How do you know it works?

– How do you improve it?

(HEQC, 1994)

These questions are deceptively simple. They are relatively easy to answer if no evidence is required, but if it is, then gaps and anomalies become glaringly obvious.

HEQC auditors examine *procedures* for quality assurance, the assumption being that if systems and procedures are in place – *and* being implemented – the quality of provision is likely to be enhanced. They do not see any teaching, but the Higher Education Funding Council for England (HEFCE) assessors do, and it is the HEFCE which holds the purse strings. HEFCE has made a number of changes to its procedures in the light of assessor experience, but the present approach demonstrates clearly that failure to reach what is regarded as a satisfactory standard is likely to mean loss of funding HEFCE (1994). On 4 November 1994, *The Times Higher Educational Supplement* reported as follows on the changes planned to take effect between April 1995 and September 1996:

- University departments that fail any aspect of new quality assessment gradings will face funding council sanctions unless they can show an improvement within a year.

- This week the Higher Education Funding Council for England accepted plans for a graded scale of assessment under which departments will receive a mark on a one to four scale on each of six core aspects of provision.

- If none of the core aspects is graded one (lowest) the department will be approved. If any receive a one the department will be judged inadequate and issued with a 'yellow card' warning.

- Assessors will revisit yellow card institutions within 12 months. Graeme Davies, chief executive of HEFCE, said : 'We would expect that if they did not make the grade within the time available to them, the yellow card would develop into a red one with withdrawal in whole or part of their funding.' The six core aspects to be assessed are:

  – Curriculum design, content and organisation

  – Teaching, learning and assessment

  – Student progression and achievement

  – Student support and guidance

  – Learning resources

  – Quality Assurance and Enhancement.

- Professor Davies said it was likely that a numerical scale would be used. 'It has so many advantages, including paralleling the research selectivity exercise'.

The HEFCE clearly means business and this announcement is likely to cause a degree of consternation to some universities who may still not have taken the quality issue seriously. Will these sanctions improve quality and value for money? Well, possibly, as long as the quality of the assessors is maintained, the visits are well planned and the reports fair.

There have already been some interesting outcomes. Heads of some university departments have reported that in spite of early objections and irritation at being distracted from what they saw as more important work, the outcomes of the exercises have, in most cases, been valuable. One reported that once the staff members were made aware of the fact that (a) they had no choice and (b) failure to do well meant money and could have an effect on the survival of the department, they set about the preparations – almost as an army getting ready for battle against the common enemy. Tasks were allocated and small groups reported back to the full department on student support mechanisms: criteria for assessment; procedures for monitoring the quality of teaching, laboratory work, seminars, tutorials; student admission and induction procedures; criteria for the marking and grading of student assignments; action taken as a result of external examiners' reports; links with employers and the record of student job placements. On and on. They began to ask such questions as: How do we really know the quality of lectures is good enough? What checking devices do we have? How do we know we provide good support for students? What action do we take if what should be done isn't?

The assessment proved to be an eye-opener for another head of department, who said he learnt more about what happened his department than he ever knew before. What was of particular interest was the fact that he learnt about the volume of work which had been regularly undertaken by some lecturers but which had never been publicised. During the course of the preparations for the assessment it became apparent that a small group of individuals had operated as trouble-shooters, had hidden the errors and omissions of certain others and had given large amounts of their time to help students who had failed to obtain support from their own tutors. Once they were asked, the students gave full and frank opinions about the quality of the department's provision. His advice to colleagues in other departments was 'Don't try to put on a show to impress the assessors, if what you do is different from normal practice, because the students will shop you'.

What began as an exercise planned to ensure good grades were achieved for external and financial reasons, ended by being an exercise which proved to be of the greatest value to the departments and to the staff and students in them. The work of setting up the exercise was massive, but once done, it was felt to be the basis for quality policies and procedures which were feasible, which could be reviewed and if necessary adapted each year without a great deal of additional work. It remains to be seen whether that forecast will prove to be accurate but there seems to be no reason why not. Such radical internal appraisal of provision is likely to enhance quality, even in good departments – and regardless of external imperatives, that has to be good news for present and future students.

In Wales, the HEQC and HEFC roles have been combined and there is increasing pressure for a similar merger to take place in England. Institutions assert that much of the work required for the audit visit is, or should be, required for the visit from assessors, and they complain about the cost and the time involved in separate visitations. Objectors to the HEQC approach claim that procedures, no matter how carefully constructed, count for little if the 'product' is poor. Whatever the outcome of these deliberations, it seems inevitable that audits and assessments will continue in universities in some form for the foreseeable future. Some rationalisation will almost certainly be needed, or, in the opinion of Professor John Bull of Plymouth University and a member of the HEQC Board, the time and resources being spent on quality monitoring will hamper the very activities it was designed to assess. He is reported as saying that 'it will lead to a situation where you could say that at any one time half the staff are going to be assessing the other half' (*Times Higher Educational Supplement*, 4 November 1994).

Some institutions (and not only universities) may feel that this situation has already been reached. If so, no doubt the groundswell of opinion will force adjustments but as all the evidence so far has indicated that the audit and assessment visits have done a great deal to raise awareness of the need to consider ways of enhancing quality in universities, it is to be hoped that quality visits will not disappear altogether.

The next lap

A great deal has already been done in schools, colleges and in universities to establish workable systems for monitoring performance. My great regret is that the impetus has come from outside. Central government directives, threats of yellow cards, red cards and the like have forced us to introduce formal procedures, to identify ways in which judgements can be made and to provide evidence to justify our claims for quality.

For many years we were never seriously asked to account for ourselves. As long as examination results and student recruitment were reasonable – and as long as finances were in order, few questions were asked. Times have now changed and I do not regret it. As one of Her Majesty's Inspectors, I saw the very best and the very worst of all sectors of education, and it seems only right that the best should be commended and their experience disseminated, and the worst made to take steps to improve. However, the externally initiated quality thrust is a waste of time, unless we introduce and maintain systems which are *appropriate for our own context and which support our own values and educational aims.*

There can never be one set of rules, one model to cover all circumstances and it is the task of education managers to ensure that quality assurance procedures are fit for the purpose. What is suitable for one context may not be for another, and we can all make a special case for our own circumstances.

The Lindop Report (1985, paragraph 7.4) made the valid point that 'the most reliable safeguard of standards is not external validation or any other outside control; it is the growth of the teaching institution as a self-critical community'. If that self-criticism is absent, then the institution will inevitably stagnate.

Reynolds (1986: Foreword) made a similar point when he stated that 'no society is healthy that is not subject to a sustained and informed critique of its structure and of behaviour in it', and 'the constant advance of knowledge requires constant reconsideration of the procedures that are appropriate for the maintenance of quality and standards'.

The problem we have all faced in recent years is *proving* that we carry out these procedures – that we *are* self-critical and *do* consider procedures that are appropriate for the maintenance of quality and standards in our particular context.

Quality is a management issue. Systems and procedures do not just happen. The process has to be managed. It has to be feasible, affordable and likely to gain the support of all involved. More than anything, it has to be seen to enhance quality. If it does not, then different approaches are needed. The one option which is not open to us is the option of doing nothing and of assuming that all is well when it may not be.

The early part of this chapter draws, in part, on material included in Chapter 12, 'The search for quality', in McNay, I. (1992) *Visions of Post-Compulsory Education*, Buckingham, Open University Press.

CHAPTER SEVENTEEN

Working for 'Whole School' Effectiveness in Three Different Settings

Anthony Dobell

It is one thing to debate, in the abstract, vision and values in managing education. It is another to apply vision and maintain or refine values in the practice of educational management, particularly at times of unprecedented change. At the same time, if the learners with whose education we are charged are to receive the quality service we should all wish, then education managers need flair and imagination. In this chapter, I consider three examples from the primary, secondary and tertiary sectors where these qualities have helped to enhance the educational experience of the learners concerned. In each case, a particular aspect of successful school/college management will be highlighted, which contributes significantly to the 'whole success' of a school or college. Each study is based on evidence gained from observations and interviews in the school setting.

Canklow Woods Infant School, Rotherham: involving parents as partners

Canklow Woods School serves a council estate, in a deprived area of Rotherham with few private homes. Eighty per cent of the estate's working population is unemployed, there is twice the national average of one-parent families, and many families have three or more children under the age of 5. As a result, adults tend, predictably, to lack self-esteem. Their own educational experiences have usually been unsuccessful and they are suspicious of 'authority'.

In these circumstances, it is hardly surprising that, in standardised tests, the school achieved among the lowest results in the local authority. The head, Betty Eggleston, soon realised after her appointment that urgent action was needed to stop this cycle of deprivation and under-achievement. She and her staff believed that children need high self-esteem to be successful learners. Further, her discussions with parents suggested that they were much concerned for their children's future and wanted them to be more successful than they themselves had been. These parents deserved all the support that the school could provide.

Betty Eggleston and her staff decided that effective intervention at an early age would help children to settle successfully into school, and would help prevent, or at least reduce, their social and emotional difficulties. Further, they decided that close links with parents and the community, and positive efforts to break down home–school barriers in order to raise the community's self-image, would enhance the children's potential for learning, and provide them with a supportive background. They therefore launched an initiative to achieve these objectives.

Their initial submission, to seek funds for their project from the Local Education Authority, emphasised the importance of a stimulating and secure environment to meet the physical, intellectual, social and emotional needs of young children. It also stressed the crucial role of parents in their children's early development, and the need to work with them as partners. Parents needed the confidence that they could contribute positively to their children's education.

Whole staff commitment to parental involvement had already resulted in a number of initiatives. Parents' Room activities included a Parent and Toddler group, a Toy Library, a 'Drop in and Chat' group, a Keep Fit class and several sewing groups. Parents were always warmly welcomed in the school, and the Nursery allowed parents open access. They were encouraged to drop in with younger children and join in activities. Parental involvement in the classroom was encouraged, warm relationships developed, and parents were beginning to see education as a positive element in their lives.

The school's application for funding for the project was successful; LEA and external funding was provided for a Home–School Liaison Teacher for 2½ years. Wide discussion determined that the Liaison Teacher's input would be basically educational and, where possible, curriculum-led, with a view to enhancing children's development. The Liaison Teacher would mirror the school in listening to problems, and then indicate to parents how and where they could be solved, rather than trying to solve them herself. It was decided that the role would have three main thrusts:

(a) Individual case work.
(b) Inter-agency and parents' room activity.
(c) Enriching the curriculum through parental help.

Individual case work

This consisted of visiting all children at home in the term before they began at the Nursery. All children were included and no parent refused this opportunity – indeed they asked when it was their turn. A range of materials was made available for each play session; parents were encouraged to join in and repeat activities between sessions. The activities included creative, constructional and imaginative experience, and a shared book session. Materials were left at home, and progress regularly monitored. About eight appointments each week were made, but, since younger children were encouraged to participate, over 20 children a week could be involved.

As a result of this work, parents became aware of the importance of giving young children the opportunity to experiment with a wide range of materials. They began to gain skills of intervention, to develop concepts to build relationships with their children, and to build up confidence in their relations with the school. Language skills of reasoning, predicting, projecting and conceptualising began to merge. Parents became excited by their children's development, because they could share in their success.

Inter-agency work and parents' room activity

The school has long been involved in inter-agency work. The creation of the Home Liaison Teacher's post meant that there was now someone available to act as a focus for their work. The information gained from the work of other agencies in the community enabled the school to become even more closely involved in the concerns of parents. As a result the school is now often able to refer parents with problems to a named person, rather than an impersonal agency, which again increases confidence and trust.

The parents' room was brought into use, as falling rolls created extra space. Activities are varied and mirror the interests of different groups of parents. Different activities attract parents of different age groups, but all promote positive community attitudes to the school. Early activities took the form of Further Education outreach classes and sewing. Later, a more open-ended approach was found more productive than the relatively structured FE activities. This embraced a range of informal activities such as the Parent and Toddler Group and the 'Drop in and Chat group'. The new approach resulted in a freer use of the room. Parents now use it as a community facility for various purposes. Refreshments are available. Re-decoration gave each group the chance to contribute something for their room – a clock, plants, ornaments, a vacuum cleaner. Thus ownership, and pride of ownership were created. Visitors were greeted with a smile and a ready explanation of their role in the school. Parents began to see themselves as partners, and self-worth flourished. They began to feel positive about their families – sometimes for the first time.

Enriching the curriculum through parental help

The school has long had an open policy towards parents. They have been encouraged to visit the school, and made to feel welcome. However, initial attempts to involve parents in the school's daily work were disappointing. An early strategy was to invite individual parents to join school visits. They were then invited to help with follow-up work. Having experienced the initial visit, they became more confident in supporting subsequent work. Initial 'don't ask me to do any writing' was replaced by support for a variety of activities, such as sewing, painting, looking at books, and even computer work, science experiments, and shared writing. Gradually they developed the confidence to support all areas of a broad, balanced, relevant and differentiated curriculum. Eventually some were willing to suggest possible kinds of follow-up. The school then decided to extend and, to a degree, formalise curriculum involvement for the parents. Each week, classes took their turn to organise a coffee morning for their parents. Teachers and parents met informally and, alongside the social chat, opportunities were taken to discover what areas of school life interested the parents. The following week, the class teacher invited parents to the Parents' Room to discuss a specific topic, while the Home Liaison teacher took the class. In this way a whole range of topics were covered with parents, including reading, maths, computer work, visits, writing, classroom organisation, school organisation, language, and discipline.

This increasing dialogue on general educational topics led to a sharing of National Curriculum documents with parents, and explanations of how the working of the Education Reform Act affected the school. Ideas as to how the National Curriculum was to be implemented were also shared. Parents offered an extra dimension to such planning, particularly as a result of their knowledge of local and community resources. For example, one mother offered to bring her goat into the school, while another provided an introduction to a keeper of Angora rabbits and to a handler of birds. Local expertise offered the children a new first-hand experience while, again, self-esteem was enhanced.

Through this initiative, the school and the community gradually developed greater mutual understanding and respect. Children's learning was enriched through their parents' deep interest in the curriculum. The initiative produced a number of valuable outcomes:

- Academic standards improved (as evidenced by the quality of children's work).

- The confidence of children and parents increased (as evidenced by their willingness to consult with teachers and with the head).

- Shared process of planning, implementation, reflection and evaluation brought parents and teachers even closer.

- The approach became increasingly collegiate, with all staff – teaching and non-teaching – determined to maximise educational opportunities for the children.

An interesting development from the initiative was a project run jointly by the School, the Workers' Educational Association and the Rotherham Local Education Authority, supported with funds from the Urban Programme, entitled *Parents as Partners*. The project aimed to:

- bring parents together in an informal setting, to discuss their children's education, and the changes taking place in schools today;

- foster an understanding of schools – how they are organised, how decisions are made – and the roles of governing bodies;

- enable partners to play a greater part in the life of the school and in managing change;

- build confidence and esteem;

- offer 'openings' for further educational opportunities, both in the community and elsewhere.

The project created a programme of work covering 20 sessions in the late autumn, spring and early summer terms of 1993–94. The sessions included various aspects of learning, curriculum planning, measuring progress, learning in the real world (via visits), parental contribution, behaviour, staffing, school governance, staff and development, and equal opportunities.

Eleven parents participated in the project (all mothers). A final evaluation session revealed that parents felt they had learned a great deal about the process of schooling. They were able to suggest a range of future possible activities. A particular revelation for them was through confronting financial constraints that the school had to face. The parents were unanimous in their wish to be given opportunities to hear children read in school. Further plans to enable parents to help (including fathers), for example with repairs to equipment, or gardening, were discussed.

This project was a valuable opportunity to carry forward the work of the early initiative, with a new generation of parents. Lack of funds has meant that the full impact of the initial work has been lost, but its spirit continues, through the regular programmes and curriculum of the school. The WEA project was a means of giving a new impetus to the school's work, which is rooted in deeply felt values with regard to quality of provision for a group of considerably disadvantaged young children, and the vision to set out to achieve that quality by imaginative programmes of development.

New College, Pontefract: achieving 'whole school' responsibility amongst staff

This sixth-form college opened in 1987. It was formed by combining the sixth forms of three schools. Its founding Principal, David Machin, wished to create an institution with high ideals and achievements. In a later staff handbook, he reminded the staff of the need for:

- teaching excellence;

- optimism about current and future success, and drive in achieving it;

- open-mindedness in accepting students of whatever background;

- real interest in guiding them;

- flexible personal organisation and a capacity to learn new concepts;

- willingness to liaise with other institutions as equal partners in education.

He added:

> Normally, you can expect to participate in negotiations over major college development and decision making.

> You may also wish to further your experiences and interest by taking part in one or more major responsibilities in college organisation. Directors of Studies will be directly responsible for one such area (working to a Vice Principal). All other teachers may also be involved if they wish.

Clearly, David Machin wanted, at the outset, a highly committed staff and he now places considerable emphasis on this. However, when the college was being created, he confronted a dilemma. As the college was being formed by combining three sixth forms in existing schools, the majority of the staff would be recruited from these schools. Further it would be logical to expect more senior staff with substantial sixth form experience to apply for posts in the college. This might well include heads of the same subject department in each of the schools. The dilemma, then, was that if one of these were appointed to a head of department post, then the other two would be disappointed, if not disenchanted. However, they might well still wish to become part of the college in order to retain their sixth form teaching. As a result, the initial college staff – that crucial element in establishing a successful institution – might well contain a number of influential but disenchanted members.

Machin realised that subjects were increasingly diversifying, through a range of cross curricular approaches and initiatives. The need for heads of department in the traditional sense was therefore diminishing. Further, teachers had, from choice, always undertaken a range of 'whole institution' roles for which they had no direct financial reward, deriving any 'allowance' from head of department, second in department or year tutor appointments. Schools may wish to move from this framework but, trapped in the existing structure, had no opportunity to realign allowances and responsibilities, in order to put greater emphasis on whole school/college roles, as opposed to departmental/pastoral roles.

Since he was creating a new college with a new structure, Machin had no such restrictions. His solution was simple, but radical. He created a structure in which responsibility allowances were available for whole college responsibilities. Departments would elect a 'chair' annually, who would act as head of department. The structure was:

	Three	Scale A–E	Teams of Staff
Principal ←	Vice Principals	← Teachers with College Duties	← interested in assisting

In the event, the mathematics department decided that it needed a permanent chair. At the outset, all other allowances were offered for those who held college responsibilities. Some of these were permanent posts while others were targeted to specific tasks, and ceased to exist when a particular initiative had run its course or was in place. Even with permanent posts, staff were not necessarily tied to them; they could move on to other responsibilities in order to extend experience and develop new interests.

Initially, staff had doubts about the structure, but with hindsight, almost without exception they speak warmly about the opportunities it has created, and the richness of provision it has made possible. By 1993, college responsibilities included the following:

- public examinations
- college finances
- capitation finance
- college environment, displays, exhibitions
- religious observance
- academic reporting and reporting: study skills
- student guidance and facilities
- student action planning; college diploma
- resources including library, AV, computerisation
- performing arts
- sports and recreation
- into Europe
- community and charity work
- accommodating the disabled
- equal opportunities
- liaison with a local special school (college twinned school)
- Duke of Edinburgh award scheme
- curriculum development
- timetable
- BTEC and TVEI co-ordinators
- core enrichment programme
- self-study materials
- general studies
- Advanced Level Information System (ALIS)
- industry/business links

- off-site visits
- enterprise activities
- news and publicity links
- induction programme
- links with high schools
- pre health link with local hospital

- work experience programme
- college marketing
- careers and HE programme
- student information systems
- stock control
- site management

It may be claimed that many of these functions would exist in a college without this structure. Yet responsibilities would be unlikely to be so widely disseminated, not only among those who hold responsibility posts in the college, but also among teams of staff who support many of these activities. Each post holder works to one of the Vice Principals or the Principal, so that line management structures are clear.

Of course, structures and systems develop over a time, and, as the college has grown in size, more departments have felt that it would be beneficial to have permanent or longer term chairs. The situation in 1993/4 was:

Annually Elected Chairs:	*Longer Term Chairs:*	*Permanent Chairs:*
Geography	Chemistry	Mathematics
Geology	English Language	Music
Biology	English Literature	Classical Civilisation
Physics	Theatre Studies	Religious Studies
Computing	Business Studies	Textiles
Economics	Secretarial Studies	Design
Politics		Health Studies
History		Modern Languages
Art		Sociology/Psychology
Sports Studies		Law
		Home Economics

Building on David Machin's vision in creating this imaginative structure, the College was able to develop a successful collegial approach to management. Teams emerged either by design or as a natural development. Team members became stake-holders in the college's development and felt ownership for the area to which they were contributing. They were the decision makers within that area, provided that their decisions were in harmony with the college's overall ethos. This sense of ownership meant that staff morale remained high as the college was established and developed. The goodwill that members of staff bring to a new institution, their keenness to make it work, was harnessed and put to effective use. Ultimately, of course, the students received the benefits of the collaborative energy that was engendered in the staffroom.

Again, vision had created values which were translated into an enriching educational experience.

Prince William School, Oundle: a study in successful delegation

Chris Lowe was the first head to be appointed to Prince William School, Oundle, in 1971. It was newly built on a green field site, and was one of the first comprehensive schools in Northamptonshire.

The school opened with what was, in those days, an innovative structure with heads of faculties and heads of year. The heads of faculties had one of the deputies as line manager, the heads of year had a second deputy as line manager, while the third deputy dealt with whole school issues such as finance and staff development.

This is essentially the structure that exists today. It has seen the school grow in numbers as the bulge years moved through it, and then decline in numbers as falling rolls followed, so it has provided stability as well as proving to be flexible during these successive changes.

Of course, the school has seen considerable developments during this time, which have been guided through task groups. This has produced some inequalities, in that it has been possible to offer financial reward to some working party chairs, but not others. For example, national initiatives such as TVEI and the Low Attainers Project brought with them external funding. This meant that it was possible to finance paid co-ordinators. At the same time, other groups such as the Whole School Development Working party were internally generated for internal purposes, and therefore carried with them no external funding. It was not, then, automatically possible to offer financial recognition to the chairs of such groups, even though their work might be central to the school's development. Thus, the new groups which were carrying forward developments in the school were not adequately reflected in the school's staffing structure, in the financial sense. Appropriate rewards were restricted by previous practices and appointments, which did not have the flexibility to respond to new needs.

In fact, it has sometimes been possible to offer at least temporary upgrading for specific tasks. For example, a gap in the structure enabled a head of department to be offered a senior teacher scale for 3 years to lead the Whole School Development Working Party. Again, the cash-backed Initial Teacher Training Initiative (1992) enabled a head of year to be offered a senior teacher post in order to co-ordinate this work.

In this way, a whole range of staff teams has emerged, which have made various contributions to the school's development. As a result, numbers of staff have obtained management experience, and a stake in a variety of developments. No one is directed to serve on a working party, but all may volunteer to do so. They thus increase the range of their experience, and enhance their professional satisfaction and prospects.

Managers in education are likely to accept that their responsibilities include 'boundary' management, too, as part of their duties in managing a school or college. However, in an even wider sense, education managers may have a role to play at a national and sometimes an international level. For many years, Chris Lowe has played a significant role on this wider stage. He has been a member of the Northamptonshire Education Committee. He was a leading local member of the Heads Association, and then of the Secondary Heads Association. He was elected a Council member of SHA, served as a member of its Executive Committee, and as its Legal Secretary. He then became President, the Association's highest office. He is Chair of the Royal Opera Education Committee, and a Director of the Royal Opera. In 1992, he became President of the European Secondary Heads Association. This role involves him in regular international visits, and he also contributes regularly to advanced courses on management in education (such as the Sheffield University MEd course).

This wide range of experience can bring considerable benefits to a school. At one level, groups of students have had opportunities to attend schools performances at the Royal Opera. Chris Lowe's interest in opera has been a factor in the development of opera productions in the school – *Carmen* and *The Bartered Bride* are recent examples. These productions have sometimes been supported by Royal Opera personnel. The productions are often taken abroad – for example, to Germany – not simply for performance, but so that workshop sessions can be organised with local schools. Thus, participating students are getting a valuable arts experience, which is then further enriched by an international dimension.

At another level – of educational leadership – Lowe's leading roles in SHA have involved him in debate and negotiation at the highest levels, with government ministers and senior planners. As well as enabling him to exert influence in educational developments at national level, the quality of this experience gives him a dimension in leading his own institution which few headteachers can enjoy. His colleagues and pupils benefit from this wide experience – as long as delegation continues to be genuinely effective.

In one sense, such responsibilities have a disadvantage for the institution: the head will be away from school more than most heads, as he or she meets the obligations which such responsibilities carry. In these circumstances, as Lowe wryly remarks, a mobile phone becomes an important management tool. In coping with this potential disadvantage, the school has had the benefit of a relatively stable senior management team, with staff who are used to working together, and who have learned to know how each colleague is likely to react to any situation. However, in such circumstances, the manager has to know that the structure will be sufficiently stable, and, at the same time, sufficiently flexible to drive the institution forward. In this way, students can benefit from the potential gains that the wide range of responsibilities and experience will bring, without too many strains caused by discontinuity and fragmentation.

To conclude

In some ways, these examples of aspects of management that involve values and vision are very different, yet they have common threads. The opening chapter of this book claimed that educative management is about getting things done in the right way for individual institutions. Leaders need to take account of the context in which they are operating and, within that context, provide leadership which 'communicates a sense of excitement, originality and freshness in an organisation'. Each of these managers has achieved that.

Further, each of them builds on a central fact – that the quality of the teaching staff is the most valuable resource that the institution has. When interviewed, Chris Lowe suggested that good teachers, by the very nature of their job, are using a wider range of skills than most managers in industry. They must be effective classroom managers, with a duty to motivate; they require a range of interpersonal skills; they must react quickly and effectively to the unexpected; they must differentiate. He cited the case of a deputy head who joined British Telecom and, within 4 years, became responsible for all management development programmes (at a significantly higher salary than he could have possibly enjoyed by remaining in education). The former deputy disclosed that this is not because he is any better, but simply that he is used to exercising a range of skills that his colleagues may well have, yet who may not realise how transferable their skills may be to what may seem to be more challenging contexts.

In one sense, then, vision in successful management simply involves recognising the strengths which are available in one's colleagues, and providing opportunities for those strengths to be released. This will mean creating a vision to which all can relate, and providing opportunities for teams to develop, and to realise that vision. This will produce fulfilled and committed staff, who feel valued and who have ownership of the ideals and practices of the school or college in which they work. The benefits of this commitment will be enjoyed by their 'clients', the learners. In different ways, each of the headteachers discussed in this chapter has succeeded in realising this potential.

CHAPTER EIGHTEEN

Managing the School Curriculum for the New Millennium

Jon Nixon

The purpose of this chapter is to consider some of the broader management issues that schools will have to face in finding ways to sustain effective curriculum practice among teachers and to monitor the success of that practice. We start as always with questions – a lot of them – but also with some serious reservations about the British National Curriculum and the policy framework within which it is developing. Thanks primarily to the 1988 Education Reform Act (ERA), the school curriculum in England and Wales has been well and truly removed from its secret garden and is now very much in the public domain. Yet that challenge to school practice leads to a larger challenge: Why should the curriculum 'belong' to government any more than it used to 'belong' to individual schools? The curriculum has individual, regional, national and international dimensions. As Lynne Chisolm (1994: 149) argues, for example, the widespread restructuring of education in the USA, Europe and Australasia has been driven to conform with 'policy solutions favoured by government for political – and not intrinsically educational – reasons'.

A major management task for the future, therefore, will be to ensure that, as the curriculum moves into the public domain, schools go on being places where teachers can think about their own teaching – and about what it means to learn – and so contribute to developing the curriculum in such a way that it meets the needs of all young people (*see* Nixon, 1992). Local and professional partnerships are, I shall argue, vital in providing effective support for curriculum development and for encouraging innovative styles of teaching and learning. Such partnerships are also necessary in order to ensure a unified service with strong continuity between the school curriculum and post-compulsory education provision.

The latter, although beyond the scope of this chapter, is an area of immense importance and subject to many of the same pressures that are currently operating upon schools (*see* Nixon, 1995; 1996).

Back to basics: questioning the policy framework

One of the lessons schools have learnt over the last 10 years is that the curriculum needs to be well managed if it is to add up to a set of learning experiences that is meaningful and coherent for the student. This should not be taken to imply that the curriculum can be reduced to an object of bureaucratic control. On the contrary, curriculum management is concerned with the process by which curriculum translates into learning, and the outcomes of that process are always unpredictable and often surprising. The task of management is not to render predictable the unpredictable or make mundane what is inherently surprising. The task is to build common understandings and shared purposes: to construct a community of learning. It is this aspiration towards mutual understanding and a sense of common purpose that enables us to distinguish management from the crude mechanisms of managerialism.

That distinction has become somewhat blurred, however, in recent years. There is a strong sense that within England and Wales the National Curriculum now constitutes the parameters of the debate on curriculum; that, as David McNamara (1990: 226) puts it, 'there is little point in continuing to challenge the philosophical and educational basis of the national curriculum (in so far as these exist)'. From this perspective the traditions and practices of curriculum development and evaluation are circumscribed by the first chapter of the first part of the 1988 Education Reform Act. Even those who (like David McNamara above) have reservations, offer these in the form of a negative, resigned support for what is acknowledged (in parentheses) to be wrong-headed (that is, having little or no 'philosophical and educational basis'). This is undoubtedly a recipe for despair: for educationists to be constructing their agendas around a notion of curriculum to which they have deeply ambivalent responses.

That ambivalence cuts deep. Some 20 years ago (Thursday 14 October 1976, to be exact) the then Secretary of State for Industry recorded in his personal diary the following comment:

> Cabinet at 10. I asked Shirley about the reports that Jim is going to make a major education speech and she passed me a note saying. 'Tony, no question of any change in emphasis on comprehensives. It's mainly on maths, why not enough kids are doing engineering, etc. A bit about standards. Curriculum will be the main row.' (Benn, 1989: 626)

Curriculum is still, of course, 'the main row'. But, like most rows, it has a history. This particular row reaches back beyond Thatcherism, beyond even the Great Debate and its aftermath (*see* CCCS, 1981: 208–27). It has its roots in the ideal of comprehensivisation and the need to work through the curriculum and pedagogical implications of that ideal. As early as 1961, Raymond Williams was heading us in this direction when, in *The Long Revolution*, he attempted to define 'the minimum to aim at for every educationally normal child'. It is interesting, 30 years on, to glance back at Williams's (1965: 174–75) version of a national, 'common' curriculum:

- extensive practices in the fundamental languages of English and Mathematics;

- general knowledge of ourselves and our environment, taught at the secondary stage not as separate academic disciplines but as general knowledge drawn from the disciplines which clarify at a higher stage...;

- history and criticism of literature, the visual arts, music, dramatic performance, landscape and architecture;

- extensive practice in democratic procedures, including meetings, negotiations, and the selection and conduct of leaders in democratic organisations ... and in the use of libraries, newspapers and magazines, radio and television programmes, and other sources of information, opinion and influence;

- introduction to at least one other culture, including its language, history, geography, institutions and arts, to be given in part by visiting and exchange.

It is all there: the core, foundation and cross-curriculum elements; balanced science; and, by implication, citizenship. There is nothing new under the sun; which is perhaps one of the reasons (there are, of course, others) why opposition to the National Curriculum (as opposed to its attendant assessment procedures) has been at best sporadic. The idea of some kind of entitlement curriculum connects only too well with the urge towards a common curriculum that has been at the forefront of educational debate for the last quarter of a century. The National Curriculum as it is shaping up may be a poor parody of an older, more egalitarian idea, but parodies (even poor ones) present a difficult target.

Particularly so when, as in this case, they are able to exploit a centuries old semantic tension implicit in the word 'common'. For that word may be used to denote something shared or to describe something ordinary; something 'low' and 'vulgar'. There are considerable and persistent overlaps in these uses and Williams (1976: 61) again points up the difficulty of disentangling them historically:

> In feudal society (negative) attribution was systematic and carried few if any
> additional overtones. It is significant that members of the Parliamentary army

in the Civil War...refused to be called 'common soldiers' and insisted on 'private soldiers'. This must indicate an existing and derogatory sense of 'common', though it is interesting that this same army were fighting for 'the commons', and went on to establish a 'commonwealth'. The alternative they chose is remarkable, since it asserted, in the true spirit of their revolution, that they were their own men.

The row rumbles on. Is the National Curriculum really about people becoming their own persons? Or is it (in defensive recoil, perhaps, from that derogatory sense of 'common') about the 'privatisation' of education? Does it indicate social division or social cohesion: 'a whole group or interest or a large specific and subordinate group'? (Williams 1976: 61). What does the National Curriculum really mean for the teachers who have to implement it and the pupils who are having to pass through it?

In approaching these questions we need to remind ourselves that the National Curriculum is part of a legislative package which not only 'represents the biggest quantum leap in direct control over detailed pedagogy and classroom activity ever undertaken' (Fletcher 1990: 68), but also aims at radically changing the ethos and culture of schooling. The Education Reform Act of 1988 is, as Stephen Bates (1990) points out, 'an uneasy amalgam of interventionist regulations (464 additional powers for the Secretary of State) and free market rhetoric'. The introduction of the National Curriculum and testing at 7, 11, 14 and 16 must be set against the revised arrangements for the admission of pupils to state schools (ERA, Part 1, Chapter 2), the system of delegated school budgets (Chapter 3), the procedures to enable schools to opt out of Local Education Authority (LEA) control (Chapter 4), the establishment of 'city technology colleges' (Chapter 5) and the abolition of the Inner London Education Authority (Part 3).

The inconsistency inherent in this package was neatly summed up by John Sayer (1989: 55):

> There appears to be a view in government which is alternatively centralistic and anarchic: central government will determine in detail what should be taught and examined in schools in the public service; but every encouragement should be given for either schools or individual parents to opt out of that service, and to exercise collective and individual parental choice even if that disrupts the planning of educational provision for the local community, or is socially divisive.

The long-term effect of the changed policy framework within which the National Curriculum is now set is difficult to gauge. It is, however, undoubtedly increasing the inequalities between schools. It is also, in spite of resistance by many teachers and head teachers, creating a competitive climate in which corporate planning across schools will become much more difficult. This lack of regional planning is undoubtedly having an impact on the provision of in-service education and training. With LEA advisory services being pulled towards an inspectorial role and the logistics of teacher secondment becoming that much more complex, the traditional patterns of inservice provision are being put under increased pressure.

Any serious attempt to establish innovative curriculum practice among teachers will have to relate to these broader policy developments and, in so doing, hold open the option of 'continuing to challenge the philosophical and educational basis of the National Curriculum (in so far as these exist)'. If those working in schools are to understand what is happening in and across their institutions, they will need to address a broad range of policy issues and to insist on the relevance of those issues to the task of effective management. That insistence, moreover, is likely to become increasingly difficult to maintain as curriculum management becomes more closely associated with monitoring, and responding to, the cumulative data drawn from successive waves of Standard Assessment Tasks.

Schools, then, will need to address some basic questions about the ways in which the policy framework established by the 1988 Education Reform Act is influencing their work. How, for example, is 'open enrolment' affecting their ethos and culture? What effect is opting out – or the possibility of it – having on collegial relationships and supportive networks across schools? What is the Local Management of Schools doing to roles and designated responsibilities within particular institutions? What is happening to the curriculum of those schools whose catchment areas and traditional communities are changing beyond recognition? Establishing the conditions necessary for addressing such questions is a prime management task.

Managing the middle ground between school and community

That task is central to the creation of what Nicholas Beattie (1990: 39) defines as

> a new 'culture of education' in which curriculum is better supported and understood by the community. What that culture will look like is difficult to predict, but it will certainly...require the forging of new alliances between educational professionals and other groups, a redefinition of teacher roles and professional autonomy, a greater willingness to communicate and negotiate.

The nature of these 'new alliances' will be an important factor affecting the involvement of schools in the overall management of learning. Any group of teachers adopting a collegial approach to curriculum practice will eventually want, and need, to think through that practice with other teachers, including those from neighbouring schools and colleges. In the past there have been mechanisms – teachers' centres, teacher secondments, LEA inservice sessions – whereby this kind of cross-institutional sharing and corporate planning has been at the very least a possibility in almost all areas. Now, many of those mechanisms are at risk.

Working for Success through Local Partnerships

LEAs, which in the past have provided that kind of regional planning and overview, are under particularly severe threat. Always vulnerable, the traditional partnership between schools, LEAs and central government is now under severe strain. Changes in legislation regarding school government together with the delegation of school budgets have now established a significant shift in the locus of authority. The possibility of schools opting out of LEA control and assuming grant-maintained status – and the financial inducements offered by central government for them to do so – has confirmed this shift and placed LEAs in an increasingly difficult position.

The effect of these changes has been to dislocate various occupational groups from their own traditional practices and, in some cases, their professional values. As Philippa Cordingley and Maurice Kogan (1993: 101) have suggested, 'over time, power distributions change, and it should not be unexpected that a period of strong local and professional rule will be followed by centralisation and de-professionalisation'. Equally, however, it should not be unexpected that this process of de-professionalisation will have a significant impact on the morale and outlook of the groups concerned, particularly when it is accompanied by 'an all-but-pathological hatred of LEAs and educationists' (Kogan, 1993). Teachers, head teachers, teacher educators and LEA personnel have all suffered the demoralising side-effects of the increasingly centralised control of an education service whose professional expertise has been treated with open disdain by government ministers.

A significant strand of central government thinking over the last few years has been that LEAs constitute a kind of mezzanine that only serves to overload the system as a whole and thereby render it less efficient. Would it not be easier just to do away with LEAs altogether and have schools funded directly by, and accountable directly to, central government? Could not the kind of consortia that have been developed, to sometimes good effect, under the Technical and Vocational Education Initiative (TVEI) extension scheme fulfil the functions of the LEA? Who, in short, needs an LEA?

Margaret Maden (1990) has challenged that particular line of thought, on the grounds not only that it ignores 'the importance of links between education and social services, physical and economic planning systems and sports, parks, museums and libraries', but also that it fails to make sense in terms of the internal management of the education service. In short, it is just plain silly to ignore local and regional contexts of education. That silliness, she points out, is highlighted if we consider how a consortium would decide whether or not a new school needed to be built:

> Presumably the consortium would need something approximating to a local authority near at hand so that longer term demographic and housing developments could be established before reaching their decision? The consortium would then, one assumes, negotiate with neighbouring consortia on the realisation of capital assets and manage the borrowing requirements and debt repayments needed for such a capital scheme to proceed? At this point, I would think the consortium would be begging for an LEA to be reinvented.

It would be an error to assume, therefore, that the abolition of LEAs necessarily follows from the devolution of financial responsibility to schools: 'this is the error of the abolitionists ... They risk the bureaucracy of a centralised system because they overlook what schools cannot and should not be made to do' (Bill Dennison, 1990). Dennison goes on to highlight four main functions which schools 'should not be made to do' and which, taken together, define for LEAs a continuing and 'indispensable role': *strategy* ('deciding the number of schools, their location, their size and age range'); *monitoring* ('the curriculum, standards of teaching and quality of accommodation'); *arbitration* ('between parents and a school over a disciplinary matter, when a teacher has an employment grievance, where a school's admission's policy is contested, and so on'); and *services* ('meals, a curriculum advice, salary payments, structural repairs and so on').

This insistence on the continuing role of the LEA is not to deny the importance of schools grouping together to share and to plan beyond the immediate needs of the individual school. After all, as Margaret Maden (1990) acknowledges, such groupings 'provide a practical structure within which constructive links and mutual dependencies could be realised'. Whether or not they will be realised must depend, however, on whether LEAs are allowed to continue in a supportive role; and that, in turn, will depend in some measure on the determination of schools to use every facility available to ensure that those 'constructive link and mutual dependencies' are strengthened and extended.

Thus although the power base of schooling has shifted significantly away from LEAs, their still considerable influence on local and regional planning and on the development of an effective curriculum and staff development programme is of immense and continuing value. Neil Fletcher (1990: 70) reinforces the earlier point made by Margaret Maden when he argues that, 'if LEAs had not already existed,...Kenneth Baker would have had to invent them in order to provide a credible means of implementing his reforms'. The question remains, however, as to how schools can, and should, respond to – and help construct – what will be a new set of alliances and partnerships.

In responding to that question schools need to remind themselves of the extent to which effective policy-making relies on local knowledge of local needs. Conditions vary significantly from one locality to another: from urban to rural, from inner city to suburbs, from multicultural areas to those that are culturally homogeneous, from areas of high unemployment to those where most adults have jobs. 'Such variants', as Anne Phillips (1994: 13) reminds us, 'affect the scale of priorities, as well as the range of considerations that should be brought to bear on any one decision'. The argument for local partnership, therefore, is an argument for using this local knowledge, and (argues Phillips) 'taking maximum advantage of people's experience and imagination and expertise'.

Working for Success through Professional Partnerships

Central to this new sense of interconnectedness is the aspiration towards greater understanding between schools, LEAs, parents and the local community concerning the nature and purposes of education. The responsibilities laid upon LEAs to secure the implementation of the National Curriculum requires, as the Audit Commission's (1989: 17) report on the role of LEA inspectors and advisers pointed out, 'the development of more systematic monitoring, with more intensive direct observation of teaching and learning and better record-keeping'. A survey conducted by David Nebesnuick (1990: 8) suggested that there are three main paths an LEA can take in order to fulfil these responsibilities: 'it can rely very heavily upon self-evaluation methods within the schools or it can adopt an external inspection system or quite possibly it can pursue a combination of the two'.

Based upon the evidence of 50 LEAs, the survey found that 25 of these inclined towards a system which emphasised the importance of 'local internal mechanisms'. Moreover, several of these LEAs 'referred to the need for individual schools to develop school-based performance indicators relevant to their local needs and circumstances', rather than being dependent upon 'comprehensive authority-wide indicators' (Nebesnuick, 1990: 6-7). Although the evidence of the survey suggests that the 'local internal mechanisms' that are being established vary considerably across authorities, it presents a far from depressing prospect of the way in which in-school procedures might become a significant element within authority-wide systems (*see* Nixon and Rudduck, 1994).

If teachers are to use these procedures as a means of achieving what Peter Ribbins (1990:91) has termed 'interdependent professionalism', they will need to ensure that whatever system is developed is consistent with their own professed values. While curriculum management may be subsidiarily concerned with questions of efficiency, cost effectiveness and value for money (the shibboleths of current orthodoxy), its prime concern must be to focus upon the education process itself. In so far as curriculum management is value driven, its values must be the professed values of the educator. A key concern, therefore, for all those involved in managing the curriculum must be to define its distinguishing features; to make explicit, in other words, what it is that is *educational* about the management of education.

As 'interdependent professionals' teachers will need to address this concern in partnership with a wide range of professional groups. Colleagues working in institutions of higher education, for example, can offer valuable support in terms of curriculum consultancy and school-focused developmental work. As Jean Rudduck (1991: 141) points out, 'schools and universities need to plan how best they can work together in a spirit of determination and common commitment'. The notion of an educational community that can facilitate and to some extent resource 'a shared commitment to clarifying values, principles and purposes, and to understanding the social and political contexts in which those values, principles and purposes are set to work' is of paramount importance.

In helping to create such a community, teachers would not only be developing a version of professionalism, which relies on something other than either the appeal to teacher autonomy or the claims of externally imposed accountability. They would also be claiming for themselves a future role in the middle ground of curriculum management: the largely unmapped and highly contested terrain between centre and periphery. To that extent the notion of 'interdependent professional' denotes a significant departure.

Towards a pedagogy of partnership

None of the partnerships we have mentioned so far has any meaning, educationally speaking, unless the idea of partnership is itself translated into pedagogical practice. That is the prime task facing curriculum management: to operationalise the curriculum in such a way that learning becomes an experience of shared endeavour among learners, between learners and teachers and between teachers, parents and learners. To approach learning in this way means, not only developing more open and mutually supportive relationships within school, but also creating links across institutions so as to ensure continuity between phases and between the practices of school and those of the wider local and business community (*see* Table 18.1).

David Hargreaves (1994: 43–44) has claimed that 'schools are still modelled on a curious mix of the factory, the asylum and the prison'. Their social organisation, in other words, focuses on repetition, segregation and surveillance: important themes which inform many of the

Table 18.1 Partnership and the processes of learning

Partnerships	*Processes*
Agents	
Learners	Collaborative learning
Learners and teachers	Negotiated learning
Teachers	Interdisciplinarity
Teachers, parents and learners	Home–school liaison
Institutions	
Schools	Cluster planning
Schools, colleges and HE	Continuity
Schools and business	Work-related learning

organisation, curriculum and assessment practices of contemporary schooling. Yet, argues Hargreaves, the workplace is changing radically, with modern businesses looking very unlike the heavy-industry factory: 'We are glad to see the end of the traditional factory; why should we expect the school modelled on it to be welcome to children?'. If schools are to resemble contemporary institutions, they must feel less like schools; and that, he suggests, means building on experiments conducted by a few pioneering institutions:

> those restricting conventional lessons to the morning, and using the afternoons for project work and independent study; abandoning the conventional school day or week for integrated, complex and real-life problem-solving projects with students working in supervised teams in a variety of settings; flexi-time arrangements that give teachers and students more control and reduce the sense of oppressive routine and predictability; restructured days giving teachers space to devote more time to planning and preparation; parents abandoning their conventional prejudices about what schooling must mean when they see new structures enhancing the commitment, motivation and achievement of their children.

While there may be some disagreement over the specific proposals put forward by Hargreaves, most commentators agree that in the future it will be increasingly important for young people to be able to work together in teams, to adapt to new tasks and challenges, and to take greater control of their own learning and of their own development as learners. The National Commission on Education (1993) helped focus this emergent consensus through its emphasis on 'applied intelligence'. In a world where constant adaptation to change is the order of the day, the individual's capacity to *apply* knowledge, skills and understanding will be crucial. Schools can help in this task by encouraging young people to learn together, to monitor their own progress in consultation with their teachers and to think across the restricting boundaries of subjects and disciplines. The task of curriculum management is to strengthen and establish partnerships in such a way as to enhance the processes of learning.

Those partnerships must also include institutional links with other schools, colleges, institutions of higher education and, crucially, business and industry. Schools do not and should not have a monopoly on learning. They are important sites of learning and (along with institutions of further and higher education) are unique in the primacy of their concern for the individual as learner. This does not mean, however, that there are not other institutional sites on which significant learning takes place. Increasingly, we shall need to think not of a school curriculum, but of a curriculum which is supported by the school in partnership with a range of other institutions. In a society that aspires to be 'a learning society', the task of school management must be to ensure that these partnerships are strong and vibrant and that they are centrally concerned with learning.

Conclusion: more questions

To set about the task of curriculum management is not just a matter of setting up systems and procedures; it is a matter also of creating a certain kind of context and asking certain kinds of questions. Among the questions that schools, in concert with their professional partners, will need to address in making such a start, are the following:

- What, if anything, is distinctively educational about curriculum management?

- What institutional conditions must be met before curriculum management can fairly claim to be educational in its principles and procedures?

- What constraints operate against those principles and procedures and by what means, if any, can these be overcome?

- What values inform and sustain the practice of curriculum management?

These, of course, are not the only questions that need to be considered. But they are some of the most important. Starting from these, any school could begin to develop a clear perspective on its management task and to communicate that perspective to other schools and professional groups. They are pitched at a high level of generality as a reminder that behind the technical and procedural issues so often associated with management lie some very big questions about values and purposes.

Schools will, of course, have to answer these questions for themselves. Nevertheless, it might be useful to offer some starting points whereby schools can begin to define for themselves what it is that is educational about curriculum management and, in doing so, work towards a common approach:

- Curriculum management is *necessarily collegial in spirit*. It is the means by which the teaching profession tries to improve its own practice in the light of those values which it espouses.

- It is centrally concerned with the *quality of teaching and learning* and on the impact of these activities across a wide range of pupil achievement. Although clearly addressing the concerns of policy makers as well as practitioners, it should be distinguished from managerial approaches which focus exclusively on policy matters.

- It should also be distinguished from those approaches which focus exclusively on the outcomes of education. Curriculum management is *concerned with both pedagogical and organisational processes*, with unpre-specified as well as pre-specified outcomes, and with the conditions pertaining within particular institutional settings.

- Curriculum management is *enquiry led*; which is to say that its decisions and planning procedures are based upon evidence that has been gathered systematically and analysed according to procedures that can be made explicit.

The National Curriculum may, in retrospect, be seen to have reinforced the derogatory sense of 'common': prove, that is, to be less about commonalty and sharing than about social division; less about entitlement than about the further subordination of what Raymond Williams (1976: 61) characterised as that already 'large specific and subordinate group'. It is, after all, for all its interventionism, part of a legislative package that is strung together with 'the privatiser's market ideology' (Lawton 1989: 38). This gloomy prognosis is less likely to prove reliable, however, if schools adopt an approach to curriculum management which takes as its point of departure the need for teachers to go on thinking and learning about the processes of learning and about the contexts which frame and constrain these processes.

If schools are to take seriously the task of supporting innovative practice, those who manage them will have to challenge many of the presuppositions of the current policy framework within which they currently operate. An approach to curriculum management based on partnership and shared enquiry will undoubtedly help in this task. In its emphasis on open dialogue, it must, even if only by implication, counter the insidious drift towards a competitive free for all in which each school is out for itself. Against that demeaning norm, schools may yet prove to exert a civilising and deeply educative influence. It is against this alternative standard that school effectiveness should be judged. The successful school is the school that makes partnership a reality and that, in doing so, reconstructs itself around a shared concern for the quality of learning.

CHAPTER NINETEEN

Value-Added Aspects of Managing School Effectiveness

David Jesson

There are at least two distinct dimensions to the debate about the assessment of schools' performance, each of which articulates apparently distinct agendas. These, while actually *complementary* to each other, have tended to be pursued as though the importance of one so outclassed the other that *it* was the only one to which attention should be directed.

The first of these – *accountability* – has dominated the political (and public) debate in Britain in recent times. It raises questions about *why schools' outcomes differ* from each other. The arguments about this have been particularly intense when set in a political context where 'comprehensive' organisation of schooling has been alleged to be the cause of much poor educational achievement in Britain. The, often explicit, contrast with 'selective' systems which 'clearly obtain better results' has set the tone for many of the legislative actions which ensure that schools' examination results became the focus of public attention about how well schools were serving the nation. 'Performance Tables' listing schools' examination outcomes were imposed centrally with the objective of making 'easy', if crude, comparisons possible between schools' achievements.

The second dimension – *to aid school self evaluation and improvement* – has had rather less attention paid to it. On the questionable assumption that schools would only respond to overt public pressure, mechanisms have been put in place to inform the public only about the *outcomes* which schools have achieved. Such information, it was implied, would assist parents in making a 'market' choice – exerting pressure on 'low performing' schools and leading, inexorably, to the closure of the 'bad' ones, whilst the 'good' would recruit more pupils and ultimately would need to be enlarged. The implication was that schools had to be 'called to account' in dramatic ways, by public pressure, rather than be encouraged to improve themselves by 'professional' review.

And yet, properly pursued, both dimensions are capable of deriving from a single framework of performance evaluation. Until 1994 government had dismissed such attempts as 'excusing the inexcusable' (since the framework indicated that not *all* the differences in achievement shown in the Performance Tables were due to 'poorer' educational provision in the 'lower' achieving schools).

In the early 1990s, therefore, the accountability dimension was the predominant mode of discussion of schools' examination performance. The annual publication of *School and College Performance Tables* (DFE, 1992, 1993a, 1994) set out, school by school in each local authority, the percentage of pupils achieving certain defined levels of examination result (at present limited to examinations for pupils aged 16 or over, but in principle to be extended to younger age groups).

That the Performance Tables appeared to offer useful comparisons between schools in simple terms is unfortunate because it is misleading. Although published with schools listed in *alphabetical* order, no official attempt was made to contest the media's reproduction of these in *numerical* order. Instead, there was an apparent connivance with 'interpretations' which were then placed upon these ranked orders of schools' examination results. Talk of 'high standards' was often unfairly associated with schools at the 'top' of these revised 'league tables', whilst the term 'failing schools' was retained for those at the 'bottom'. Thus there was a meretricious refusal to discriminate between *'achieving more of something'* and *'being a good school'* or *'achieving less'* and *'being a poor school'*. This, perhaps more than any one single other factor, soured both the quality of the debate about schools' performance and also the relationships between schools and government. In the meantime it did nothing to assist schools in the purposes which most, quite clearly, see themselves in the business of achieving: that is to raise the standards of attainment of the pupils they teach.

The sad thing about this 'debate' is that it was sterile and flawed from the start. Its nemesis was reached in 1991 with the publication of the results, in each local education authority, of the Key Stage One assessments on pupils aged seven (DES, 1991b). That Richmond-on-Thames, Surrey, Sussex and the leafier suburbs came out 'at the top', whilst inner city areas such as Newham and Bradford 'came bottom' surprised no one, due to the very different characteristics of the pupils which these areas served – but the occasion was used by the then Secretary of State for Education to mount an intemperate attack on schools in these latter LEAs for their 'poor standards' and for 'failing their pupils'. The widespread rejection by teachers of the testing regime (which were seen as giving more opportunity for attacks of this kind) was an almost inevitable outcome of these prejudicial attitudes.

These events conspired to make the effective use of examination (and assessment) results much less developed in the middle 1990s than they might otherwise have been. In this chapter I seek to redress that balance and look at ways in which schools might utilise the wealth of information to which they now have access – but within a 'fair' framework, and one which offers the possibility of learning, collaboratively, from the successes and failures of other schools in seeking to 'get the best' out of the young people they educate.

With the publication of the SCAA Report *Value-Added Performance Indicators for Schools* (SCAA, 1994) the 'Value Added' assessment of schools' examination results achieved its rightful place. It is this framework which offers the possibility of making 'fairer' comparisons between schools (thus satisfying the accountability dimension of this debate) whilst at the same time making possible the comparative evaluation of performance within individual schools (with its potential for highlighting areas for improvement).

The measurement of value-added aspects

In principle this refers to the amount that the individual school contributes to pupils' educational outcomes – once allowance has been made for the effects of factors which are not directly controlled by the school. I shall restrict its use here to test score outcomes, and specifically to GCSE examination results. This is not because they are the only important aspects of schooling, but because of their ready availability in comparable form for all schools.

Essentially a value added framework requires *three* key elements:
1. A measure of pupils' starting points $\Big\}$ data on *individual* pupils
2. A measure of pupils' outcomes
3. The average 'progress' made within the time scale spanned by 1 and 2.

Whilst we do not, as yet, have National Curriculum Assessments for all pupils on a longitudinal basis to allow measures such that (1) and (2) above could be based on a *common scale*, many groups of schools have adopted serviceable alternatives – such as the use of standardised scores on reading tests, non-verbal reasoning tests and other widely available instruments, providing a 'normative' view of the starting points of pupils. Once these measures of 'prior attainment' are linked to the outcomes these pupils achieve in their GCSE examinations it becomes possible to see how they can act as 'indicators' of potential later examination performance.

The assessment of a school's 'value-added' characteristics has developed more rapidly in Britain than anywhere else in the world, and is being routinely applied in a wide variety of contexts – from rural counties such as Shropshire and West Sussex to metropolitan districts such as Barnsley, Wakefield and Wolverhampton. In each of these LEAs a set of practices is developing which has a consistency and coherence, and which, whilst it takes the 'accountability' element seriously has moved a long way further in utilising information in value added form, to address a variety of issues related to school improvement.

The key aspect of using information in a value-added context is to identify what are the reasons why pupils' examination outcomes differ, and hence to establish what are 'reasonable' expectations of pupils with differing characteristics. Differences over and above these need to be assessed and associated with the particular effects which school membership has on each school's pupils.

What key factors are related to differences in pupils examination scores?

Over the past 5 years the following six factors have emerged consistently:

1. *Pupils' prior attainment score* (those with higher prior attainments 'do better').

2. *Gender* (girls 'do better' than boys).

3. *Socio-economic factors* (pupils on 'free school meals' do less well than others).

4. *The season of a pupil's birth* ('summer' born pupils generally do less well than others).

5. *The number of examinations entered* (the more entries the 'better' the outcome).

6. *The actual subjects taken in examinations* (subject 'difficulties' vary substantially).

The first four of these are characteristics over which few schools have control, so differences related to these factors need to be clearly identified. The other two are matters which it is useful to know about, and, although they generally represent the result of long-term decisions taken by the school it may be that some of these are open to change in the interests of obtaining better performance. When these factors have been 'taken account of' it becomes a matter of some importance to identify a seventh which lies at the heart of the search for school improvement:

7. *The quality of teaching in particular subjects*, and its organisation across the school.

How to set about establishing an 'information database' to guide the search for 'effectiveness' and to identify areas for 'improvement'

One useful by-product of the data collection exercise undertaken to produce the Performance Tables is the existence of a single body which collates *all* the examination results for all Year 11 pupils in every school in the country. The National Consortium for Examination Results (NCER, based in Cheshire County Council), in collaboration with the University of Bath, produces two linked 'files' of information from which each school's detailed examination result profile for each pupil can be derived.

Each local authority maintained school can obtain the relevant information on its own pupils through its LEA (provided the LEA has paid its participation subscription to NCER) whilst grant maintained and independent schools may need to make their own arrangements to the same end. Many schools, with differing funding arrangements however, have authorised the local authority to be the recipient of their information. In these cases it simplifies the building of a collaborative context within which such data, and its uses, can be shared.

By whatever means it is established, the outcome of obtaining such information should be the creation of a detailed spreadsheet of individual pupil characteristics and examination results for each school. It should comprise the following elements: first, a list of pupils by name; second, basic information relating to them such as gender, date of birth, numbers of examinations entered; and third, stretching to the right as a series of individually referenced 'columns', the examination results for each pupil in each of the major subjects taken within the school. Each school can create its own such database, but it is clearly in the interests of comparability for there to be a common format, so that different schools can compare their results directly.

Examples of 'differences' between pupils' outcomes

We look at each of the seven issues identified above through a series of figures, showing the relationship between each and pupils' examination outcomes. Each derives from studies which have been undertaken with large, representative groups of pupils over the past year.

Pupils' prior attainment scores

Figure 19.1 shows the relationship between pupils' 'prior attainment' scores (measured at or around their time of entry to secondary school) and their later examination scores. For the latter we have adopted the common practice of assigning 7 points to a GCSE grade of A or A*, 6 to a B down to zero for an 'unclassified' pass or failure to take the examination for which the pupil had been entered.

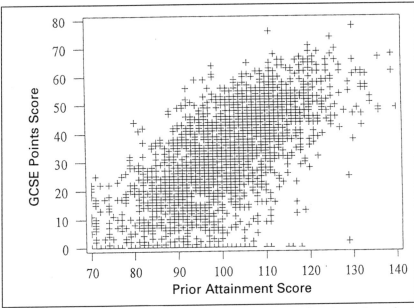

Figure 19.1 GCSE points score for sample pupils plotted against prior attainment score

The figure shows both the overall relationship between pupils' prior attainment scores and outcomes (in a form which can be quantified by a 'prediction formula'). It also shows the extent to which pupils vary around these predicted levels. One useful test, therefore, for a school would be to plot its own results in a similar fashion to see whether 'their' pupils on average score more 'above prediction' than below it. The more this occurs, the greater the evidence that this school is 'adding additional value' over and above that which is achieved in most other schools. (There are technical methods of doing this with greater precision, but in principle, once the nature of the relationship between 'intake' and 'outcome' has been established over a wide range of pupils, it would be sufficient to plot one's own school's points and superimpose them on the 'general' graph).

There are basically three possible results of an exercise such as we have described – first, your own school's points may lie quite close to their predicted values – or at least there will be about equal numbers of them 'above' and 'below' the line. This should be taken as evidence that the school is helping its pupils gain examination results in a similar way to most other schools. Clearly there is some need for guidance about what constitutes 'close enough to expectation' – but it has been found that somewhere between one half and two thirds of schools fall into this category.

Alternatively, the school's results may fall substantially 'above' the line – suggesting 'better' performance, or 'below' it suggesting 'worse'.

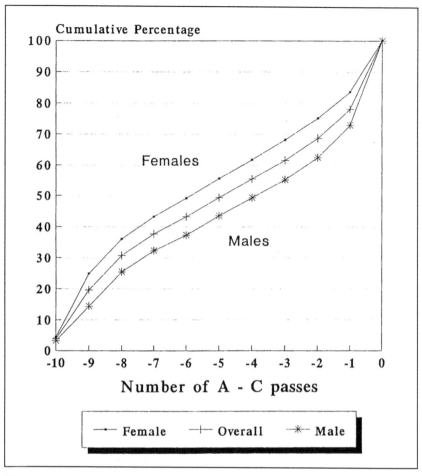

Figure 19.2 Number of A – C passes in GCSE exams for County pupils

Clearly this activity alone can provide a first useful indicator of the overall state of examination performance within the school – based as it is on comparisons with similar pupils in other schools.

Gender

Figure 19.2 shows the percentage of girls and boys achieving A, B or C grades. The outperforming by girls of boys is particularly marked in the middle ranges of achievement – which will have substantial representation in most schools. Knowing this general tendency, the information provided by Figure 19.3 is salutary – gender differences do not apply evenly between schools. It would obviously be helpful to explore the 'gender gap' in each school, if only to discover whether it was wider than normal in a particular school. Its narrowing in some instances

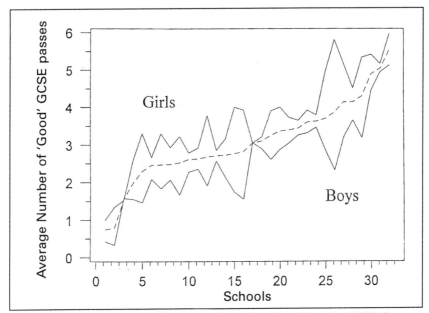

Figure 19.3 Gender differences in achieving 'Good' GCSE Passes (By school)

would also be of interest – and depending on whether this was due to 'better than expected' performance by boys (in the sense of the Section above) or 'worse than expected' by girls – might offer pointers to improvements in overall performance.

Gender issues permeate the results of assessments in the 11–16 age group. In some circumstances particular practices can minimise the differences due to these, whilst others exacerbate them. One of the purposes of acting collaboratively with other schools would be to discover what evidence there might be, which might help inform profitable changes in a school's practices.

Socio-economic factors

Figure 19.4 shows the number of grades A, B or C gained by pupils in receipt of free school meals, contrasted with the same outcome for other pupils. Clearly, overall, the 'free school meal' group do much less well than the others – although this is not true for all of these pupils.

It is helpful for schools to recognise the extent to which 'economic' stress (for which the receipt of free school meals is a proxy) affects pupils' performance, particularly when seen in a wider context than those specifically educated in a particular school. We should beware of 'talking down' pupils' potential – but equally, be prepared to recognise the specific educational disadvantage faced by many pupils in this category.

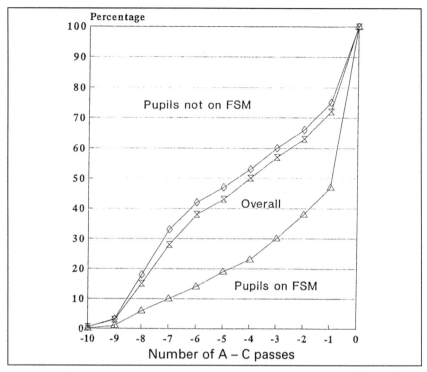

Figure 19.4 Number of A – C passes in GCSE exams for County pupils by free school meal (FSM) status

Birthdate

Figure 19.5 is an enhanced version of Figure 19.4 and shows the extent to which the term in which a pupil was born appears to have a continuing impact on the achievement of each level of examination performance at GCSE.

One matter which may be checked straightforwardly is the extent to which 'summer-born' pupils predominate in the lower sets within the school. In many cases these pupils are more able than their current levels of performance suggest – yet by placing them with others for whom a lower of achievement is expected, the school may reinforce their own perception of themselves as 'failures'.

Two factors over which schools have considerable control are: the numbers of examinations for which pupils are entered and the particular 'mix' of subjects available to them.

Entry to examinations

Figure 19.6 gives an indication that, at pupil level at least, entering for more examinations rather than less is associated with higher examination scores. There is, of course, nothing particularly surprising about these

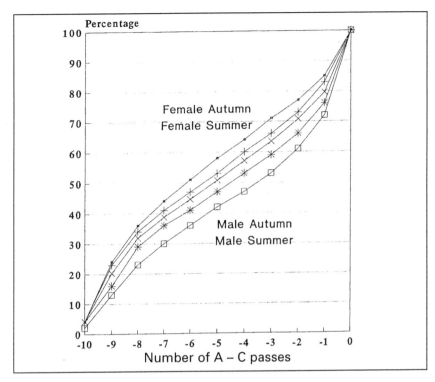

Figure 19.5 Number of A – C passes in GCSE exams for County pupils

basic facts; the unexpected element is presented in Figure 19.7, where schools' average entry rates are presented alongside their average examination scores. The degree to which schools make different decisions in respect of examination is brought sharply into focus – and thus, each school might usefully question whether its own procedures are those most appropriate for its pupils.

The situation is, however, not quite as clear-cut as the simple equation 'more entries equals more examination success' might imply. In Figure 19.7 it is clear that schools making similar decisions on entry policy nevertheless obtain widely varying levels of outcome. Part of the explanation of this may be that schools entering pupils for similar numbers of examinations differ substantially in the prior attainments of their pupils – as is indeed evident from Figure 19.8. However, a further differentiation arises here – in that even schools with similar prior attainment profiles enter pupils for substantially different numbers of examinations. Whichever representation appears most compelling, both show that the number of examinations which school policy results in pupils entering is certainly *associated* with higher examination scores but is by no means a full explanation of them.

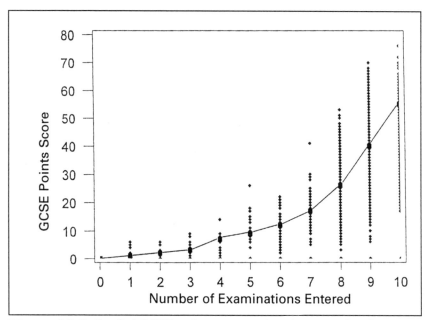

Figure 19.6 Pupils' GCSE points score related to examination entry rate

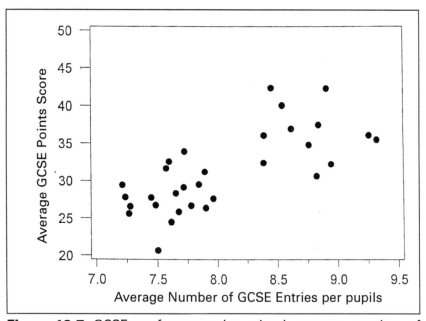

Figure 19.7 GCSE performance by school average number of exam entries

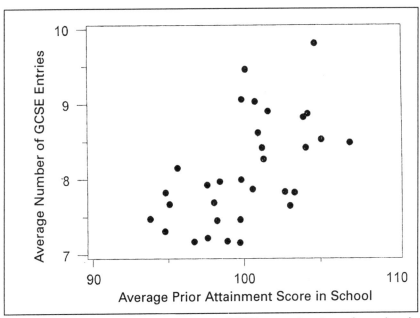

Figure 19.8 Average entry rate to GCSE examinations for schools with pupils of differing prior attainment scores

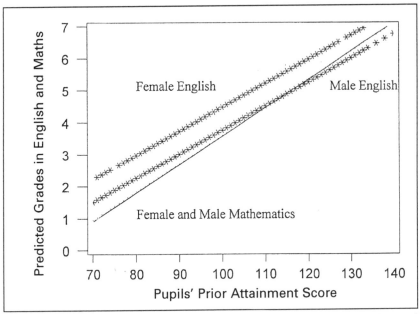

Figure 19.9 Predicted GCSE grades for pupils in English and mathematics

Differing subject difficulties

Nationally, in 1994, well over 50% of pupils obtained grades A, B or C in English GCSE examinations, whereas only around 40% managed this in mathematics. This could be because the teaching in English courses was superior to that in mathematics, but equally the explanation may lie elsewhere.

A basic framework for exploring the apparent differences in subject difficulty is provided by comparing the performance of 'typical' pupils in each of them. Figure 19.9 shows the level of GCSE English performance for a large sample of pupils, whilst superimposed on this is the performance of identical pupils in mathematics.

The first thing to note about English performance is the consistent bias towards higher outcomes for girls: at every level of prior attainment score they 'outperform' (on average) boys of similar characteristics. The level of difference is around 0.7 of a grade in favour of girls.

When performance in mathematics is compared with that of English, it is clear that girls, as well as boys, perform less well. There appear to be no major gender differences in outcomes in mathematics, so although boys do worse in their mathematics than their English, the differential is much less marked for them than it is for girls. Thus, the concept of subject 'difficulty' needs to be expressed differentially in terms of gender – and this is what Table 19.1 presents. The description of this offers a relative ranking of subject 'difficulty' for girls and boys and separately. Table 19.1 shows that there is a 'hierarchy' amongst subject 'difficulties', and that this hierarchy differs for boys and girls.

Similar observations apply to each of the subjects listed in Table 19.1 – for example, double science, which is now the scientific subject taken by the great majority of pupils, appears 'harder' than English for girls, but slightly 'easier' for boys. Also this is one of the few subject areas which does not show a significant advantage in performance for similar pupils of girls over boys. The final column of Table 19.1 shows the rate at which grades change with changes in prior attainment scores – and these allow similar 'subject lines' to be drawn for each of the areas listed.

When this is done, as for example in Figure 19.9, it is clear that the level of relative difficulty for subjects is not constant for all pupils. Thus mathematics appears a grade and a half more difficult for low prior attaining girls than English, but this is reduced considerably (although still giving the edge to English) for girls with higher prior attainment scores.

Uses of value-added evaluations as a means of identifying 'good practice'

Given the evaluations of subject level performance by boys and girls,

Subject	Entries	Grade	Gender	PAttain
English	C Core	4.67	−0.71	0.075
Maths	C Core	3.75		−0.086
Double science	C Core	4.07		0.073
Single science	1000's	3.19		0.066
CDTTec	100's	3.36		0.066
DesCom	100's	4.05	−0.66	0.057
DesReal	100's	4.35	−0.81	0.048
Design & Technology	10's	3.96		
Business studies	1000's	4.37	−0.40	0.071
HE food	100's	3.87	−1.00	0.056
Art	1000's	5.00	−0.71	0.050
Geography	1000's	3.95	−0.32	0.079
History	1000's	4.02	−0.55	0.098
Religious studies	100's	4.00	−0.91	0.084
Literature	1000's	4.47	−0.70	0.075
Drama	100's	5.13	−0.72	0.052
French	1000's	3.64	−0.62	0.078
German	1000's	3.90	−0.61	0.082
PE/Sport	100's	3.82		0.071

The table shows the grade achieved by a female of average prior attainment score (not in receipt of free school meals) in each of the subjects listed.

Table 19.1 Relative performance levels in differing curriculum areas (estimates based on a female of average prior attainment, not on free school meals)

separately, as indicated in Table 19.1 it is possible to evaluate the degree to which subject departments within a given school offer performances which differ from those in most other schools. The grade in each subject area which individual pupils are *predicted to achieve* can be compared

246

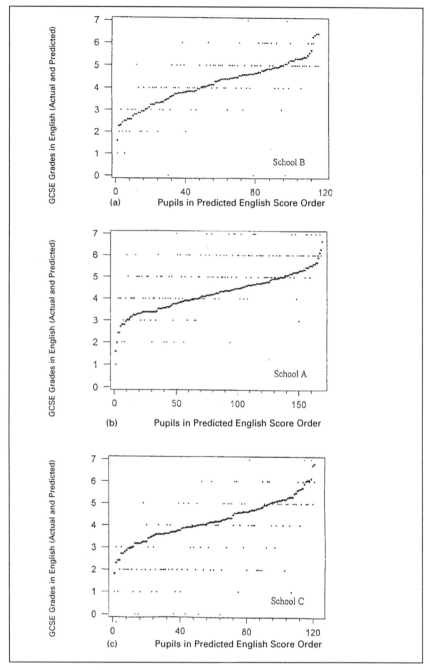

Figure 19.10 (a) English GCSE results compared with predicted grades for a school with 'around average' results (b) English GCSE results compared with predicted grades for a school with 'better than average' results (c) English GCSE results compared with predicted grades for a school with 'below average' results

with *the grades they actually obtain* – and this comparison should allow any significant differences to be identified.

An application of these ideas to the assessment of performance to three schools' English departments is shown in Figure 19.10. Here the results for both boys and girls are shown together since the predicted scores take account of the large difference in the 'expected' results between them.

The 'solid' lines in Figure 19.10 running from bottom left to top right represent the grade in English which each pupil was predicted to achieve. Pupils are then listed in order of this predicted grade – their names would constitute the horizontal axis, but in Figure 19.10 these have been suppressed in the interests of confidentiality. The other symbols represent the actual performance achieved by these pupils.

The extent to which the predictions and actual scores 'match' each other is shown (crudely) by the number of points above and below the solid line. If there are many more above than below the solid line, this provides evidence that performance for these pupils in this school is better than would be expected to occur in many other schools, and that pupils in this school outperform their counterparts in English in other schools. (The situation in School A.) In other words this suggests that this situation describes the results of 'more effective' teaching. Conversely, more points below the line than above would provide evidence of lower levels of performance than similar pupils would achieve elsewhere – and hence be indicative of 'less effective' teaching (as indicated in School C). Either way the indication provided by this form of representation is indicative of outcomes which are 'unusual' and so worthy of more detailed investigation. The 'normal' situation is represented by School B.

However, the value of this form of representation for focused enquiry does not end there. Any tendency, for example, for boys to do worse than girls even after taking account of the known characteristics of the examination itself, can be directly accessed. So also can the situation in respect of different 'sets' be established. Simply by identifying each set with a reference category, results can be sorted into 'set' order and the tendency for 'over' or 'under' performance can be established. This might even give some evidence of the effectiveness of teaching of individual teachers – although preferably one would need evidence collected over a number of years before such conclusions could be reasonably said to be established. None the less, the capacity for analyses of the kind reported here to generate much useful management information has been clearly identified.

There is, of course, a need to keep a sense of perspective in all this – and to this end it can be helpful if the limits (or the extent) of what constitutes 'normal' practice can be identified. To this end a collaborative grouping of schools, within which results are shared, can be a valuable asset in setting one's own school's results in an appropriate relative context. In fact this is already happening in many of the local areas mentioned above – and has given rise to further focused enquiry about what practices might be associated with 'good' as opposed to 'poor' outcomes for particular subject areas.

Much of this may in the first instance be speculative and exploratory – but the purpose behind it is very much in line with the goal of school improvement. By focusing on comparisons where there is evidence of consistently 'good' outcomes, schools may be helped to identify some of the characteristics which are associated with these favourable outcomes. Equally, practices which appear to disfavour pupils may also be identified in schools where the outcomes indicate that teaching (in a particular subject area) is 'less effective'.

Threshold issues: increasing the percentage of those who achieve five or more grades A* to C

One final aid to technical 'improvement' should not be overlooked. Since the 'Performance Tables' utilise discrete criteria to identify the outcomes of schools' examination results, and since the most often utilised measure is that which reports the percentage of pupils gaining five or more passes at grades A*, A, B or C, discovering what potential there might be for helping more pupils over that particular threshold would seem to be a useful additional strategy.

D Grades → ↓A – C Grades	0	1	2	3	4	5+
0	21	10	8	8	6	4
1	7	6	4	3	3	2
2	5	5	3	4	2	3
3	1	3	2	1	2	2
4	0	1	3	2	1	3

Table 19.2 The number of pupils not achieving five or more grades A to C and the number of additional D grades

Table 19.2 has as its framework, in the vertical dimension, the number of 'A* to C' passes achieved by those who did *not* achieve five or more, and, in the horizontal direction, the number of 'D' grades obtained.

The use of this table is as follows: fill in each cell with the initials of the pupils to whom it refers. In the printed version we have simply identified the number of pupils in each of the cells. The lightly shaded cells represent potential candidates whose achievements might be boosted to cross the 'five or more' threshold. Clearly, a pupil who has already gained four 'good' passes and who has four further 'D' grades should (had attention been given to this particular purpose) have been encouraged to give particular effort to one or more of these latter subject areas with a view to achieving five 'good' passes.

Identifying, first of all, who the pupils are who fall into the 'potential' achievers category is obviously important – but then, as a second stage in the exercise the subject by subject results of each of these pupils should be obtained. It is likely that this will show that in some subject areas more than others, a disproportionate number of 'potential achievers' exist. Clearly, this would suggest an opportunity for a departmental focus on these pupils in order to maximise their chances of passing this subject with an enhanced grade.

What is possible here can be further explored within the 'predicted' and 'actual' grade framework which we have discussed above – for clearly there may be greater scope in some subject areas for these 'advances' to be made.

Even though Table 19.2 is retrospective in its focus, it has helped many schools to use the 'mock' examinations taken some months before GCSE, to target particular subjects and particular pupils with a view to helping them, together, to agree courses of action aimed at enhancing the possibility of turning potential 'D' grades into something better.

This form of action is, of course, not limited to improvements at the grade D/C boundary – it can be used as a diagnostic to encourage *all* pupils to aim higher. Schools must clearly avoid the temptation to direct additional resources to 'some' potential improvers at the expense of others. Equity requires that all pupils be given the opportunity to achieve the very best they are capable of. Experience with 'threshold' groups such as those identified in Table 19.2 suggests that this has potentially powerful implications for the 'culture of achievement' across the whole school. Taken together with all the actions outlined earlier, this would complement schools' use of a value added framework in helping actively to manage their own effectiveness.

CHAPTER TWENTY

Understanding Contemporary Leaders and Leadership in Education: Values and Visions

Peter Ribbins

Identifying issues

At the time of writing, Chris Woodhead, Chief Inspector of Schools for England, was in the news. His first annual Inspection Report (OFSTED 1995) laid claim to novelty. In his preface, Woodhead noted he had 'broken with convention and identified a number of secondary schools which have both received very positive inspection reports and achieved an improvement of around or greater than 10% in their examination performance between 1992 and 1994'. He suggested that 'the vision, commitment and expertise of the teachers who work in such schools deserve the widest possible praise', and concludes by stressing his belief 'that all children deserve access to the quality of education provided by these schools' (OFSTED, 1995: 2).

If the Report is innovative in some respects, its explanations for successful education are robustly traditional, in their replication of two of the key findings common to many reports of research into school effectiveness conducted in the UK and elsewhere over the last two decades (Ribbins, 1993a, b). Firstly, that the quality of teaching matters in determining levels of pupil achievement. Secondly, that the quality of headship matters in determining the quality of the teaching which takes place within a school. In the light of these claims, in this chapter I shall draw upon my researches into headship to consider three main issues. Firstly, to examine some of the claims made in the Chief Inspector's Report. Secondly, to propose a new approach to the study of heads and headship. Thirdly, to consider the place of values and vision in the exercise of leadership and to illustrate what this might mean for headship, drawing upon some of my own research into this theme.

Teaching and leadership matters

Commenting upon the wealth of inspection evidence presented in his Report, Woodhead claims that the 'largest single factor' in determining 'pupils' standards of achievement' is 'the quality of teaching' (p.5). Given that 'the content of the National Curriculum has been settled by the Dearing review, it is issues of *teaching methodology* which ought, nationally and in individual schools, to be high on the agenda for discussion' (p.6). This is so, it is suggested, because 'it is the values and expectations, the theoretical assumptions and the professional expertise of the individual teacher that will determine whether the words on the pages of the National Curriculum order have any impact' (p.6). Happily, what constitutes 'good teaching' is not a mystery. Indeed, OFSTED comments on this matter amount to no more than a statement of the obvious: 'children achieve more when they are taught by teachers who have high, but realistic expectations; who have a firm understanding of the subject content they are teaching; who are able to explain things clearly and to use questions effectively to assess pupil knowledge and challenge their thinking; and who can deploy an intelligent balance of strategies' (p.6).

If the quality of teaching matters in determining levels of pupil achievement, it is often claimed that headship matters a great deal in determining the quality of a school and of the teaching which takes place within it. This belief is widely shared amongst the general public, educational professionals and even amongst politicians. It is replicated in reports of studies of school effectiveness from a growing number of countries, and is the norm in the literature on headship in education published in this country and elsewhere. There are some exceptions. From a survey of the findings of school effectiveness research in the Netherlands, Scheerens (1992: 65) concludes that:

> variables like … 'educational leadership' show few consistent associations with achievement. 'Education leadership' even correlates negatively now and then with educational achievement. As a possible explanation of these results one could think of a more amicable, as opposed to a more managerial, concept of a school head within Dutch schools.

Lynn Davies takes this issue further in a forthcoming paper, where she argues 'The Case for Leaderless Schools', based upon 'a vision of a school without a head at all'. This may not be quite such an eccentric idea as it might at first seem. Certainly there are precedents for it in other parts of the world including the Netherlands, Portugal and Switzerland. In some schools in the Netherlands, the principal is an elected office of relatively short duration. In Portugal, school principals tended to be seen as creatures of the Salazar regime. Following its demise, they were discredited and the system disestablished, although there have been recent demands in favour of re-establishing the role of the principal within schools. Finally, in Switzerland, some small primary schools located in German cantons do not have a principal.

But these are minority views and rare examples. In most countries, the need for the transformational leadership, which only a head is thought to be capable of offering, is assumed. Peter Gronn's forthcoming article 'Greatness re-visited: the current obsession with transformational leadership' documents this in great detail. In a personal communication he comments that 'the energy being given over to this sort of stuff (leadership studies of all kinds) by commentators is mind boggling. I have been wading through mountains of it...'.

How is this 'obsession' to be explained? As Kenneth Baker (1993: 199) once put it:

> All too often educationalists (want) to explain away the poor performance of, say, an inner-city school by reference to the socio-economic circumstances of the area in which the school was located. Certainly one should not discount such factors entirely.... On the other hand, even in these areas there can be very good schools with high levels of achievement. It depends essentially upon the leadership of the Head and the quality of the teaching.

Early in his Report, Woodhead takes such a view even further, by proposing that if the quality of teaching is the single most important influence on the standards of pupils' achievement within schools, it is 'the *leadership provided by the headteacher* which is the critical factor in improving the quality of teaching in today's schools' (OFSTED, 1995: 6). In making judgements on standards of management within a school, the Report stresses the importance of:

> the creation of an ethos and a sense of purpose which promotes standards of achievement, a high quality of pupil education and pupils' moral, social and cultural development. Account is taken of the quality of working relationships, the effectiveness and efficiency of administration, and the means of organising work and of planning, implementing and evaluating change in schools (p.23).

On the basis of such criteria, and using evidence drawn from the inspection of some 900 secondary schools, the Report concludes: 'Evidence shows that most headteachers are successful in developing a shared vision and a sense of purpose amongst staff. Relationships run for the most part smoothly and day-to-day administration is usually efficient' (p.6).

Yet, if the Report claims that in 'the majority of schools, headteachers (have) succeeded in creating a strong school ethos and effective working relationships with staff and parents' (p.23), it also suggests that many have been less successful in other aspects of their work. It is, for example, noted that

> Relatively few headteachers…spend sufficient time evaluating the quality of teaching and learning. Many should play a stronger part in curriculum development, and, in particular, should review the implementation of new initiatives to ensure that the original objectives are being achieved (p.6).

In partial mitigation of this regrettable state of affairs, it is acknowledged:

> It may be that headteachers do not at present see these tasks as key responsibilities. It may be that the responsibility is accepted, but thought, because of other pressures, impossible to discharge…it is certain that the right sort of training, before and during headship, has not been available. (p.6)

For a study which draws upon some 900 inspection reports, these latter speculations – on what might or might not be the views of secondary headteachers, on what they might or might not regard as their key responsibilities as educational leaders during a period of intense change – are curiously tentative. It may also be that some of the findings presented in the Report are questionable. Consider, first, the degree of significance which headteachers attach to their curricular responsibilities, as compared with their other tasks.

Much recent writing on the role of the contemporary secondary headteacher has tended to suggest that, in attempting to cope with implementing the many innovations arising from the unrelenting pace of recent educational reform, many secondary headteachers tended, initially at least, to focus on their 'administrative' rather than on their 'curricular' functions. Writing in the wake of the Education Reform Act of 1988, Williams (1988: ix, xi), for example, predicted that

> The daily life of English headteachers in the 1990s will be very different from their predecessors a generation earlier…. Much of the curriculum responsibility of heads will be taken away and guidelines about the implementation of the National Curriculum will be issued from government agencies…. Heads will become managers of an imposed curriculum rather than partners in curriculum development. However, at the same time schools and their heads are to be given greater financial autonomy, and they will have to consider economic issues such as the most effective and efficient ways to deliver a given curriculum. Financial skills such as drawing up budgets, control of budget management and management information systems will loom large in the day-to-day life of headteachers and their senior colleagues as the Education Reform Act is implemented.

From such a perspective, the role of the headteacher is seen as shifting from that of the school's 'leading professional' to that of its 'chief executive' (Hughes, 1975). As such it is based upon a model which has had its exponents amongst both practitioners and researchers. This model makes two assumptions. Firstly, that the orientation which headteachers bring to their work can be defined in terms of the role response which they make to a continuum of responsibility. Towards one polar end of this are located a set of administrative tasks, and towards the other a set of curriculum duties. Secondly, that as heads emphasise one aspect of their role they must do so at the expense of the other. I have argued elsewhere (Ribbins, 1993a: 35) that these assumptions seem unduly restrictive, and that an alternative might be to see the two dimensions as largely independent of each other. As such it is possible to envisage headteachers as taking a high (or low) orientation to either, or both, their administrative or curricular functions. In practice, I discovered that teachers and headteachers had little trouble in using this model to classify heads whom they knew.

I also found some headteachers who felt that recent developments had forced them to reduce their role as active managers of development and quality in the curriculum. As one put it:

> With an increasingly detailed and prescriptive National Curriculum being imposed on schools I feel myself a curriculum functionary ... I am also busy trying to ensure the school survives in the kind of competitive world the Government have created. I have to spend more and more time on marketing and managing our inadequate budget. This means I cannot give the curriculum as much of my attention as I want to and as I used to.

However, other headteachers have increasingly contested the idea that recent reforms have established a much greater priority to the administrative dimension of their work. In doing so, they commonly make one or both of two main points.

Firstly, that coming to terms with the new administrative and budgetary responsibilities, which they were forced to carry in the wake of the 1988 Act and subsequent legislation, had been a demanding experience yet, within just 2 years, many of them had managed to achieve this. As one pointed out:

> It was quite difficult at first. I did not come into headship expecting to carry the detailed financial, staffing, marketing and other administrative responsibilities I am now expected to exercise. I did find I had to spend a lot of time on this in the early days but we got a lot of help from the LEA and once I understood what needed to be done and had some experience in doing it I have not felt so swamped by it. When I talk to other colleagues I get the impression that most of them feel the same way.

Secondly, some heads believe that those who have emphasised the administrative, at the expense of the curricular dimension of their role, have often chosen to do so. This view was forcefully expressed by one experienced headteacher. Speaking even before the publication of the Dearing curriculum review he said:

> Achieving a worthwhile curriculum today is possible and very demanding. It is not surprising that some heads are more comfortable retreating into their

administrative duties ... They do so because they want to. But to allow yourself to be trapped into an administrative role is a road to isolation. It sets up barriers. If you see yourself as an administrator you can hardly hope to be a leading professional as well.

In summary, most of the headteachers I have studied have sought to play a major role in evaluating the quality of teaching and learning within the classroom and have given great emphasis to the curricular aspect of their responsibilities.

Furthermore, whilst the OFSTED Report stresses the importance of such concepts as values and vision in the expression of leadership within the secondary school, the reader is given remarkably little help in understanding what these might actually mean for the theory, practice and praxis of headship. These are important and sometimes misused concepts, which are worth some reflection. The distinctions they entail, as Hodgkinson (1991: 42–43) has noted, were first made by Aristotle:

> who taught what our present day schools of administrative theory...seem to have forgotten, namely there are three ways of knowing and dealing with the world, three modes of action. He called them *theoria (theory), techne* (technique) and *praxis*. Aristotle intended *praxis* to mean ethical action in a political context, or purposeful human conduct, or behaviour informed and guided by purposes, intentions, motives, morals, emotions and values *as well* as the facts or 'science' of the case.... It implies a duality in action....one of consciousness or reflection...and one of action and commitment....Praxis suggests the conscious reflective intentional action of man, as opposed to mere reflex....The educational leader whose time is spent dealing with emergent problems...is not likely to be involved in praxis.... Such an administrator is not leading and, more important, is following or being led.

Since the late 1970s, I explored these and related themes in my studies of leadership in education. My research can by no means match the weight of classroom based observations produced by the hundreds of inspectors who have gathered the evidence upon which the Chief Inspector's Report is based. However, it has the possible compensating advantages of having used a wide range of research methodologies and having attempted to focus specifically on exploring in some depth the personal, professional and managerial attitudes and actions of more than thirty secondary headteachers.

At this point the reader, knowing that no other role within the British system has been investigated with such sustained intensity as that of the secondary headteacher, may shudder at the prospect of reading yet another theory, purporting to justify the need for yet another new approach to the study of leadership in education. Those who feel this way will be in distinguished company. In an interview with Christopher Hodgkinson on the occasion of his impending retirement I asked him what he was trying to say in his justly famous book on *The Philosophy of*

Leadership (1982). He replied:

> I set out to explore the swamp of literature on leadership. It goes on and on and ranges from the sublime to the ridiculous with little in between. Taken as a whole it is a shambles, a mess full of philosophical confusion. If you could burn words at the stake in the same way the Nazis burnt books, the first word I would suggest is leadership. It is full of word magic of the worst kind. I was moved to write a book on leadership to get this message across. (in Ribbins, 1993a: 21).

If this was not the answer I had anticipated from one of the most distinguished, and prolific, students of leadership of recent times it did make me wonder if I might not give a somewhat similar answer, were I to be asked to comment upon the extant literature on headship.

The case for a new approach

Secondary headship has long attracted the attention of researchers within the UK. This dates from the last century, when it mainly took the form of accounts of the careers and views of some of the foremost headmasters of the day, including Arnold of Rugby, Butler of Shrewsbury, Keate of Eton and Thring of Uppingham. Curiously, with a few exceptions, such as Thomas and Bailey's wonderful *Letters to a Young Headmaster* (1927), little of note took place in the study of post-Victorian headship during the first 70 years and more of this century. Since then, research into the nature of contemporary heads and headship has grown apace. The literature can be classified in various ways (*see* Ribbins and Marland, 1994: 3–4). It includes numerous surveys, autobiographies, autobiographical statements, biographies and case studies of schools which, to a greater or a lesser extent, are concerned with the role of the headteacher. Given the existence of this extensive, rich and varied literature, what is the case for yet more studies of headship? I offer two justifications.

Firstly, much of the available literature, within the UK at least, draws on research conducted in the 1970s and before. Yet, as Reynolds and Parker (1992: 178) have noted:

> The complexity of the contemporary situation in which he or she is likely to be, the overload of pressures – all these are likely to call for a style of effective headteacher very different from the one-dimensional creatures that stalk through the present day literature within school-effectiveness.

What we 'know' of headship, it can be argued, relates largely to a bygone age. However, there is another sense in which heads have been presented as 'one dimensional creatures', that offers a further justification for more studies of headship. It may be that methods used to study headship in the past have led to the depiction of headteachers in monochrome. John Rae, in *Delusions of Grandeur: A Headteacher's Life* (1993: 11–12), sets out 'to explore, through my own experience, the role of the English public school headmaster'. He claims that existing biographies and autobiographies 'do not tell you much about what it is really like to do the job' (p.11). In his view 'fiction has been more successful in entering the headmaster's mind' (p.11). Even so, for Rae, 'Auchincloss is the only author who understands how the master's personality influences the way he will play the role *and* how the demands of the role draw out particular aspects of his personality (p.11). Furthermore, it might be equally interesting to note the ways in which the personality of a headteacher shapes, and is shaped by, the ways in which he or she enacts the role.

To tackle such issues requires not just more research, but new methods of research. I have listed (Ribbins, 1993b) six propositions which, taken together, might offer a 'new' and potentially helpful framework for the study of contemporary headship during a period of radical educational reform. At the core of this approach is the idea that we need evidence which is contemporary in its relevance and that, to collect this, we may need to augment traditional methods with a new approach to the study of headship in the 1990s. Such an approach might enable the production of accounts of headship which *contextualises* in three main ways.

Firstly, as a *situated perspective*. Many accounts of headship are based upon surveys which typically claim to be more or less representative of the views of headteachers as a whole. From these surveys the researcher extracts composite, glossed accounts of key issues which may represent more or less accurately the views of the sample as a whole, or the ideas of a particular head on one or more topics. Whatever its merits, it is still hard to see how this approach can possibly offer a rich and comprehensive understanding of the *perspectives* and *styles* heads bring to their role. For this to be possible the reader must be offered a much fuller access to the *views* and *actions* of individual headteachers across a representative range of *issues* and *events*.

Such an approach would present a set of portraits of individual heads each reported in depth. It can take a variety of forms. Mortimer and Mortimer (1991) invited a small number of headteachers to respond *in writing* to a set of issues specified by the researchers. Marland and I (Ribbins and Marland, 1994) recorded a series of *face-to-face* interviews in preparing for *Headship Matters*. This approach has proved so effective that with another head, Brian Sherratt, I have used it in a study of political leadership and national policy making entitled *Conservative Secretaries of State and Radical Educational Policies*. I plan to use it again in studies of leadership in primary education. This approach has been used with great effect by Kogan and his collaborators, in interviews with ministers of education (1971) and chief education officers (1973).

Secondly, as a *contextualised perspective*. Traditional reports of headship *decontextualise* in the way which has been described above, but also sometimes do so, in so far as they do not attempt to locate what heads say within a context of the views of *significant others* (senior and other staff, pupils, parents and governors) within the *community of the school*. A contextualised perspective would seek to give the reader some access to such information.

Thirdly, as a *contextualised perspective in action*. Few extant studies explore what heads say (as described above) in the context of what they do. To offer a contextualised perspective in action the researcher must do four things. Firstly, to observe heads as they enact their role in relevant situations. Secondly, to discuss with heads what they are trying to do and why. Thirdly, to set these accounts against the views of significant others. Finally, to compare and contrast the available evidence, in the hope of producing the kind of enriched portrait of headteachers and of headship that is sought. Without fully being aware of every aspect of these arguments, I have come to realise that, in practice, I have been employing a kind of third level approach to the study of heads and headship, since the mid-seventies and our research at Rivendell. Our published account of that research takes the form of a long chapter on 'Management, Continuity and Change' in which we explore the characteristics of three regimes of headship at the school, in terms of the educational and managerial vision and values which three successive headteachers claimed to espouse; how these claims were regarded by others within the school; and, how far three very different heads sought to enact their vision and values in practice, and with what effect (Best *et al.*, 1983).

It is possible, and worthwhile, to engage in research into headship in each of these ways. It is also possible to regard them taken together, as amounting to a comprehensive research programme made up of *three levels* in which the second level subsumes the first and the third level subsumes the second and the first. Since 1989 I have been involved in such third level research at Great Barr which, with 2300 pupils of between 11 and 18, is the largest school in the UK. At first, this research was informed by the ideas we had begun to develop at Rivendell, and which I had sought to refine elsewhere. As such, the study at Great Barr was planned to focus on an examination of the way in which a large urban comprehensive school was responding to the educational reform agenda initiated by the 1988 Education Act. However, as the research progressed I became increasingly interested in the role of the head as an interpreter and enactor of change. With the headteacher, Brian Sherratt, I have tried to develop a novel third level approach to the study of headship, based upon an elaboration of the ideas outlined above. In this version the head becomes both the principal subject of the research and also a full partner within it. As such the research we are jointly engaged in is *autobiographical*, in so far as it requires and enables the head, as *internal researcher*, to reflect systematically and critically upon his *praxis* during a period of intense reform. He has done this in a variety of ways including over 30 interviews with me, the production of a frank diary of his everyday life as a head and the systematic collection of relevant documentation. The study is also biographical in so far as I, as external researcher, have recorded interviews with well over 200 significant others including teachers and other staff, pupils, parents and governors and have observed a variety of events related to the exercise of his management in practice. We have almost completed the field research and have just begun what is likely to be an exhaustive process of writing it up.

I hope readers will suspend judgement on the merits of the approach as a whole until they can consider our final report on *Brian Sherratt at Great Barr School.* Yet it is already possible to examine what a first level study might look like, by reading the portraits of the seven very different headteachers reported in *Headship Matters,* and in doing so, to consider its merits as a means of developing an understanding of the vision and values of Sue Benton, Valerie Bragg, Peter Downes, Elaine Foster, Michael Marland, Brian Sherratt and Harry Tomlinson. In this context, my final section returns to an examination of the place of values in educational leadership.

The place of values in educational leadership

In their introductory chapter to their book, Bell and Harrison stress the significance of the role played by Thomas Greenfield and Christopher Hodgkinson, in rediscovering the centrality of the place of values in the praxis of educational leadership. They are surely right to call our attention to this but, whilst Greenfield and Hodgkinson have much in common, there are also interesting differences between their positions, which seem worth pursuing further.

Both urge more reflection in leadership. Greenfield made the point powerfully (*see* Greenfield and Ribbins, 1993: 262) when commenting upon the classic work, *The Consolation of Philosophy,* he said:

> The story of Boethius is touching. He was a Christian who stood at the hinge between the Roman World and the Middle Ages. He is an administrator, one caught between the Emperor and the Pope. He is condemned, and as he awaits his death he thinks back on his career and writes, thus bringing a new insight to the administrative task. Few of us will face the horror that Boethius did, but I am convinced that potentially there is that same dimension in all administrative rule, a kind of horror. The wielding of power is terrible, and the more power, the more terrible. If there is to be some kind of humanizing of that power a contemplative, philosophical dimension must and should be brought to it. Perhaps to do the thing at all requires … a need for a meditation on values.

Greenfield believed that if such a meditation is to take place then:

> the ultimate training of a leader would be a kind of philosophical withdrawal

to look at the larger issues in fresh perspective.... A deeply clinical approach to the training of administrators in needed, as it is for teachers. Our training is disjointed, reflection is separated from action, thinking from doing, praxis from the practical. Why do we merely throw people at these jobs, expecting them to do well with almost no experience of them, offering them no *analysis* of their experience.

In developing these ideas, he notes that:

One of the things I have sensed in speaking to leaders in education, is how impoverished their real world is. They don't see beyond a narrow horizon. They don't see the problems of education, except in rather technological terms, or if they do see it, if they talk about it in larger terms, they are sentimental and platitudinous. We need leaders in education who can think about the larger issues.... But it will be an uphill struggle to bring them to such contemplation .... The headlong pressure to act, to do, to be the leader militates against a reflective attitude – a stance that is needed for the growth of worthwhile values, of character. That is what I see as the ultimate in the nurture of leaders through training. It would be aimed at persons in power, fostering awareness of values and of the value choices that face them, and thereby perhaps assisting character growth. (pp.258, 259).

As such, in making decisions about their selection and training:

All we can do is work with the character of leaders. This is a distinction Hodgkinson makes. Whereas studies of leadership in the positivistic mode have looked at the characteristics of leaders, what is important is their character. (p.259)

In so far as Greenfield implies that leaders are reluctant to reflect on value issues, this does not square with Hodgkinson's experience or with my studies of heads and other educational leaders. As Hodgkinson notes:

From the beginning I have had an obsession with administrative man and the concept of values. Real life administrators are often thought to have a minimal attention span, a contempt for all things intellectual and a pride in their tough images, but I have found that when you start talking about values you can establish an instant rapport with them. Values are the key to their interest. They know what you are talking about. You are onto something which is important to them. (in Ribbins, 1993a:15)

Certainly, all the heads interviewed for *Headship Matters* talked a good deal of their efforts to achieve a shared vision for the school, and the struggle to clarify and apply their values as leading educators in practice. Brian Sherratt, for example, saw 'building the ethos of the school and... working at it daily' as 'absolutely crucial'. Such an ethos, he emphasises, must be expressed in the values *and* the procedures of the school. It is:

because we have these *values* this is the way we do these things.... On the whole teachers are not very happy with philosophical talk. They tend to say 'That's philosophy, it's nothing to do with ... the realities of the job'; but it can

be, and if they can see the principles which drive the way the institution wants to do things, and if this can be broken down into the things they do in the classroom and the yard … they will accept that this stress on values can be helpful. (Ribbins and Marland, 1994: 170).

In thinking about the nature of the good leader and of effective headship, I am reminded of Greenfield's account of St Paul:

He shows us what it is to be a good leader. His combination of vision with untiring effort and endless recipes and advice for making things work, seeing where values require taking a stand on what matters, and working out their implications for practical reality.… That's leadership, and it has a political element woven with the visionary. He is filled with concern for the world as it is and how to change it and organise it but at the same time he is touched by…a transcendental vision. (Greenfield and Ribbins, 1993: 260)

With this in mind, re-reading my many interviews with heads before and after *Headship Matters*, I am struck again and again by the unending commitment so many expect of themselves as a matter of course. As Sue Benton says:

In a sense it is an impossible job, but…I would not want to do anything else. We could all do with 48 hours in the day but these are not available so we have to do the best with the twenty four that we can.… This is a job which could easily become your life. It takes up such a lot of your time and energy. (Ribbins and Marland, 1994: 55)

Brian Sherratt, when asked how he deals with pressure responded, 'I cope with it by working. I work long hours by virtue of necessity. During the week my life is Great Barr and at the weekends what I try to do is to be a good husband and father' (p.181). Peter Downes casually notes:

I have to confess that I probably work too hard. I think I probably work about 75-80 hours a week.… The difficulty in working such long hours is that I find myself having to make certain decisions without having given the matter enough thought or without having read widely enough. (p.99)

A final reflection

In this final chapter, I have noted some claims made about the relationship between the quality of leadership, particularly that of the headteacher, within secondary schools and the quality of schooling and pupil achievement. In doing so, I have stressed the centrality of values to the praxis of leadership and have sought to illustrate, in a preliminary way, the merits of a *three-level approach* relevant to the study of headship within the contemporary secondary school.

In a concluding reflection on leaders in education, Hodgkinson observed that, 'History is the biography of great men, but educational administration is the biography of ungreat men' (in Ribbins, 1993a:24).

As a summary of what he really thinks, this characteristically wry comment should probably be treated with some caution. In any case it does not accurately reflect my own experience of educational leaders. In particular, amongst the headteachers, primary and secondary, I have known and studied more than 20 years, I can think of many I would not scruple to describe as 'great men', or as 'great women'.

References

Adler, S., Laney, J. and Packer, M. (1993) *Managing Women*. Buckingham: Open University Press.

Argyris, C. (1991) 'Teaching Smart People How to Learn', *Harvard Business Review,* May–June.

Argyris, C. and Schön, D. A. (1974) *Theory in Practice: Increasing Professional Effectiveness*. London: Jossey-Bass.

Aspin, D., Chapman, J. and Wilkinson, V. (1994) *Quality Schooling*. London: Cassell.

Assistant Masters and Mistresses Association (AMMA) (1987) *Teacher Stress: Where Do We Go From Here?* London: AMMA.

Assistant Masters and Mistresses Association (AMMA) (1990) *Managing Stress. Guidelines for Teachers*. London: AMMA.

Audit Commission (1985) *Obtaining Better Value From Further Education*. London: HMSO.

Audit Commission (1989) *Assuring Quality in Education: The Role of LEA Inspectors and Advisers*. London: HMSO.

Auld, R. (1976) *William Tyndale Junior and Infants Schools Public Enquiry*. London: ILEA.

Bailey, D. and Sprotson, C. (1987) *Understanding Stress*. Part Three. London: HMSO.

Baker, K. (1993) *The Turbulent Years: My Life in Politics*. London: Faber and Faber.

Barber, M. (1992) 'Practising Fearlessness: Quality in Professional Development in the 1990s', *British Journal of In-Service Education,* **15** (1), 29–31.

Barnett, C. (1986) *Audit of War: the Illusions and Reality of Britain as a Great Nation*. London: Macmillan.

Bartlett, F.C. (1932) *Remembering. A Study in Social Psychology*. London: Cambridge University Press.

Bates, S. (1990) 'A crumbling right wing revolution born of revenge or a guilty conscience', *Guardian,* 23 November.

Beattie, N. (1990) 'The wider context: are curricula manageable?', in Brighouse, T. and Moon, B. (eds). *Managing The National Curriculum: Some Critical Perspectives*. Harlow: Longman/BEMAS.

Beave, H., Caldwell, B. and Millikan, R. (1989) *Creating an Excellent School*. London: Routledge.

Becher, T. (1989) 'The National Curriculum and the Implementation Gap', in Preedy, M. (ed.). *Approaches to Curriculum Management*. Buckingham: Open University Press.

Becher, T. and Kogan, M. (1992) *Process and Structure in Higher Education,* 2nd edn. London: Routledge.

Bell, L. (1992) *Managing Teams in Secondary Schools*. London: Routledge.

Benn, T. (1989) *Against the Tide (Diaries 1973–76)*. London: Hutchinson.

Bennett, N., Glatter, R. and Levacic, R. (eds) (1994) *Improving Educational Management*. London: Paul Chapman/Open University.

Bennis, W. (1989) *On Becoming a Leader*. California: Addison-Wesley.

Best, R., Ribbins, P., Jarvis, C. and Oddy, D. (1983) *Education and Care*. London: Heinemann.

Bigelow J. D. (ed.) (1991) *Managerial Skills Explorations in Practical Knowledge*. London: Sage.

Birch, D. (1988) *Managing Resources in Further Education: A Handbook for Managers.* Blagdon: Further Education Staff College.

Blackburn, K. (1975) *The Tutor.* London: Heinemann.

Blackburn, K. (1983) 'The Pastoral Head: A developing role', *Pastoral Care in Education.* **1(2)**, 18–24.

Blackmore, J. (1989) 'Educational Leadership: a Feminist Critique and Reconstruction', in Smyth, J. (ed.). *Critical Perspectives on Educational Leadership.* London: The Falmer Press.

Bloch, A. M. (1978) 'Combat neurosis in inner city schools', *American Journal of Psychiatry,* **135**, 189–92.

Bolam, R., McMahon, A., Pocklington, K. and Weindling, D. (1993) *Effective Management in Schools. A Report for the Department of Education via the School Management Task Force Professional Working Party.* London: DFE/HMSO.

Bolman, L. G. and Deal, T. E. (1984) *Modern Approaches to Understanding and Managing Organisations.* San Francisco: Jossey Bass.

Bolman, L. G. and Deal, T. E. (1991) *Reframing Organisations. Artistry, Choice and Leadership.* San Francisco: Jossey Bass.

Bottery, M. (1992) *The Ethics of Educational Management.* London: Cassell.

Bottery, M. (1994) *Lessons for Schools?* London: Cassell.

Boyd-Barrett, O., Bush, T., Goodey, J., McNay, I. and Preedy, M. (eds) (1983) *Approaches to Post-School Management.* London: Harper and Row.

Bradley, F. H. (1962) *Ethical Studies.* 2nd revised edn. Oxford: Oxford University Press.

Bradley, J., Chesson, R. and Silverleaf, J. (1983) *Inside Staff Development.* Windsor: Nelson/NFER.

Bridges, D. (1994) 'Parents: Customers or Partners?', in Bridges, D. and McLaughlin, T. H.(eds) *Education and the Market Place.* London: Falmer.

Brighouse, T. (1991) *What Makes a Good School?* Stafford: Network Educational Press.

Brown, M. and Ralph, S. (1992) 'Towards the identification of stress in teachers', *Research in Education,* **48**, 103–110.

Brown, M. and Ralph, S. (1994) *Managing Stress in Schools.* Plymouth: Northcote House.

Burridge, E. and Ribbins, P. (1994) 'Promoting Improvement in Schools: Aspects of Quality in Birmingham', in Ribbins P. and Burridge E. (eds). *Improving Education: Promoting Quality in Schools.* London: Cassell.

Burrows, R. and Loader, B. (1994) *Towards a Post-Fordist Welfare State?* London: Routledge.

Bush, T. and West-Burnham, J. (eds) (1994) *The Principles of Educational Management.* Harlow: Longman.

Caldwell, B. J. and Spinks, J. (1986) *Policy-making and Planning for School Effectiveness.* Hobart: Education Department: Tasmania.

Caldwell, B. J. and Spinks, J. (1992) *Leading The Self-Managing Team.* London: Falmer Press.

Calvert, M. and Henderson, J. (1994) 'Newly Qualified Teachers: Do We Prepare Them for their Pastoral Role?', *Pastoral Care in Education,* **12(2)**, 7–12.

Campbell-Evans, G. (1993) 'A values perspective on school based management', in Dimmock, C. (ed.) *School-Based Management and School Effectiveness.* London: Routledge.

Cantor, D. and Bernay, T. (1992) *Women in Power: The Secrets of Leadership.* Boston: Houghton Mifflin Company.

Carlson, R. (1975) 'Environmental constraints and organisational consequences: the public school and its clients', in Baldridge, J. V. and Deal, T. E (eds). *Managing Change in Educational Organisations.* Berkeley: McCutchen.

CCCS (Centre for Contemporary Cultural Studies) (1981). *Unpopular Education: Schooling and Social Democracy in England Since 1944.* London: Hutchinson (in association with CCCS).

Chervin, R. (1986) *Feminine, Free and Faithful.* San Francisco: Ignatius Press.

Chin, R. and Benne, K. (1974) 'General Strategies for effecting changes in human systems', in Bennis, W., Benne, K. and Chin, R. (eds). *The Planning of Change.* New

York: Holt, Rinehart and Winston.

Chisolm, L. (1994) 'Lessons from Europe? On the political curriculum of shadow boxing', in Lawrence, I. (ed.) *Education Tomorrow*. London: Cassell.

Clark, B. R. (1983) *The Higher Education System: Academic Organisation in Cross-national Perspective*. Berkeley: University of California Press.

Clark, C. K. M.(1992) 'Teachers as designers in self-directed professional development', in Hargreaves, A. and Fullan, M. (eds). *Understanding Teacher Development*. London: Cassell; and New York: Teachers College Press.

Cohen, A. R., Fink, S. L., Gadon, H. and Willits, R. D.(1976) *Behaviour in Organisations*. Homewood, I. Irwin-Dorsey.

Cohen, M. and March, J. G. (1986) *Leadership and Ambiguity – The American College President*. Bolton: Harvard Business School Press. First published in 1974 by McCraw-Hill, New York.

Coleman, M. (1994) 'Women in Educational Management', in Bush, T. and West-Burnham, J. (eds). *The Principles of Educational Management*. Harlow: Longman.

Constable, J. and McCormack, R. (1987) *The Making of British Managers*. London: BIME,CBI.

Cooper, B. and Shute, W. (eds) (1988) *Training for School Management*. London: Bedford Way Paper 35.

Cordingley, P. and Kogan, M. (1993) *In Support of Education: the Functioning of Local Government*. London: Jessica Kingsley Publishers.

Cowham, T. (1994) 'Strategic Planning in the Changing External Context', in Crawford, M., Kydd, L. and Parker, S. (eds). *Educational Management into Action*. London: Paul Chapman/Open University Press.

Cox, C. B. and Dyson, A. E. (1969) *Black Paper One: The Fight for Education*. London: Critical Quarterly Society.

Cox, C. B. and Dyson, A. E. (1970) *Black Paper Two: The Crisis in Education*. London: Critical Quarterly Society.

Cox, T., Cox., S, Farnworth, W. and Boot, N. (with Walton, C. and Ferguson, E.) (1989) *Teachers and Schools: A Study of Organisational Health and Stress*. London: NUT.

Crawford, M., Kydd, L. and Parker, S. (eds) (1994) *Educational Management into Action*. London: Paul Chapman/Open University Press.

Crosby, P.(1979) *Quality is Free*. New York: Mentor Books.

Darking, L. (1991) 'The Equalizer', *The Times Educational Supplement*, 3 May, 1.

Davidson, M. J. and Cooper, C. C. (1992) *Shattering the Glass Ceiling: The Woman Manager*. London: Paul Chapman.

Davies, B., Ellison, L., Osborne, A. and West-Burnham, J. (eds) (1990) *Education Management for the 1990's*. Harlow: Longman.

Davies, J. L. (1992) 'Developing a strategy for internationalisation in universities: towards a conceptual framework', in Klasek, C. B. (ed.). *Bridges to the Future: Strategies for Internationalizing Higher Education*. Carbondale, Illinois: AIEA.

Davies, J. L. and Morgan, A. W. (1983) 'Management of higher education institutions in a period of contraction and uncertainty', in Boyd-Barrett, O., Bush, T., Goodey, J. McNay, I. and Preedy, M. (eds) *Approaches To Post-School Management*. London: Harper and Row.

Davies, L. (1990) *Equity and Efficiency? School Management in an International Context*. London: The Falmer Press.

Davies, L. (unpublished paper) 'The case for leaderless schools'.

Davis, O.L.(1990) 'Who is the Curriculum Customer?' *Curriculum*, 11(1), 38–42.

Day, C. (1993) 'Reflection: a Necessary but not Sufficient Condition for Professional Development', *British Educational Research Journal*, 19(1), 83–93.

Day, C. (1991) 'Quality Assurance and Professional Development', *British Journal of In-Service Education*, 17(3), 189–94.

Day, C. and Gilroy, D. P. (1993) 'The Erosion of INSET in England and Wales: Analysis and Proposals for a Redefinition', *Journal of Education for Teaching*, 19(1), 66–93.

Dennison, B. (1990). 'Jobs for the middlemen', *Times Educational Supplement*, 19 October.

DES (Department of Education and Science) (1977) *Education in Schools: A Consultative Document,* Cmnd 6869. London: HMSO.

DES (1978) *Special Educational Needs,* (Warnock Report). London: HMSO.

DES (1989) *Standards in Schools 1987–88: The Annual Report of HM Senior Chief Inspector of Schools.* London: DES.

DES (1990) *Developing School Management: The Way Forward.* Report by the School Management TAsk Force. London: HMSO.

DES (Department of Education and Science) (1991a) *School Teacher Appraisal.* Circular 12/91. London: HMSO.

DES (1991b) *Testing 7 year olds in 1991: Results of the National Curriculum Assessments in England.* London: DES.

DES (1991c) *Education (School Teacher) Appraisal Regulations.* London: HMSO.

Department of Education and Science and Welsh Office (1987) *Managing Colleges Efficiently.* London: HMSO.

DFE (1992, 1993a, 1994) *School and College Performance Tables.* London: Department for Education.

DFE (1993b) *Effective Management in Schools. A Report for the Department for Education via the School Management Task Force Professional Working Party,* compiled by Bolam, R., McMahon, A., Pocklington, K. and Weindling, D. London: HMSO.

Drucker, P. (1988a) *Management.* London: Pan Books.

Drucker, P. (1988b) 'The coming of the new organisation', *Harvard Business Review,* **Jan/Feb,** 45–53.

Duignan, P. A. and Macpherson, R. J. S. (eds) (1992) *Effective Leadership. A Practical Theory for New Administrators and Managers.* London: Falmer.

Duignan, P. and MacPherson, R. (1993) 'Educative Leadership: a Practical Theory', *Educational Administration Quarterly,* **29(10),** 8–33.

Dunford, J. (1993) *Managing the School for Inspection.* London: Secondary Heads Association.

Dunham, J. (1992) *Stress in Teaching.* London: Routledge.

Dunlap, D. and Schmuck, P. (1995) *Women Leading in Education.* Albany: State University of New York Press.

Earley, P. (1992) *Standards for School Management: The School Management Competences Project.* Slough: School Management South and NFER.

Ellison, L. (1990) 'Managing Stress in Schools', in Davies, B., Ellison, L., Osborne, A. and West-Burnham, J. (eds). *Education Management for the 1990s.* Harlow: Longman

Eraut, M. (1994) *Developing Professional Knowledge and Competence.* London: The Falmer Press.

Eraut, M. (1986) 'Friends or foes?' *Times Educational Supplement,* 4 September, 4.

Fielden, J. (1975) 'The decline of the professor and the rise of the registrar', in Page, G. F. (ed.). *Power and Authority in Higher Education.* Guildford: SRHE.

Fitz-Gibbon, C. (1994) 'Performance Indicators, Value Added and Quality Assurance', in Ribbins, P. and Burridge, E. (eds). *Improving Education: Promoting Quality in Schools.* London: Cassell.

Fletcher, N. (1990) 'The Education Reform Act and Educational Politics', in Morris, R. (ed.). *Central and Local Control of Education after the Education Reform Act 1988.* Harlow: Longman/BEMAS.

Freire, P. (1972) *Cultural Action for Freedom.* London: Penguin.

Friedman, M. and Rosenman, R. (1974) *Type A Behaviour and Your Heart.* Fawcett, Conneticutt: Greenwich Publications.

Fullan, M.(1991) *The New Meaning of Educational Change.* London: Cassell.

Fullan, M.(1992) 'Visions that blind', *Educational Leadership,* **49(5),** 19–22.

Fullan, M. (1993) *Change Forces. Probing the Depths of Educational Reform.* London: Falmer Press.

Fullan, M. and Hargreaves, A. (1992) *What's Worth Fighting for in Your School?* Buckingham: Open University Press/Ontario Public School Teachers' Federation.

Management, and Careers in the 1990s. London: Unwin Hyman.

Ketteringham, J. (1987) 'Pupils' Perceptions of the Role of the Form Tutor', *Pastoral Care in Education*, **5(3)**, 206–217.

Kim, W. C. and Mauborgne, F. A. (1992) 'Parables of Leadership', *Harvard Business Review*, **July-August**, 123–128.

Kogan, M. (1971) *The Politics of Education: Edward Boyle and Anthony Crossland.* Harmondsworth: Penguin.

Kogan, M. (1973) *County Hall LEA: The Role of the Chief Education Officer.* Harmondsworth: Penguin.

Kogan, M. (1993) 'Cut out the blather'. *Times Educational Supplement,* 16 July.

Lakomski, G. and Evers, C. (1994) 'Greenfield's Humane Science', *Educational Management and Administration,* **22(4)**, 260–69.

Lally, V., Knutton, S., Windale, M. and Henderson, J. (1992) 'A Collaborative Teacher-centred Model of In-service Education', *Educational Review,* **44(2)**, 111–26.

Lang, P. (1983) 'How Pupils See It: Looking at How Pupils Perceive Pastoral Care', *Pastoral Care in Education,* **1(3)**, 164–75.

Langland, E. and Gove, W. (1983) *A Feminist Perspective in the Academy: the Difference it Makes.* Chicago:The University of Chicago Press.

Lawrence, I. (1994) *Education Tomorrow.* London: Cassell.

Lawton, D. (1989). *The Education Reform Act: Choice and Control.* London: Hodder and Stoughton.

Leat, D. (1993) *Managing Across Sectors.* London: City University Business School.

Lindop Report (1985) *Academic Validation in Public Sector Higher Education.* Report of the Committee of Enquiry into the academic validation of degree courses in public sector higher education. Cmnd 9501. London: HMSO.

Lorriman, J. L. and Takashi Kenjo (1994) *Japan's Winning Margins: Management, Training and Education.* Oxford: Oxford University Press.

MacNamara, D. (1992) 'The Reform of Teacher Education in England and Wales: Teacher Competence: Panacea or Rhetoric?' *Journal of Education for Teaching,* **18(3)**, 273–87.

Macpherson, R.J.S. (1992) 'Educative Leadership and the Co-option of Corporate Managerialism and Oligarchic Politics', in Simkins, T., Ellison, L. and Garrett, V. (eds). *Implementing Educational Reform. The Early Lessons.* Harlow: Longman/BEMAS, pp.277–92.

Maden, M. (1990). 'Danger in DIY democracy', *Times Educational Supplement,* 30 November.

Marland, M. (1989) *The Tutor and the Tutor Group.* London: Longman.

Marsh, C. (1994) 'An Analysis of Selected School Improvement Practices', in Bennett, N., Glatter, R. and Levacic, R. (eds). *Improving Educational Management.* London: Paul Chapman/Open University.

Maslow, A. H. (1954) *Motivation and Personality.* New York: Harper and Row.

McGill, I. and Beaty L. (1992) *Action Learning: A Practioner's Guide.* London: Kogan Page.

McGuiness, J. (1989) *A Whole-School Approach to Pastoral Care.* London: Kogan Page.

McMullen, H. (1991) 'The Role of Appraisal in Staff Development', in Bell, L. and Day, C. (eds). *Managing the Professional Development of Teachers.* Buckingham: Open University Press.

McNamara, D. (1990). 'The National Curriculum: an agenda for research', *British Educational Research Journal,* **16 (3)**, 225–35.

McNay, I. (1988) *Coping with Crisis.* London: Longman.

McNay, I. (ed.) (1992) *Visions of Post-compulsory Education.* Buckingham: Open University Press.

McNay, I. (1994) *Universities Going International: Choices, Cautions and Conditions.* Paper given to the EAIE Conference, London, November.

McNay, I. (1995a) *The University as an Organisation.* Option Module 1, MA Higher Education, Middlesex University.

McNay, I. (1995b) 'From collegial academy to corporate enterprise: the changing cultures of universities' in Schuller, T. (ed.). *The Changing University.* Buckingham,

SRHE/Open University Press.

Men's Health (1991) July/August.

Meriwhether, C. (1984) *Women in Educational Administration in Israel and the US.* Unpublished PhD thesis, University of Minnesota.

Middlehurst, R. (1993) *Leading Academics.* Buckingham: SRHE/Open University Press.

Mixon, D. (1989) *Obedience and Civilization: Authorized Crime and the Normality of Evil.* London: Pluto Press.

Morgan, C. and Murgatroyd, S.(1994) *Total Quality Management in the Public Sector.* Buckingham: Open University Press.

Morris, R. (ed.) (1990) *Central and Local Control of Education after the Education Reform Act.* Harlow: Longman/BEMAS.

Mortimer, J. and Mortimer, P. (1991) *The Secondary School Head; Roles, Responsibilities and Reflections.* London: Paul Chapman.

Murgatroyd, S. and Morgan, C. (1992) *Total Quality Management and the School.* Buckingham: Open University Press.

National Commission on Education (1993) *Learning to Succeed: A Radical Look at Education Today and a Strategy for the Future.* (Report of the Paul Hamlyn Foundation National Commission on Education). London: Heinemann.

National Union of Teachers (NUT) (1990) *Health and Safety. Teachers, Stress and Schools.* London: NUT.

Nattrass, S. (1991) 'Beating Stress', *Teachers' Weekly*, **13(8)**, 7.

Nebesnuick, D. (1990). *Monitoring and Evaluation and the 1988 Education Reform Act.* Slough: NFER.

Nelson, J. (1983) *Between Two Gardens:Reflections on Sexuality and Religious Experience.* New York: The Pilgrim Press.

Nelson, L. (1949) *The Socratic Method of Critical Philosophy*, selected essays. Translated by T. K. Brown. New Haven: Yale University Press.

Neumann, L. F. (1982) 'The Importance of Critical Ethics for the Social Sciences', *Ratio*, **XXIV(1)**, 11–27.

Nixon, J. (1995a) 'Markets, towers or meeting places? Higher education for a learning society', *Studies in Higher Education* (in press).

Nixon, J. (1995b) 'The University as a Place of Learning: Perspectives on the "Quality" Debate', in Carrotte, P. and Hammond, M. (eds). *Learning in Difficult Times: Issues for Teaching in Higher Education,* Sheffield: Committee of Vice Chancellors and Principals of the Universities of the UK, Universities Staff Development Unit, (CPCV/UCoSDE), 46–54.

Nixon, J. (1996) 'Professional Identity and the Re-structuring of Higher Education', *Studies in Higher Education*, **21(1)** (in press).

Nixon, J. and Rudduck, J. (1994) 'Professionalism, judgement and the inspection of schools', in Scott, D. (ed.). *Accountability and Control in Educational Settings.* London: Cassell.

Nixon, J., Martin, J., McKeown, P. and Ranson, S. (1995) *Encouraging Learning: Towards a Theory of the Learning School.* Buckingham: Open University Press.

O'Brien, K. (1994) 'Primary Schools and Their Teachers', in Lawrence, K. (ed.). *Education Tomorrow.* London: Cassell, pp.53–64.

Office for Standards in Education, (1992; 1993b; 1994b) *Handbook for the Inspection of Schools.* London: OFSTED.

Office for Standards in Education (1993a, 1994a) *Framework for the Inspection of Schools.* London: OFSTED.

Office for Standards in Education and Office of Her Majesty's Chief Inspector of Schools (Wales) (1994c) *Improving Schools.* London: HMSO.

Office for Standards in Education (1994d) *A Focus on Quality.* London: OFSTED.

Office for Standards in Education, (1995) *The Annual Report of Her Majesty's Chief Inspectors of Schools: Standards and Quality in Education.* London: HMSO.

Oldroyd, D. and Hall, V. (1991) *Managing Staff Development – A Handbook for Secondary Schools.* London: Paul Chapman.

Oldroyd, D., Smith, K. and Lee, J. (1984) *School-Based Staff Development Activities: A*

Handbook for Secondary Schools. York, Harlow: Longman.

Peake, G. (1994) *Mission and Change. Institutional Mission and its Application to the Management of Further and Higher Education.* Buckingham: SRHE/Open University Press.

Pedler, M. (1994) 'Applying self-development in organisations', in Mabey, C. and Iles, P. (eds). (1994) *Managing Learning.* London: Routledge.

Pedler, M., Burgoyne, J. and Boydell, T. (1986) *A Manager's Guide To Self-Development.* London: McGraw-Hill.

Pedler, M., Burgoyne, J. and Boydell, T. (1991) *The Learning Company: A Strategy for Sustainable Development.* London: McGraw Hill.

Peteet, J. (1991) *Gender in Crisis: Women and the Palestinian Resistance Movement.* New York: Columbia University Press.

Peters, R. S. (1968) *Perspectives on Plowden.* London: Routledge.

Peters, T. and Waterman, R. (1982) *In Search of Excellence.* New York: Harper and Row.

Peters, T. (1992) *Liberation Management.* New York: Knopf.

Peterson, M. and Ingalls, Y. (1993) *Palestinians in Profile: A Guide.* Jerusalem: Panorama Centre.

Pfeffer, J. (1992) *Managing with Power: Politics and Influence in Organisations.* Boston, Ma.: Harvard University Press.

Phillips, A. (1994) *Local Democracy: The Terms of the Debate.* (Commission for Local Democracy Report No. 2). London: Commission for Local Democracy.

Pigors, P. (1935) *Leadership or Domination.* London:George Harrap & Co.

Plowden Report (1967) *Children and Their Primary Schools: A Report.* Central Advisory Council for England. London: HMSO.

Price, C. (1994) 'Piloting higher education change: a view from the helm', in Weil, S. (ed.). *Introducing Change from the Top in Universities and Colleges: Ten Personal Accounts.* London: Kogan Page.

Rae, J. (1993) *Delusions of Grandeur: A Headmaster's Life, 1966–1986.* London: Harper Collins.

Rees, F.(1989) *Teacher Stress: An Exploratory Study.* Windsor: NFER, NAS/UWT.

Reynolds, P. A. (1986) Foreword to the report of the CVCP group on academic standards, *Academic Standards in Universities' Methods and Procedures for Maintaining and Monitoring Academic Standards in the Context of the Quality of their Teaching.* London: CVCP.

Reynolds, D. and Parker, A. (1992) 'School effectiveness and school improvement in the 1990s', in Reynolds, D. and Cuttance, P. (eds) *School Effectiveness: Research, Policy and Practice.* London: Cassell.

Ribbins, P. (1990). 'Teachers as professionals: towards a redefinition', in Morris, R. (ed.). *Central and Local Control of Education after the Education Reform Act 1988.* Harlow: Longman/BEMAS.

Ribbins, P. (1993a) 'Conversations with a *condottiere* of administrative value', *Journal of Educational Administration and Management,* **8(1)**.

Ribbins, P. (1993b) 'Towards a prolegomenon for understanding what radical educational reform means for principals', Keynote Paper to the *Annual National Conference of CCEA/ASSP.* Adelaide, September 1993 (unpublished).

Ribbins, P. (1994a) 'De Quistibus non est Disputandum', *Educational Management and Administration,* **22(4)**, 218–22.

Ribbins, P. (1994b) 'Telling Tales of Secondary Heads: On Educational Reform and the National Curriculum', in Chitty, C. (ed.). *The National Curriculum: Is It Working?* London: Longman.

Ribbins, P. and Marland, M. (1994) *Headship Matters: Conversations with Seven Secondary School Headteachers.* Harlow: Longman.

Riches, C. and Morgan, C. (eds) (1989) *Human Resource Management in Education.* Milton Keynes: Open University Press.

Ricoeur, P. (1991) *A Ricoeur Reader. Reflection and Imagination.* Edited and translated by M.J. Valdes. Hemel Hempstead: Harvester Wheatsheaf.

Riley, R. E. (1994) '*Educational Evolution; the on-going creation and re-creation of the head of faculty role in an 11 to 18 Catholic Comprehensive School'*, unpublished. M.Ed. thesis. University of Sheffield: Division of Education.

Roderick, C. (1993) 'Becoming a learning organisation', *Training and Development*, **11(3)**.

Rowland, S. (1993) *The Enquiring Tutor. Exploring the Process of Professional Learning.* London: Falmer.

Rudduck, J. (1991) *Innovation and Change.* Buckingham: Open University Press.

Russell Report (1973) *Adult Education: A Plan for Development.* Report by a Committee of Inquiry appointed by the Secretary of Stage for Education and Science under the chairmanship of Sir Lionel Russell, CBE. London: HMSO.

Russell, C. (1993) *Academic Freedom.* London: Routledge.

Ryan, H. (1992) 'BS 5750: Is the Standard Appropriate for Education?', *Management in Education*, **6(3)**, 9–10.

Sayer, J. (1989) *Managing Schools.* London: Hodder and Stoughton.

Scheerens, J. (1992) *Effective Schooling: Research, Theory and Practice.* London: Cassell.

Schön, D. (1983) *The Reflective Practitioner.* New York: Basic Books.

Schön, D. (1987) *Educating the Reflective Practitioner.* San Francisco, Oxford: Jossey-Bass.

School Curriculum and Assessment Authority (1994) *Value Added Performance Indicators for Schools.* London: School Curriculum and Assessment Authority and Central Office of Information.

Schratz, M. (1993) *Qualitative Voices in Educational Research.* London: The Falmer Press.

Scott, W. G. (1985) 'Organisational Revolution: An End to Managerial Orthodoxy', *Administration and Society*, **17(2)**, 149–70.

Selye, H. (1956) *The Stress of Life.* New York: McGraw-Hill.

Semler, R. (1993) *Maverick!* London: Century.

Senge, P. M. (1990a) 'The leaders' new work', *Sloan Management Review*, **Fall**, 7–23.

Senge, P. M. (1990b) *The Fifth Discipline – The Art and Practice of the Learning Organisation.* New York: Doubleday.

Serey, T. T. and Verderber K. S. (1991) 'Beyond the Wall: Resolving Issues of Educational Philosophy and Pedagogy in the Teaching of Managerial Competences', in Bigelow, J. D.(ed.). *Managerial Skills: Explorations in Practical Knowledge.* London: Sage.

Shakeshaft, C. (1987) *Women in Educational Administration.* California:Sage Publications.

Shaw, M. (1994) 'Current Issues in Pastoral Management', *Pastoral Care in Education*, **12(4)**, 37–41.

Shipman, M. (1990) *In Search of Learning.* Oxford: Blackwell.

Shotter, J. (1984) *Social Accountability and Selfhood.* Oxford: Blackwell.

Showers, B. (1985) 'Teachers Coaching Teachers', *Educational Leadership*, **42(7)**, 43–49.

Simkins, T., Ellison L. and Garrett, V. (eds) (1992) *Implementing Educational Reform. The Early Lessons.* Harlow: Longman/BEMAS.

Slack, P. and Cornelius, P. (1995) 'To Walk the Red Road as School Leaders', in Dunlap, D. and Schmuck, P. (eds). *Women Leading in Education.* Albany: State University of New York Press.

Slee, P. (1995) 'Using Total Quality Management as a management tool in educational support services', in Slowey, M. (ed.). *Implementing Change from Within Universities and Colleges: Ten Personal Accounts.* London: Kogan Page.

Slowey, M. (ed.) (1995) *Implementing Change from Within Universities and Colleges: Ten Personal Accounts.* London: Kogan Page.

Smyth, J. (1993) *A Socially Critical View of the 'Self-Managing School.* London: Falmer Press.

Stewart, R. and Barsoux, J.-L. (1994) *The Diversity of Management: Twelve Managers Talking.* London: Macmillan.

Stillman, A. B. (1989) 'Institutional evaluation and LEA advisory services', *Research Papers in Education*, **4(2)**, 3–27.

Stodgill, R. (1981) *Handbook of Leadership: a Survey of Theory and Research*. New York: Free Press.

Stott, K. and Walker, A. (1992) 'The Nature and Use of Mission Statements in Singaporean Schools', *Educational Management and Administration*, **20(1)**.

Tajfel, H. and Fraser,C. (1978) *Introducing Social Psychology*. Harmondsworth: Penguin.

Taylor, J. (1995) 'Accessibility and institutional change', in Slowey, M. (ed.). *Implementing Change from Within Universities and Colleges: Ten Personal Accounts*. London: Kogan Page.

Thomas, W. and Bailey, C. (1927) *Letters to a Young Headmaster*. London: Blackie.

Thompson, M. (1989) 'Appraisal and Equal Opportunities', in Evans, A. and Tomlinson, J. (eds). *Teacher Appraisal*. London: Jessica Kingley.

Tiles, J. G. (1987) 'Meaning', in Gregory, R. (ed.). *The Oxford Companion to the Mind*. Oxford: Oxford University Press.

Torrington, D. and Weightman, J. (1989) *The Reality of School Management*. Oxford, Blackwell.

Trethowan, D. M. (1991) *Achieving Quality Schools Through Performance Management*. London: Paul Chapman.

Trott, C. (1994) *Women and Appraisal*. Unpublished MA dissertation, University of Leicester.

Tse, K.K.(1985) *Marks and Spencer: Anatomy of Britain's Most Efficiently Managed Company*. Oxford: Pergamon.

Turner, G. and Clift, P. (1988) *Studies in Teacher Appraisal*. London: Falmer Press.

Universities Association for Continuing Education (1995) *Handbook for Quality Assurance in University Continuing Education*. UACE Working Paper No. 6.

Van de Pitte, M. (1991) 'Are Academic Administrators to be Trusted?', *Educational Management and Administration*, **19(3)**, 142–49.

Wallace, M. (1991) *School Centred Management Training*. London: Paul Chapman.

Wallace, M. and Hall, V. (1994a) 'Promoting Collaboration among Schools and Colleges', Lawrence, I. (ed.). *Education Tomorrow*. London: Cassell, pp.100–115.

Wallace, M. and Hall, V. (1994b) *Inside the SMT. Teamwork in Secondary School Management*. London: Paul Chapman.

Warren, R. (1994) 'The Role of the Assistant Headteacher', in Crawford, M., Kydd, L. and Parker, S. (eds). *Educational Management into Action*. London: Paul Chapman/Open University Press, pp.185–98.

Weaver, T. (1979) 'Department of Education and Science: central control of education?', Unit 2, E222. *The Control of Education in Britain*. Milton Keynes: The Open University.

Weeks, R (1994) 'The Deputy Head and Strategic Planning', in Crawford, M., Kydd, L. and Parker, S. (eds). *Educational Management into Action*. London: Paul Chapman/Open University Press, pp.251–63.

Weick, K. (1976) 'Educational organisations as loosely-coupled systems', *Administrative Science Quarterly*, **21(1)**. (Reprinted in Westoby, A. (1988). *Cultures and Power in Educational Organisations*. Milton Keynes: Open University Press.)

Weightman, J. (1989) 'Women in Management', *Educational Management and Administration*, **17**, 119–22.

Weil, S. (ed.) (1994) *Introducing Change from the Top in Universities and Colleges: Ten Personal Accounts*. London, Kogan Page.

West-Burnham, J. (1994) 'Strategy, Policy and Planning', in Bush, T. and West-Burnham, J. (eds). *The Principles of Educational Management*. Harlow: Longman/University of Leicester.

West-Burnham, J. (1992) *Managing Quality in Schools*. Harlow: Longman.

West-Burnham, J. (1992a) 'Total Quality Management in Education' in Bennett, N., Crawford, M. and Riches, C. (eds). *Managing Change in Education*. London: Paul Chapman.

West-Burnham, J. (1990) 'The Management of Change', in Davies, B., Ellison, L. Osborne, A. and West-Burnham, J. (eds). *Education Management for the 1990s*. Harlow: Longman.

274

Westen, D. (1985) *Self and Society. Narcissism, Collectivisim and the Development of Morals.* Cambridge: Cambridge University Press.

Whitaker, P.(1993) *Managing Change in Schools.* Buckingham: Open University Press.

Wilcox, B. and Gray, J. (1994). 'Reactions to Inspection: a study of three variants', *Cambridge Journal of Education,* **24(2)**, 245–59.

Wilkinson, A. and Willmott, H. (eds) (1995) *Making Quality Critical: New Perspectives on Organisational Change.* London: Routledge.

Williams, R. (1965) *The Long Revolution.* Harmondsworth: Penguin.

Williams, R. (1976). *Key Words.* London: Fontana/Croom Helm.

Williams, G. (1988) 'Foreword', in Cooper, B. and Shute, W. (eds). *Training for School Management.* London: Kogan Page (Bedford Way Paper 350.

Wilson, A. (1994) 'The management of change in a large civic university', in Weil, S (ed.). *Introducing Change from the Top in Universities and Colleges: Ten Personal Accounts.* London: Kogan Page.

Woodcock, M. (1979) *Team Development Manual.* London: Gower Press.

Wragg, T. (1994) 'Under the Microscope', *Times Educational Supplement,* 9 September.

Index